The Life of
James Hamilton
(1788-1825)

The Life of
James Hamilton Stanhope
(1788-1825):

Love, War and Tragedy

By

Mark Guscin

Cambridge
Scholars
Publishing

The Life of James Hamilton Stanhope (1788-1825):
Love, War and Tragedy

By Mark Guscin

This book first published 2021. The present binding first published 2023.

Cambridge Scholars Publishing

Lady Stephenson Library, Newcastle upon Tyne, NE6 2PA, UK

British Library Cataloguing in Publication Data
A catalogue record for this book is available from the British Library

ISBN (10): 1-5275-9517-X
ISBN (13): 978-1-5275-9517-0

This book is dedicated with fond memories to Julia Mosquera Froix (Tana), who left us just before I completed it.

TABLE OF CONTENTS

ACKNOWLEDGEMENTS

As could not be otherwise, this book has seen the light of day thanks to the help of other people. I would like to thank, in no particular order,

Rebecca Gladders, Adam Rummens and everyone else at Cambridge Scholars, who make things much easier than they might otherwise be.

Andrew V. Wright from the Cumbria Archives for his interest and generosity.

Armando Sánchez Ramos for his help turning over hundreds of pages of manuscripts while I took photographs.

Lara Joffe, Jennifer House and everyone else at the Kent History and Library Centre in Maidstone.

Jane Hewitt, a family researcher.

Hristina Krastanova from the Travellers Club.

The staff at Kenwood House.

Dr. Allison Goudie at the Iveagh Bequest.

Colonel Alastair Mathewson from the Chevening Trust.

Norman Poser, author of the biography of the first Lord Mansfield.

Louise Cooling, Assistant Curator, Kenwood, English Heritage.

The Chevening Trust, for their permission to reproduce images from the Stanhope Manuscript Collection, and in particular, Colonel Alastair Mathewson for his wise suggestions to improve the text.

FOREWORD

It is recorded that on the night of 16th January 1809 the body of Major the Hon. Charles Stanhope, still wearing the new epaulettes he had put on earlier that day, was buried on the field of Corunna. It must therefore be the old pair he set aside that morning that now rests, together with his sash and shoe buckles, in a tin in the library of Chevening House in Kent. The small change from his pocket is also at Chevening, wrapped in hand-written scraps of paper that commend the coins firstly to Charles's sister Hester, and then later to the children of their youngest brother. Together the tin and the coins form an eloquent testament to grief and with it a tangible link to a long-dead generation of the Stanhope family.

It was that youngest brother, James Hamilton Stanhope, himself present at the Battle of Corunna, who brought Charles's effects home and it is he who is the subject, and as will soon become apparent to some extent the co-author, of this fascinating book. The memoirs of the great can be illuminating about the past but the memoirs of bystanders to greatness, observant flies on famous walls, can add authenticity and immediacy to long-familiar people and events. Lieutenant Colonel the Hon. James Stanhope MP had access to a remarkable range of famous walls. He was nephew to William Pitt the Younger, brother to Lady Hester Stanhope, heir to the botanist Sir Joseph Banks, aide-de-camp to Sir John Moore and later to Prince Frederick, "the Grand Old Duke of York". He witnessed, and describes with a keen eye, action in the Peninsular War and at the battles of Quatre Bras and Waterloo. His account of the death of Pitt the Younger, written within three days of the event, is regarded as authoritative. He was witness to the death and burial of Sir John Moore at Corunna. His recollections of the Duke of Wellington's views on the tactical decisions taken by Napoleon and Marshal Grouchy at Waterloo, expressed soon after the battle to a French officer following dinner in a restaurant during the occupation of Paris, form a valuable contribution to a subject of enduring historical interest.

Born and brought up at Chevening House in Kent, the youngest child of the intellectually brilliant "tyrannical freedom-lover" Charles, 3rd Earl Stanhope and his "stiff and frigid" second wife, James did not go to school. His eccentric father, an inventor of genius and, as "Citizen" Stanhope or "The Minority of One" a considerably less successful radical politician, was a product of the Enlightenment who among many more valuable and enduring inventions created a wooden "Demonstrator" to illustrate the mechanical basis of logical thought. He took charge of his children's education through a succession of hand-picked tutors, one of whom, a devoted republican, was arrested at Chevening and taken to the Tower of London on a charge of high treason when James was about six. His five elder siblings left home as soon as they were able and he met them quite rarely thereafter. In the absence of practical, pecuniary, or emotional support from their parents they all relied heavily on William Pitt, described by James following the prime minister's death in 1806 as "our only protector, who had reared us with more than parental care".

From these pages emerges a more nuanced and interesting figure than a mere observer of his times. James Hamilton Stanhope, in contrast to his father, is a figure of the Romantic era, a soldier, artist, and poet. His love for Lady Frederica Murray, his wife of only 30 months, is immortalised in her tomb in St Botolph's Church, Chevening (he lies in it too, but at his insistence it remains outwardly hers). The simple white marble sarcophagus is said to have been considered by its sculptor, the prolific Francis Chantrey, to be his best work. With "Freddy", and with her family at Kenwood and at Scone, he seems to have found all too briefly the love, stability and family life missing in his upbringing. While James's verse, with its tramping columns of sometimes relentless couplets, never scaled the heights of Parnassus (as he might have phrased it), his watercolours suggest a strong and romantically coloured imagination.

In company he could shine. As one acquaintance saw it

> "What an extraordinary person is Stanhope! If you happen to be in a frivolous mood, he will say foolish things, and will inspire folly in others. If you are in a serious vein, his conversation becomes interesting, and in the highest degree instructive. If you feel sentimental, his wonderful memory will supply poetical images from the finest passages in poetry."

But there was at the same time a brooding side to his character, noted from childhood by his sister Hester.

For the last third of his life he suffered recurring physical torment from a war-wound, a ball of grape-shot lodged deep in his upper back which no surgeon was ever able to remove, probe for it as they regularly did. His early death, plausibly attributed to the mental anguish engendered by a terrible promise made in a moment of grief, is a Romantic trope. His sister Hester's reaction to it, bricking herself up for the rest of her life in a remote hilltop monastery in Lebanon, is another.

In the immediate aftermath of his wife's death in 1823, Colonel Stanhope set down the structure and sources for a book to be published at some period after his own death. It was to be a compendium of his historical and military memoirs and an anthology of his poetry, culminating in a panegyric to the great love of his life and their blissful but tragically short Christian marriage. Dr Mark Guscin, already the biographer of Lady Hester Stanhope, has adopted that structure for the book that follows and augmented the sources through his own scholarship. In his sympathetic hands James Hamilton Stanhope has at last found a worthy literary collaborator, editor, and amanuensis to tell his story.

Alastair Mathewson
Chevening, November 2020

INTRODUCTION

Just two months after his wife's death in 1823, James Stanhope expressed in writing his desire to write the story of his own life, a wish he conceived when making copies of his deceased spouse's correspondence. The document[1] is dated 9 March 1823, and was written at Kenwood[2], his parents-in-law's home where he now spent most of his time. Stanhope himself entitled it "My wishes about my papers and Freddy's letters, journal etc. etc. 1823"

> Kenwood, 9 March 1823
> On writing out extracts of my beloved wife's letters, I am come to a determination that some day or other this benefit shall not be confined to myself or my family, but that my country shall see what it ought to regard with equal pride and advantage.
> I bequeath these inimitable emanations of the purest and best of mortals to every child, that they may learn and appreciate their duties to a parent; that they may see how a mother should be loved; to every wife that they may imitate her devoted attachment, her utter want of self, her fidelity and her virtues! To every Christian that they may see the blessed fruits of the religion they profess, and in following her steps may learn to live and die like her!
> To my executors and to my son if he survives me, I leave the charge of executing this subject to their judgement and to my son's wishes as to the time, certainly not for many years – if he wishes it not till after his death.
> To connect it I mean to write a short memoir of my early life and I wish the arrangement to be as follows:
> My early life up to 1810, with an account of Mr. Pitt's death, already written.

---

[1] Kent History and Library Centre, Maidstone, U1590 C262/4.
[2] The name is sometimes spelt Caen Wood, but as Earl Mansfield, James' father-in-law, who lived there, used the spelling Kenwood, I too have adopted this spelling, except of course when quoting others who prefer the alternative spelling.

2 volumes of military journal, from 1810 to 1815, now in South Audley Street[3], to be illustrated, with extracts from the speeches in the Cortes taken by myself and by miscellaneous correspondence of that time.

Freddy's acquirements – discovery of cubes – her letters/if it is wished illustrated by extracts from my own.

My account of her last illness.

Her last letter.

In an appendix any parts of my poetry and translations and all or part of Freddy's journal now in the possession of Lady Mansfield[4].

Neither James himself nor his son James Banks ever fulfilled this wish, and apart from his military diary[5] the rest of these documents have remained unpublished until now. My intention in this biography, almost two hundred years later, is to bring James' wishes for his written work to fruition. All the documents he mentions are included[6], not in the same order he expressed (e.g. excerpts from Lady Frederica's diary are included in their chronological order, not in an appendix[7]) and of course with much more information taken from other sources.

James Hamilton Stanhope, however, was contradictory in numerous episodes in his life, and this document expressing his wishes for his biography is no exception. Immediately after his wish to see his life in print he adds the following words, written two weeks later:

On reflection, I think they should not be published, but only collected and arranged in the order I have mentioned. If my son has children I wish them to descend in his family. If my direct line is extinct I leave it to the eldest branch of Lord Mansfield's family to be kept at Scone or Kenwood.

---

[3] James' address in London; he had evidently not given up the lease on the house.

[4] The journal was from the Grand Tour of the family in 1819 and 1820; James made an exceedingly fair copy for his mother-in-law, although the originals are also preserved.

[5] Edited and published by Gareth Glover, Gareth Glover, *Eyewitness to the Peninsular War and the Battle of Waterloo – The Letters and Journals of Lieutenant Colonel the Honourable James Hamilton Stanhope, 1803 to 1825, recording his service with Sir John Moore, Sir Thomas Graham and the Duke of Wellington* (Barnsley, 2010).

[6] Although given its length and the fact that it has already been published, the military diary is not included in its entirety.

[7] I am currently working on an illustrated edition of Frederica's diary as written on her Grand Tour of 1819 and 1820.

James Hamilton Stanhope, March 24th 1823
I wish all Freddy's letters to me in Ireland (which are put up in several parcels and numbered) to be burnt without being opened and I wish also all Hester's letters to be burnt unopened and I leave this in trust to my executors to fulfil.

This declaration is something of a mystery. In all the surviving documentation related to the lives of James, Hester and Frederica, there are no letters from Frederica to James in Ireland, and none of Hester's letters to James either, so maybe they were indeed burned or otherwise destroyed. Hester indeed had not written to James for some years, but we may assume that her letters sent and received before this date in 1823 had been opened and read; maybe James still expected to hear from his eccentric half-sister and his instructions were to burn any letters that might yet come. This in turn would imply that he knew, or suspected, that he would die before Hester did.

Another unusual point is the reference to Frederica's letters to James when he was in Ireland; any such letters must of course have been written after the two started corresponding. The earliest correspondence still surviving is from Frederica's Grand Tour in 1819-1820, although this in itself does not mean that there was nothing before this (the argumentum ex silentio has always been fallacious). There is only one reference to James having been in Ireland (so at least we know that he was there), but the reference itself is problematic.

James was planning to go to Ireland with his sister Hester in 1809, but Hester at least never got past Wales, and it is unsure whether James crossed the sea. In any case, Frederica at the time would have been nine years old. The reference in question is a letter from James to his mother, dated just 15 January, and written from Dublin. No year is given on the letter, which in itself is unusual. The letter is included in a file[8] which is entitled "Letters to Louisa Dowager Countess Stanhope from her son James"; Louisa became the dowager countess when her husband died in 1816, but this is no clue as to the dates of the letters in the file as they contain correspondence from as early as 1806, ten years before the death of the third Earl. The letters are ordered immediately after others sent in April 1816, which could suggest they date from this year, as all the dated letters are filed in chronological order except for the very first one; this, however, would not in itself constitute proof as the letters might have been rearranged, and whoever put them in the order they are now in might have been mistaken.

---

[8] U1590 C 270.

There are two ways in which the year of the letter could be deducted, and hence the time when James was in Ireland (which must have been more than a few days if there was time for Frederica to write to him several times and for the letters to get there). The first is by eliminating years when we know where James was on 15 January, or thereabouts. The second is from the internal content of the letter itself.

The first method becomes unnecessary when the second is applied, as in the letter James says:

> Freddy is recovering very well, has had no pain or fever and writes in good spirits – our little boy is heavier and bigger on dit[9] visibly and is now a great man for he can show a tooth though he cannot bite. Freddy desires me to thank you for your kind message.

Their little boy was their son James Banks Stanhope, born on 13 May 1821. In January 1823 James was at home while Frederica was in labour again, which means that the letter from Dublin was necessarily written on 15 January 1822, which also makes perfect sense of the reference to the baby's teething.

Whatever letters Frederica sent him while he was in Ireland, he would surely have opened and read them himself; what he probably means by his intructions to have them burnt unopened is that the parcels he had made with them should not be opened again but rather destroyed. Either way, his wishes in this aspect seem to have been fulfilled. The letters were no doubt very personal, written so soon after the birth of the couple's first child, although as tends to happen, James' exclusion of these letters from what he initially wished to be published (and the apparently successful destruction of the letters) only arouses all the more our curiosity as to why he saw them as so different from the rest.

In writing this biography I have of course paid heed to James' first wish, and not his afterthought. This is because I wholeheartedly agree with him that there is plenty to learn from both his own life and that of his wife; plenty to learn about war, the tragedy that can unexpectedly afflict us at any time, and the pure and carefree love they felt for each other and which shines out above any other part of their short lives.

As with any life, there are inevitably references to other people that need to be put in context in order to understand them. Other people in James' family lived fascinating lives; his father, his brothers, and above all his half-

---

[9] James often included in his letters phrases, sentences and even complete paragraphs in French and Spanish; "on dit" was one of his favourite expressions.

sister Lady Hester. I have given certain details about all these people and not simply assumed that everyone knows who they are and what they did. The documentary research involved in this book has been considerable, and rather than summarize or rephrase what James, his parents, brothers and sisters and wife wrote, I have preferred to quote from their original writings whenever possible[10]. The characters in this biography tell their own story much better than I could ever hope to do.

---

[10] James was an assiduous writer, like so many other people of the time. The amount of time he spent writing letters, journals and poetry must have been so much longer than the time we tend to spend writing e-mails and WhatsApps nowadays; cf. a letter from his sister Hester in 1813, "I received above one hundred pages from dearest James", and Mark Guscin, *A Very Good Sort of Man* (Brighton, 2017), p. 66, quoting from the diary of Charles Lewis Meryon, Lady Hester's physician, on 16 March 1818: "I wrote to Lady Hester from 9 in the morning until 12 at night".

CHAPTER ONE

EARLY LIFE

According to the history of the Stanhope family[1], the name was derived from the "township of Stanhope in County Durham" and the Stanhopes "were prominent in the north as early as the thirteenth century". It was the first Earl Stanhope (James Stanhope, 1673 – 1721) who bought Chevening as the family residence (see Figure 1.1), after taking part in the War of the Spanish Succession. The second Earl, Philip, was James' grandfather; he married Grizel Hamilton[2] (see Figure 1.2), the origin of James' middle name[3]. Philip had only two children; Philip, known in his lifetime as Lord Mahon[4], a title used for all the heirs to the earldom until they actually became Earls, and Charles. Philip was the elder of the two sons, and always of a weak constitution. His parents took him to Switzerland in 1763 to see a well-known chest physician, Dr Tronchin. All their efforts were in vain and Philip died on 6 July, leaving his younger brother Charles as Lord Mahon and heir to the earldom.

---

[1] Aubrey Newman, *The Stanhopes of Chevening* (London, 1969), p. 15.
[2] The daughter of Charles Lord Binning and granddaughter of the Sixth Earl of Haddington. Cf. Newman, *Stanhopes*, p. 107: Grizel's grandmother "Lady Grizel Baillie was a formidable character, many of whose traits were inherited by Grizel Hamilton herself and thus transmitted to the Stanhopes", and p. 128, in reference to Grizel, James' grandmother: "She stands out prominently among the women at Chevening, and her influence has been enormous, not merely on her own immediate generation and descendants, but on all those who subsequently bore the name of Stanhope and on those who have known and loved Chevening; her portraits still dominate, pleasantly but unmistakably, all the others in the family collections there".
[3] The habit of using one of the parent's surnames as a middle name was common in the nineteenth century; cf. the famous engineer Isambard Kingdom Brunel, whose mother's maiden name was "Kingdom".
[4] Mahon is a town on the island of Menorca, captured by the first Earl in 1708 during the War of the Spanish Succession. On 3 July 1717, James Stanhope was created Baron Stanhope of Elvaston and Viscount Stanhope of Mahon, and on 14 April 1718, Earl Stanhope.

Figure 1.1 – Chevening, the Stanhope family house where where James grew up

Figure 1.2 – Grizel Stanhope, née Hamilton, James' grandmother

Much has been written about the third Earl (see Figure 1.3); he is one of the best known figures in the Stanhope family history. Charles "Citizen" Stanhope[5] was an eccentric inventor who believed so much in the principles of the French Revolution that he reportedly slept on the floor with the windows open in winter and sent his children to do manual work in an attempt to make himself (and his family) equal to the majority of his countrymen[6]. He exercised a great interest in science; he invented a printing press which remained in use until the early twentieth century, a system for fireproofing houses (which he tried out once on his unsuspecting guests by herding them into a wooden hut and setting fire to it) and also worked on trying to produce a steamship, although he never managed to convince the Navy[7]. He married William Pitt the Younger's sister, Hester, and had three daughters by her; Hester in 1776 (see Figure 1.4), Griselda in 1778 and Lucy in 1780. Lucy was born in February, but her mother never really recovered from the birth and after lingering in poor health for some months, died in July.

As often happened at the time, Mahon, the future third Earl, married again soon after being widowed, in the following March, just nine months after the death of his first wife. The bride this time was his first wife's

---

[5] Stanhope himself at this time signed his letters "fellow citizen" and even took down the coronets from the gates at Chevening; these ideas did not last long but the nickname stuck.

[6] Hester apparently had to look after geese on the common, while James was apprenticed to a cobbler, cf. Charles Lewis Meryon, *The Additional Memoirs of Lady Hester Stanhope* (ed. Mark Guscin, Brighton, 2017), p. 44: "...she who had cherished the tenderest affection for her two brothers, Charles, the eldest, and James, now in question. She had always prided herself on the success of her scheme in removing these two, and I think Lord Mahon also from their paternal home, at a time when her father's extreme radical principles and the cry of equality, to which she alludes in making James a cobbler, rendered him as it was supposed an unfit guide for his children".

[7] The Duchess of Cleveland, the third Earl's granddaughter, wrote about Charles in *The Life and Letters of Lady Hester Stanhope* (London, 1914) (p. 4): "We, his descendants, are justly and I may say exceedingly proud of his genius and achievements, and yet humbly grateful that we were not called upon to live under his roof, for, ardently as he advocated liberty and enfranchisement abroad, he was the sternest of autocrats at home". Wilhelmina was born a few years after the third Earl died, so she could never have been called upon to live under the same roof.

Figure 1.3 – The 3rd Earl Stanhope, James' father

Figure 1.4 – A miniature of Lady Hester Stanhope, James' half-sister

cousin Louisa, the daughter of Lady Chatham's[8] younger brother, James
Grenville. Louisa bore Mahon four sons; Philip Henry in 1781 (who
eventually became the fourth Earl), Banks (who was born and died in 1784),
Charles Banks in 1785 and James Hamilton on 7 September 1788. James
Hamilton Stanhope was thus the youngest child of the family, and had two
full brothers and three half-sisters.

The third Earl's granddaughter, Catherine Wilhelmina, who on her
marriage became the Duchess of Cleveland, later wrote a book about her
aunt Lady Hester Stanhope. The book was as close as could be at the time
to what would nowadays be called an official biography; she was a member
of the family and focused, as was only to be expected, on the positive
aspects of her subject. When she makes any kind of negative comment,
therefore, we can only accept it as true. This is what she has to say about the
third Earl's second wife and her relationship with her three stepdaughters[9]:

> ... the new lady Mahon did not commend herself to her
> stepdaughters. She was a worthy and well-meaning woman; but, as
> I remember her, stiff and frigid, with a chilling, conventional
> manner. They never became fond of her, and she never seems to have
> gained any influence over them – least of all over Lady Hester. As
> for their father, he did not even attempt to do so; he merely gave his
> orders and took care they were obeyed. They saw very little of him,
> for he was the busiest of men.[10]

It is never an easy task to find details and stories about the childhood of
most people in history; and even when such details are available, they tend
to be of little interest as what makes most lives interesting is what people
did in adulthood. Biographers are often forced to have recourse to
generalities about the times, or describing what happened to other people
(often adults) in the subject's life, to provide a feeling for the atmosphere
the subject grew up in, and I am no exception to this rule. There is, however,
in this case, a very touching picture of James Hamilton Stanhope as a young

---

[8] Chatham was the honorary title of William Pitt the Elder, inherited by his eldest
son, after whose death the title fell into disuse.
[9] Cleveland, *Life and Letters*, pp. 1-2.
[10] For a more neutral view of the situation cf. Newman, *Stanhopes*, p. 187: "Louisa
Stanhope ... did her duty by her stepdaughters, doing her best to bring them up
properly, and writing frequently to Lady Chatham with details of the girls designed
to delight their grandmother".

child, written in a letter many years later by his grandmother Grizel[11]. Grizel was ninety-one years old when she wrote the letter; the handwriting is spidery and there are many words missing and sentences which ramble on without concluding the idea they started with (although the general meaning is always clear). In addition to a grandmother's fond reminiscences the letter also complains about the lack of contact from James over what would seem to be a long period of time, and when she did receive news it was never good.

> I thought I saw my little strunty[12] boy, hopping like a sparrow on one leg (for you rarely went upon two), and climbing the damson trees, devouring the plumbs [sic] like a little pig, and many more such like events come to my mind of those happy days, and which only a fond grandmother could recollect about you, my dear Slyboots (as I used to call you), my dear grandson who often used to own over and dine with me; one Sunday happened to meet and went away sooner than usual after a cordial and affection (at least in appearance to one), we parted as usual. From that hour for years we not only never met, but I never heard where you were nor about you, and when I did, nothing but what gave me concern, and too often heart-breaking sorrow.
>
> …
>
> I used to dream seeing my little Hopper the same height as when hopping (and to this hour no other idea have I formed of your present figure).

A note included at the end of the letter tells us yet more about James when he was a child, and what he liked to do in his free time:

---

[11] The letter is preserved in the Stanhope Collection at the Kent History and Library Centre in Maidstone under the general catalogue number U1590. The reference number for this letter is U1590 C262/1. The letter is dated 16 May 1809, and was thus written and sent after James had returned from Corunna and the battle there on 16 January 1809. Somebody penciled the following words on the paper the letter is wrapped in, "Preserved at Revesby Abbey until February 1918, when it was sent to Chevening at the general dispersion". On the envelope (still in pre-postage stamp dates) it says "Colonel J. Stanhope from his grandmother Grizel Dowager Countess Stanhope, written in 1809, she died in 1811, in her 93rd year".

[12] Cf. John Jamieson, *An Etymological Dictionary of the Scottish Language* (Edinburgh, 1818), pages unnumbered; "strunty" means "short or contracted". Given Grizel's Scottish roots, this is no doubt the explanation for her use of the word, but cf. also John Greaves Nall, *Glossary of East Anglian Dialect, reprinted from the 2nd volume of 'Chapters on the East Anglian Coast',* Norfolk 2006 (first published 1866), p. 188: "strunty" is a version of "stunty", i.e. short or dwarfish.

I forgot to tell you that in packing your poor Aunt's gold tooth pick
case, which she left you, I found along with the precious box, it was
packed into another but you, valise[13]. I found a little clipboard made
by the same hand, and also a little box made at the same time by you,
made of cards, about 2 inches square, the door of card hinge and
fastening of strong thread, covered all over with black wax, and tho'
you often burnt your fingers you would finish it to your taste, and
then made some chopmen of cards coloured red and blue and put into
it. These are most carefully kept by me in remembrance of the
makers, whose ingenuity and handiness I used to admire.

The letter thus gives us the picture of a typical little boy; enjoying
himself hopping, climbing trees and eating the damson plums directly from
the branches. He also seems to have been something of a craftsman, making
little boxes that his grandmother fondly kept over the years.

None of the third Earl's children ever went to school; they had private
tutors at Chevening[14]. One of the documents in the Stanhope manuscript
collection is Lady Hester's mathematics exercise book[15] (see Figure 1.5); it
is safe to assume that James had to do similar exercises to the ones contained
therein. This makes it all the more difficult to understand what Charles
Lewis Meryon, Lady Hester's future physician, says about James[16]. Meryon
has described how one of Lady Hester's servants had only one eye, and adds
the following information:

Hannah had but one eye, and Lady Hester always shewed
commiseration for one-eyed persons: for before this time there had
been in her service Yusef, a boy with one eye, and now there was

---

[13] This sentence is a good example of the above-mentioned anacoluthon of James'
elderly grandmother.

[14] Cf. Cleveland, *Life and Letters*, p. 11: "They [Philip, Charles and James] were
never sent either to school or to college, but brought up with their sisters at home
and taught by their father's secretary". This private secretary and the children's tutor
was Jeremiah Joyce, who was arrested on charges of high treason for "revolutionary
principles" but released without trial in 1794. According to Frank Hamel, *Hester
Lucy Stanhope: A New Light on Her Life and Love Affairs* (London, 1913), p. 20, he
taught the children "in desultory fashion". In 1820, when James was considering
entering Parliament, his fiancée Frederica Murray says in a letter dated 20 January
"It is true no education was more neglected than yours was (perhaps I am speaking
ignorantly)".

[15] U1590 C 231.

[16] Meryon, *Additional Memoirs,* p. 297, note 469.

this cook. I conceived it to arise from a recollection of her brother James's misfortune, who had lost the sight of one eye from an arrow shot by a schoolfellow.

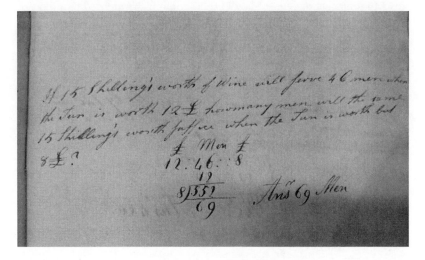

Figure 1.5 – An exercise from Hester's mathematics book

Apart from the fact that James never went to school, there are no references anywhere else to his having lost the sight of an eye. We should not forget that Meryon was over ninety years old when he wrote the Additional Memoirs, and his memory was not what it had once been. He must surely have confused James with another acquaintance, possibly also called James; if James Hamilton Stanhope had lost the vision in one eye it would surely be mentioned in the vast documentation that remains about his life.

Life at Chevening under the tyrannical freedom-lover Earl Charles soon became unbearable for all six children. Lucy was the first to leave; in January 1796, when James was just seven years old, Lucy, not yet sixteen years old herself, eloped with a local apothecary called Thomas Taylor, who had probably been an employee of the Stanhope household. This was the perfect opportunity for the third Earl to put his revolutionary principles into practice; he seems to have done so in the following letter written to a friend shortly after the event (on 25 January), although it could be possible to read the Earl's words as somewhat forced, and even then trying to raise the social standing of the man in question by calling him a surgeon, who despite having studied under the eminent Henry Cline (as did Lady Hester's physician in later years, Charles Lewis Meryon), was not a surgeon. The letter reads as follows[17]:

> My youngest daughter Lucy is soon going to be married to a most worthy man of her own chusing [sic]. Her Mind is liberal, and she despises Rank and Aristocracy as much as I do. I have seen much both here and abroad of the middling classes; and I have observed, by far, more happiness there, as well as virtue, than amongst those Ranks of Men who insolently term themselves their betters. Her Object is Felicity, and I trust that she will find it. She has behaved with the greatest propriety, and with a becoming Confidence due to an affectionate Father. The Person she has chosen is young Thomas Taylor, the surgeon at Sevenoaks.

Lucy's uncle, Prime Minister William Pitt, obtained Taylor a position as Controller-General of the Customs Office and despite his seemingly good intentions, the Earl's relationship with his daughter and son-in-law soon deteriorated, and just as with the rest of his children, dissolved into nothingness. Hester later narrated the affair to her physician Charles Lewis Meryon as follows[18]:

> But there were other events which occurred previous to Lady Hester's quitting home, and which the author must be excused for introducing, in justice to three other daughters[19] of Lord Stanhope who were compelled to leave the paternal roof.
> Mr. Taylor was an apothecary near Chevening, Lord Stanhope's seat, and was in the habit of attending his Lordship's family. Lady Hester told me the history of his marriage with her sister, Lady Lucy, in the following words.
> "Mr. Taylor was a smart-dressed man, and as my father at that time had nothing but dirty democrats around him, he wore a very respectful appearance among them. One day my father said to Lucy 'What do you think of Tom Taylor? I fancy he is in love with you. You know my sentiments on equality: so that, if you like him, don't mind saying so. Observe, the next time he enters the room where you are, if he doesn't blush'. Lucy did observe; and prepared by her father to receive the man favourably, they soon came to an understanding.

---

[17] Quoted in Newman, *Stanhopes*, pp. 188-189.

[18] Meryon, *Additional Memoirs*, p. 225.

[19] A lapsus by Meryon, as there were three daughters altogether, including Hester. The word "other" is a later addition to the manuscript, and if Meryon realized his mistake, was possibly meant to replace "three".

Some time after, when it was already settled that they should be married, Lucy saw him at a distance coming down the park. She put on her bonnet and went to meet him, and walked by the side of his horse down the road. In the course of the day my father sent for Lucy, and said to her 'Where have you been walking?' Out of modesty she did not say with Mr. Taylor, but that she had been taking a walk in the shrubbery with Hester. Lord Stanhope immediately fell into a pretended passion, and as if he had been seeking for some excuse to quarrel with her, cried 'You tell me a lie: you have been walking with Tom Taylor: but you may walk with him and marry him if you like – you must expect nothing from me'. So from that day he pretended to have withdrawn his consent and whenever she was married gave her nothing but her wardrobe".

When they were living in a very straitened way I proposed to Mr. Pitt to give him a place or some employment. Mr. Pitt wrote to me to know of Mr. Taylor's politics were such as he could trust to, and whether his talents could be turned to some purpose. So I rode over secretly to Holiwood, and alighting at the door asked to see Mr. Pitt. I told him as for politics Mr. Taylor had none, and as for skills he had as little. The place in the Custom House was then thought most fit for him.

There is a contemporary caricature cartoon of Lucy's marriage to Thomas (see Figure 1.6), published on 4 March 1796. The title is "Democratic Leveling – Alliance à la Française – The union of the Coronet and Clyster Pipe"[20]. A picture above the people depicted shows that rather than in a church, the marriage took place in the "Shrine of Equality", decorated with the image of a king (judging from the crown on his head) being guillotined; numerous other crowns lie around on the ground. Stanhope is shown as a sans-culotte. Taylor is represented by a mortar and pestle wearing the bonnet-rouge. The ministers are Charles James Fox[21], reading from the "Rights of Man", and Richard Sheridan[22], reading from "Thelwal's Lectures". Lady Hester Stanhope had mistaken memories of the caricature, as related in her conversations to her physician[23]:

[20] The coronet is Lucy, in reference to the coronets at Chevening (which her father had removed), while a "clyster pipe" is an apothecary, cf. Francis Grose, *The 1811 Dictionary of the Vulgar Tongue* (London, 1811), p. 55.
[21] The prominent Whig politician and rival of Stanhope's brother-in-law William Pitt the Younger.
[22] Another Whig, and ally of Fox.
[23] Meryon, *Additional Memoirs*, pp. 225-226.

Figure 1.6 – A cartoon of Lucy Stanhope's wedding

To such a pitch were Lucy and Griselda's minds worked up by my father's democracy, that after Lucy's marriage they were caricatured. Lord Stanhope was represented with his 24 pockets. Out of one appeared a ship to go against wind and water (my father, by the way, had hardly ever crossed the channel). Out of another a label with Liberty, Equality etc. Mr. Taylor figured as an apothecary, with a clyster pipe coming out behind. Lucy was veiled and hoodwinked. I and Griselda were the goddesses of reason and something else, I forget what.

Hester's memory was at fault here as neither she nor Griselda are depicted at all on the cartoon.

Griselda was the next to leave Chevening, also in 1796; she went to live in a cottage at Walmer, which her uncle William Pitt provided for her. In 1800 she married John Tekell, an army officer. Hester herself was the next to leave, in 1800, when James was just twelve. She went to live with her grandmother, Lady Chatham, at Burton Pynsent in Somersetshire (see Figure 1.7). At the age of twelve, all three of James' sisters had left, and his contact and relationship with them would from this time on be no more than sporadic.

A year later, Philip Henry, the Earl's eldest son and heir to the earldom, requested from his father a university education, which was duly refused. With Hester's help, he quite literally escaped from home and registered under a pseudonym as a student at the University of Erlangen in Germany. Once he had left the shores of England Hester wrote to their father to inform him of what had happened. Great help in this adventure was provided by someone referred to as T. J. Jackson[24]; in a letter written to him after Philip's escape, Hester gives her opinion as to her half-brothers, in which interestingly enough she does not even name James, referring to him as just a "second brother"[25]:

---

[24] A possible mistake for the British diplomat Francis James Jackson (1770-1814), who was in Germany at the time.
[25] Letter dated 8 March 1801, quoted in Cleveland, *Life and Letters*, pp. 19-21.

Figure 1.7 – Burton Pynsent, Lady Chatham's house

My great wish is that my darling Charles, his godson, should come in for a share of his riches[26], and therefore it is important he should know their situation. A second brother, without a profession, little application, but the finest mind, the most noble and generous spirit in the world, money would be well bestowed upon. Charles is by nature my favourite, though he has the least ability of the three, but a degree of goodness and open nature which wins every heart.

In 1802, Hester left her grandmother and went on the Grand Tour[27], making the most of the situation of peace with France. When she came back in 1803, her grandmother had died and she could no longer go back to live at Burton Pynsent; she ended up as Prime Minister Pitt's head of household,

---

[26] The riches in question were those of Sir Joseph Banks, who would later play a significant role in James' life.
[27] The Grand Tour was the seventeenth and eighteenth-century custom of a traditional trip round the continent undertaken by young upper-class Europeans of sufficient means and rank.

living at Downing Street and shocking all and sundry but delighting her uncle with her wicked tongue, until Pitt's death in 1806.

James was already in the Navy at the age of thirteen, as is evident from one of Hester's letters, written in February 1802. She writes "I heard today from James's captain (a great friend of mine): he says he never had a boy before in his ship he was so fond of".

Whatever the occasion may have been, James admits that he cried on leaving his brother[28]:

> Wednesday, Portsmouth, 9 March 1803
> My dear Mahon
> Agreeably to your desire I here send an accurate journal of my journey
> Monday
> Wept at your departure and am not ashamed to confess it, dried up my tears and went out to find Lord Bridport .... I sent in to say that Mr J Stanhope was waiting to see his Lordship, with dispatches from Burton and was immediately introduced into the dining room. I having just done dinner; the old Admiral was in an amazing good humour and behaved to me in the most polite manner, as did Lady Bridport. After he had made me drink several glasses of wine, he very politely offered me one of his servants to conduct me about Bath and accordingly on that afternoon showed me the greatest part of Bath.

Later in the year he sailed to Newfoundland, seemingly on the advice or suggestion of his brother:

> Spithead, 9 May 1803
> My dear Mahon,
>
> I coincide most perfectly with your desire of my going out to Newfoundland, once more what you say I always shall like and always obey for I assure you I always take your advice as that of a guardian angel.
> I suppose you have seen the letter from Charles or else I would enclose some parts of its contents. I am sorry to see that he expects to go the West Indies.

---

[28] U1590 C272/1.

He sailed on HMS Isis; the dates are uncertain but by November he was back, and congratulated Mahon on his marriage to Catherine Lucy Smith. In a letter dated 15 November 1803, Hester says "Little James I expect shortly from Newfoundland"[29].

By 1804, James had left the navy and was in the army, as Hester explained in a letter dated 14 January 1804: "I am at this moment alone here [at Walmer Castle] with my little brother James, who has left the Navy for the Army. He is too clever for a sailor – too refined, I mean".

Since Hester had moved in to Downing Street with her uncle, her behaviour (and especially her vicious tongue) had become too much for even her brothers. In a letter to Philip, dated Saturday 12 March 1804[30], James has the following to say about his sister:

My dear Mahon,

I this morning received your kind letter, the contents of which have equally consoled and instructed me, but I hope they are instructions that I never have violated nor ever, ever will. I do not in the least confide, rely or trust in H, nor am I the least enthralled, at least so far, but that I can relinquish at any time every appearance of confidence in her actions without the blame of any one sensible man, of any unprejudiced person, or of any man unconnected with her, by her freedom of manners and purse, a freedom which she employs to good purpose, that of retaining a few in chains as long as she can. Among that number I (thank God) am not and I want to know to whom am I indebted for every blessing I now enjoy, to whom I am indebted for the present good character I bear, to whom am I indebted for the delivering one from the worst of vices, the most formidable of all dangers, namely being subverted to her power, and being obliged to follow every mad scheme, shall I answer it? Yes! It is to you, it is to the best, to the most excellent of all brothers, to that person who has of all others most conduced not only to my personal happiness, but to the character and prosperity of the Stanhope family and name.

You may think my dearest brother that is the language of panegeric [i.e. panegyric], that my intention is to make you believe what I do not feel, but I assure, I most solemnly assure you, it is the feelings of a heart sensible of your kindness, grateful for your favour of all

---

[29] Quoted in Newman, *Stanhopes*, p. 195.
[30] U1590 C271/1.

things most desirous of making you sensible of it, and of rendering you happy by every means (alas! they are but few) in my power.

There is no ending to the letter, no signing off, and the next sheet continues with no introduction; it seems to be from the same letter. The paper is different (it is larger) and undated; it names Hester directly instead of referring to her as H. If it does belong to the same letter, it was no doubt written on a different date, as often happened with letters at the time.

The debate of last night was as you must see by the papers opened by Mr Pitt, and was continued in the most animated manner. The whole of the speeches are well given in the papers except Mr Pitt's last speech, a speech of great length (near three hours) and they say one of the best he ever delivered. He was most warmly and meanly attacked in the most personal manner by Mr Sheridan, who was quite drunk, and to whom Mr Pitt spoke something as follows: "I have been attacked most particularly by a lack of eloquence from the RHG, a meteor which has not often shown itself lately in this house, a wandering light which has not ever fixed its residence in any one particular place, but who now has darted its indignant rays upon me, but I hope the house will excuse me if I dare encounter the blaze of its face (so far being as red as that element ….

The rest of this passage is also lost. The letter seems to continue as follows on another page:

Mr. Pitt is going he believes to Walmer Kent Thursday. What a waste of time, however I will make up for it when I get there. Lady C. sends her compliments to you, and the whole of the L, and in the hope that the lure of hearing politicks might tempt you to come to town, she confesses she has been talking about nothing else the whole morning and has seen nobody but great political characters. I have a great deal to tell you, more than the compass of this letter will allow me to do, about a most unpardonable, indecent and impudent thing that Hester has done. I will shortly tell you what about, Lord C's brother upon a trifling question voted for Mr Ad. Hester sent a note to Lord C stating that "she should like to know what his brother meant by voting against her". What must be the feelings of Lord C on hearing such a malicious, gross falsehood, even if true what business had she to mention it, but more of this another day.

Now upon the subject of money, when I go if I have not enough money I will get the quantity from Coutts I want, that is to say if you approve of it. At any rate you may send a one or two pound note. You th[page torn] I am very expensive, I believe best [page torn] that I should ever injure you by it. Stop me when I do. Give my most sincere love to Lady M. and Lucy and believe me most sincerely your affectionate brother, J. H. Stanhope.

P.S. Nash is a great deal better. Forgive the infamous way I have written this in and the great length and stupid contents. JHS.

The P.S. makes us think (the mention of great length, not the stupidity of the content) that even though some of the pages are now missing, it must all be one letter, possibly written on different dates.

James lived with his tutor the Rev. John Stonard for at least part of 1804, as can be shown from a letter written by Stonard to Richard Heber[31], who also became a friend and correspondent of James:

You do not seem to have been yet informed that in addition to young Lowther[32], I have at the request of Mr. Pitt taken James Stanhope, the youngest son of my old friend Lord Stanhope, under my roof. Mr. Pitt has entirely supported him since he quitted his father's.

James became friends with Lowther, and went to stay with him at the family home in Cumberland. In an undated letter (just Friday), James asks Mahon for some spurs as his have broken; we do not have Mahon's reply, but James' reply to his brother's lost letter is telling:

[31] R. H. Cholmondeley, *The Heber Letters* (London, 1950), p. 196.
[32] William Lowther (1787-1872), the second Earl of Lonsdale. Lowther later became a renowned opera lover and formed part of the Prince Regent's (i.e. the future George IV's) group of friends. A French opera dancer, Narcisse Chaspoux, became pregnant by him, and gave birth to Frances (Fanny) Lowther in June 1818. Narcisse clearly meant no more to him than various other women: he also had a daughter called Marie Caroline, the daughter of opera singer Caroline Saintfal from Paris, who was born just a month before Narcisse gave birth, and another daughter by another French dancer at the London Opera, Mademoiselle Noblet, in 1821. In 1841 he had a son by Emilia Cresotti, a singer at the Paris Opera, and no doubt other children in the twenty intervening years, whose names are now forgotten to history. Narcisse Chaspoux also had a son in 1821 by Charles Lewis Meryon, Lady Hester Stanhope's physician and assistant from 1810 until her death in 1837; the son was called Charles Meryon and became a famed engraver in Paris, although he died in an asylum believing that by sacrificing his own life he would save the world.

Cookham, Maidenhead, 5 August

It is with the most unfeigned sorrow that I have heard of your unpleasant circumstances, I cannot indeed express the anguish that I felt at being still obliged to further add to that burthen you can but just bear. I return many thanks for your kind present, which I had not received when my last letter went away. I am sorry to have taken anything from you as it must augment your distress. The journey to Cumberland amounting to £8 or 9, I have accepted of Hester's offer of sending me some money. I shall only wish for a small reinforcement (if you can then conveniently spare it, not otherwise) before my departure from Cumberland back to this place.

PS My finger is better. ... Write to me at Lowther, you need only put Lowther, Cumberland.

This makes it clear that James was still in the south at the beginning of August, but with definite plans to go up to Cumberland. The whole family appeared to be suffering from financial problems after leaving Chevening and the Earl's money; Pitt no doubt provided for their immediate needs, but they were probably unwilling to ask him to finance their personal pleasures too.

James wrote to Mahon from the Lowther residence on 14 September 1804:

I feel my dear brother with the greatest force and see with the greatest solicitude the many snares and vices of the world in which I am soon about to enter, but hope and trust that with you for my polar star I may escape shipwreck and arrive at that end (more to be desired than human happiness), a happy immortality. Now that I have done preaching, for which I hope you will excuse me, I will conclude with most ardent wishes for your welfare ....

Which world full of snares and vices was James referring to? He was about to embark on his career in the army, but it would seem strange to refer to this as full of snares and vices; it is even less likely that he was referring to his stay with Lowther, as this was clearly temporary. It is possible that he was simply referring to leaving his childhood behind (although his time in the Navy can hardly be seen as part of his childhood) and entering adult life, as he was sixteen years old at the time.

Whatever a "normal" childhood at the time may have been for a member of the nobility, James certainly did not enjoy a peaceful one. He was the youngest child of an eccentric father and cold mother who struggled to get on with his sisters; while he was still a child his sisters all left the family house as soon as they could, while his elder brother had to escape from their father. He did not see any of them much again; they were companions of his earliest childhood and they enjoyed occasional adult contact. Later life would show James to be a sensitive, thoughtful and almost delicate character; such a childhood can hardly have been conducive to happiness for him.

In 1805 James temporarily left the army to keep on studying, as his sister Hester explains in a letter dated 3 February[33]: "James has had a commission in the Guards for more than a year; but the Duke of York has given him leave of absence to study with a private tutor".

By 1805 James had started writing verse (a habit he never gave up, but which he never really mastered either), as can be seen from a letter, dated 22 January 1805, sent to his brother Philip from Chertsey Abbey[34]:

> In return to an English letter I send you the same which I hope you will excuse; I feel very happy in your praises for the last little peice [sic] of "poesy" and have endeavoured to the best of my power to comply with your request, though the muses were not propitious last night when I wrote them, I suppose they were at a good supper or something of that kind upon the top of Parnassus. As for Lady Mahon not being able to write verses in return to those that I sent I suppose you mean it was not her pleasure to show any less sublime than Milton, or more elegant than Horace.
>
> ...
>
> I feel very happy in the idea of going abroad and having the opportunity of signalizing myself, and of returning with honour or falling with glory, in short I may say with Horace besides my motto "Pro patria non timidas mori"[35].

---

[33] Quoted in Cleveland, *Life and Letters*, p. 67.

[34] Founded in AD 666, very little of the abbey buildings now remain.

[35] The Latin means "Do not be afraid to die for your country"; James had been learning Latin and classical literature, but the quotation is not entirely accurate. Horace, *Odes* III.XIX includes the line "Codrus pro patria non timidus mori", which means "Codrus, who was not afraid to die for his country". The usual quotation for this sentiment is taken from Horace *Odes* III.II "dulce et decorum esto pro patria mori", perhaps better known from Wilfred Owen's poem about the First World War, which describes the motto as "the old lie". In another letter dated a month later James tells Mahon that he has been reading Latin; he has finished Cicero's essay *De senectute* and is now reading Virgil's *Eclogues*. He was also studying Mathematics and Grammar.

...

My most fervent prayers for the safety of the "to be".

Mahon was going to be a father; James offered to be the godfather to his nephews and nieces and was accepted. By the time James wrote again on 2 February, Mahon had had a boy. This was Philip Henry, who eventually became the fifth Earl.

The relationship between the Prime Minister William Pitt the Younger and his nephews and nieces was always one of love and trust; Hester lived with him after coming back from her Grand Tour until he died in 1806, and Charles and James were regular visitors. William Napier tells a highly amusing story of what happened on one of these visits[36]:

> Mr. Pitt likes practical fun, and used to riot in it with Lady Hester, Charles and James Stanhope, and myself; and one instance is worth noticing. We were resolved to blacken his face with burnt cork, which he most strenuously resisted, but at the beginning of the fray a servant announced that Lords Castlereagh and Liverpool desired to see him on business. 'Let them wait in the other room' was the answer; and the great Minister instantly turned to the battle, catching up a cushion and belabouring us with it in glorious fun. We were, however, too many and strong for him, and after at least ten minutes' fight, got him down and were actually daubing his face, when, with a look of pretended confidence in his prowess, he said 'Stop, this will do; I could easily beat you all, but we must not keep those grandees waiting any longer'. His defeat was, however, palpable, and we were obliged to get a towel and basin of water to wash him clean before he could receive the grandees. Being thus put in order, the basin was hid behind the sofa, and the two lords were ushered in. Then a new phase of Mr. Pitt's manner appeared, to my great surprise and admiration. Lord Liverpool's look and manner are well known – melancholy, bending, nervous. Lord Castlereagh I had known since my childhood, had often been engaged with him in athletic sports, pitching the bone or bar, and looked upon him as what indeed he was, a model of quiet grace and strength combined. What was my surprise to see both him and Lord Liverpool bending like spaniels on approaching the man we had just been maltreating with such

---

[36] William Napier, *Life of General Sir William Napier KCB, edited by H.A. Bruce MP* (London, 1864), Vol. 1, pp. 81-82. The incident is also reported in Cleveland, *Life and Letters*, pp. 62-64, and William Hague, *William Pitt the Younger* (London, 2004) p. 534.

successful insolence of fun! But instantly Mr. Pitt's change of manner and look entirely fixed my attention. His tall, ungainly, bony figure seemed to grow to the ceiling, his head was thrown back, his eyes fixed immovably in one position, as if reading the heavens, and totally regardless of the bending figures near him. For some time they spoke; he made now and then some short observation, and finally, with an abrupt stiff inclination of the body, but without casting his eyes down, dismissed them. Then, turning to us with a laugh, caught up his cushions and renewed our fight.

Lady Hester told her physician that an incident with Mr. Pitt led to the only time she ever argued with her brothers Charles and James[37]:

When Mr. Pitt was going to Bath, previous to his last illness, I told him I insisted on his taking my eider-down quilt with him. 'You will go about', said I, 'much more comfortably; and instead of being too hot one day under a thick counterpane, and the next day shivering under a thin one, you will have an equable warmth, always leaving one blanket with this quilt'. Charles and James were present, and could not help ridiculing the idea of a man's carrying about with him such a bundling, effeminate thing. 'Why', interrupted I, 'it is much more convenient than you all imagine: big as it looks, you may put it into a pocket handkerchief'. 'I can't believe that', cried Charles and James. 'Do you doubt my word?' said I in a passion: 'nobody shall doubt it with impunity', and my face assumed that picture of anger, which you can't deny, Doctor, in me is pretty formidable; so I desired the quilt to be brought. 'Why, my dear Lady Hester', said Mr. Pitt, 'I am sure the boys do not mean to say you tell falsehoods; they suppose you said it would go into a handkerchief merely as a *façon de parler*'.
    Lady Hester, when she told me this story, here interrupted herself – 'And upon my word, Doctor, if you had seen the footman bringing it over his shoulder, himself almost covered up by it, you would have thought indeed that it was only a *façon de parler*'.
    She continued. 'I turned myself to James. Now, sir, take and tie it up directly in this pocket handkerchief. There! Does it, or does it not go into it?'

---

[37] Charles Lewis Meryon, *Memoirs of the Lady Hester Stanhope, as related by herself in conversation with her physician; comprising her opinions and anecdotes of the some of the most remarkable persons of her time, in three volumes* (London, 1845), Vol. II, pp. 80-81.

'This', concluded Lady Hester, 'was the only quarrel I ever had with Charles and James. James often used to look very black, but he never said anything'[38].

Hester's comment on James often looking black hints at a dark side to his personality, which became evident in later episodes in his life, and was at times clearly shown earlier on too.

The Stanhopes' want of money is expressed in relation to Pitt's last illness, when there was no doubt he was dying, in a letter from the Rev. John Stonard to Richard Heber, dated 21 January 1806[39]:

Poor dear Pitt is I am afraid very bad, very bad indeed. They ought to have prevailed on him to resign when they found him not gaining ground at Bath. Anxiety is the most formidable enemy in the world to a gouty constitution. In the event of his decease, I apprehend the Grenvilles and Fox must come in. There does not seem to be anybody to whom the King can turn, but then the one will doubtless not come in without the other. Indeed the aspect of public affairs is extremely discouraging both at home and abroad. There is no conjecturing what is to come to pass. I am extremely grieved for the poor young Stanhopes, who will be left without a protector on Mr. Pitt's death. To Lady Hester in particular it will be a most dreadful blow, instead of being mistress of the Prime Minister's house, she must become dependent on some cool-faced friend or relation for protection. Lord Mahon is dreadfully off at present, but he had some good prospects at a short distance while Mr. Pitt continued in office. Charles I think is the best off of the family. But poor James will have to encounter a sad reverse.

Both Hester and James were with Pitt when he died early in 1806; in fact, the Prime Minister's last words were addressed to James[40]. He made

---

[38] Cf. Carola Oman, *Sir John Moore* (London, 1953), pp. 355-356: "Mr. Pitt was not looking well. He had a cough. His niece was all for bearing him off to Bath before the cold weather set in, and she wanted him to take her eiderdown quilt. James and Charles had hooted at this. They thought it was unmanly, and that the Prime Minister could not arrive at a Bath lodging carrying about such a bundling ridiculous thing. But she had thought that he could; besides it would fold up into her handkerchief".
[39] Quoted in Cholmondeley, *Letters*, pp. 209-210.
[40] Cf. Meryon, *Memoirs*, Vol. III p. 167, where Hester says "I was the last person who saw him except James".

some notes just a few days after Pitt's death, so the following can be taken as an accurate account of what happened[41]:

> I returned to Downing Street from Norman Cross, to which place I had escorted a party of French prisoners, on the night of Lord Nelson's funeral. Mr. Pitt was then on his way from Bath to Putney. I heard of his being very ill, but had not the slightest idea of the fatal event which shortly took place being so near.
>
> Among the accounts that I heard, the circumstance of Mr. Pitt having lost the deep tone and wonderful harmony which characterised his voice both in public and private, and that it had become feeble and tremulous, alarmed me the most. My sister remained entirely at Putney from Mr. Pitt's arrival till the dinner that was given at Downing Street previous to the opening of Parliament. As he was advised to be kept very quiet, and an interview which he had with Lord Hawkesbury was productive of considerable evil, I did not go to Putney till Sunday the 19th, when I went in the carriage with Hester. When we came within three hundred yards of the house, Mr. Rose stopped the carriage. We immediately conceived the most dreadful apprehensions when we perceived him in tears, and his manner exhibiting marks of the most poignant grief. He said "I fear there is danger"; and I believe these were his only words. On arriving at the house we found the melancholy intelligence but too true, and that apprehensions were entertained for his life, owing to a typhus fever which had succeeded his state of debility. On the Sunday he, however, took two eggs beaten up, and on account of their remaining on his stomach considerable hopes were entertained by Sir W. Farquhar. He passed a tolerable night, but on the Monday evening (Jan. 20) grew worse. He passed a bad night, and on the Tuesday morning (Jan. 21) was certainly considerably worse.
>
> During these days a great number of people of all ranks called to inquire after his health. Lord Chatham called on Tuesday morning, but by the advice of Sir Walter and Doctors Baillie and Reynolds (who had been sent for on the Monday) was not allowed to see him. The Dukes of Cambridge and Cumberland, besides Canning, Sturges, Steele, Rose etc. called on the Tuesday. On the Wednesday morning (Jan. 22) his pulse was at times as high as 130. He was very faint, and could not retain any nourishment he took. It was then

---

[41] Quoted in the *Life of Pitt* by the fifth Earl Stanhope (London, 1862), Vol. 4 pp. 378 ff. Cf. Wilson, *William Pitt the Younger*, p. 337.

considered necessary to acquaint Mr. Pitt with his danger, which the Bishop of Lincoln did at about eight on the Wednesday morning. Not being present myself, I cannot decidedly state the particulars of the interview; but I understood that the Bishop offered to administer the Sacrament, which Mr. Pitt declined, alleging his unworthiness of receiving it. The Bishop prayed with Mr. Pitt for some time by his bed side. Mr. Pitt received the intelligence of his own danger with unexampled firmness, and expressed to the Bishop every sentiment worthy of a real Christian. He then stated to the Bishop of Lincoln his last wishes, which I need not repeat, from their having already appeared in the public prints. Mr. Pitt attempted to write himself, but was unable. He then dictated to the Bishop, and afterwards read what the Bishop had written aloud, and signed it in the presence of three witnesses, two of whom were the Bishop and Sir Walter, the other being his own and faithful footman, Parslow.

After this was concluded, Mr. Pitt begged to be left alone, and he remained composed and apparently asleep for two or three hours. Doctors Baillie and Reynolds arrived about three, and gave us as their opinion that Mr. Pitt could not live above twenty-four hours. Our own feelings in losing our only protector, who had reared us with more than parental care, I need not attempt to describe.

From Wednesday morning I did not leave his room except for a few minutes till the time of his death, though I did not allow him to see me, as I felt myself unequal to the dreadful scene of parting with him, and feared (although he was given over) that the exertion on his part might hasten the dreadful event which now appeared inevitable. Hester applied for leave to see him, but was refused. Taking, however, the opportunity of Sir Walter's being at dinner, she went into Mr. Pitt's room. Though even then wandering a little, he immediately recollected her, and with his usual angelic mildness wished her future happiness, and gave her a most solemn blessing and affectionate farewell. On her leaving the room I entered it, and for some time afterwards Mr. Pitt continued to speak of her, and several times repeated 'Dear soul, I know she loves me! Where is Hester? Is Hester gone?' In the evening Sir Walter gave him some champagne, in hopes of keeping up for a time his wasting and almost subdued strength; and as Mr. Pitt seemed to feel pain in swallowing it, owing to the thrush in his throat, Sir Walter said: 'I am sorry, Sir, to give you pain. Do not take it unkind'. Mr. Pitt, with that mildness which adorned his private life, replied: 'I never take anything unkind that is meant for my good'. At three o'clock on Wednesday Colonel

Taylor arrived express from His Majesty at Windsor, and retried with
the melancholy [news] of all hopes having ceased. I remained the
whole of Wednesday night with Mr. Pitt. His mind seemed fixed on
the affairs of the country, and he expressed his thoughts aloud,
though sometimes incoherently. He spoke a good deal concerning a
private letter from Lord Harrowby, and frequently inquired the
direction of the wind; then said, answering himself, 'East; ah!; that
will do; that will bring him quick:' and at other timers seemed to be
in conversation with a messenger, and sometimes cried out 'Hear,
hear!' as if in the House of Commons. During the time he did not
speak he moaned considerably, crying 'O dear! O Lord!' Towards
twelve the rattles came in his throat, and proclaimed approaching
dissolution. Sir Walter, the Bishop, Charles and my sister were lying
down on their beds, overcome with fatigue. At one (Jan. 23) a Mr.
South arrived from town in a chaise, bringing a vial of hartshorn oil,
a spoonful of which he insisted on Mr. Pitt's taking, as he had known
it recover people in the last agonies. Remonstrance as to its certain
inefficacy was useless, and on Sir. W. saying that it could be of no
detriment, we poured a couple of spoonfuls down Mr. Pitt's throat.
It produced no effect but a little convulsive cough. In about half an
hour Mr. South returned to town; at about half past two Mr. Pitt
ceased moaning, and did not speak or make the slightest sound for
some time, as his extremities were then growing chilly. I feared he
was dying; but shortly afterwards, with a much clearer voice than he
spoke in before, and in a tone I never shall forget, he exclaimed 'Oh
my country! How I love my country!'[42] From that time he never
spoke or moved, and at half past four expired without a groan or
struggle. His strength being quite exhausted, his life departed like a
candle burning out.

Mr. Pitt during his illness frequently inquired after Charles and
myself, and during his wanderings often repeated our names, in the
same manner as he did Hester's after her leaving the room. At five I
left Putney for Downing Street in Mr. Pitt's carriage, where with Mr.
Adams we sealed up his books and papers etc. etc. I made these
minutes on the Sunday (January 26) and am therefore certain they
are correct[43].

---

[42] Sometimes quoted as "How I leave my country!". I prefer James' reading, as it
was written down just a few days after Pitt's utterance and by an eyewitness (the
only one), and also because as the less effective *lectio difficilior* it is preferable.
[43] The causes of Pitt's death are best summed up by Glover, *Eyewitness*, p. 251: "It
is probable that Pitt was actually suffering from either a duodenal (peptic) ulcer or

On 26 August 1806 James wrote from on board HMS Kingfisher in Plymouth to his mother; their destination was as yet unclear:

> You may have heard, my dear mother, that the destination of the expedition is changed, and that Sicily (if at all) is not the first object in view. We have a considerable train of battery cannon embarked and everything proper for a siege, a circumstance which I cannot understand and that envolves the whole in the darkest veil of mystery.

The way James signs off seems somewhat distant and formal, even taking into account the social mores of the time. With people he felt closer to he was much more expressive.

> Wherever we go, or whatever becomes of me, you may depend, my dear mother, that my affection and duty to you remains unaltered and unimpaired, and that I shall always think it the purest honour to remain your most dutiful and affectionate son,

In October 1806 Commander William Hepenstall was ordered to take HMS Kingfisher into the eastern Mediterranean, so despite his doubts, James did eventually sail for Sicily, although we learn more about what he did there from the letters written by his brother Charles than from anything he wrote himself. On 29 April 1807 Charles wrote to Hester, telling her of one of James' characteristic acts of kindness (there were many more in his life, he was so generous with his money that people often took advantage of him). The story is as follows:

> You tell me in your last to look after James so I must tell you how modestly he behaves and how much he is liked, he is a great

---

pancreatic disease and had probably contracted typhoid fever in the later stages. It has been stated that Pitt died of acute liver failure brought on by his heavy drinking. However there is much conjecture over Pitt's death and current medical thinking is that the most likely cause was a duodenal ulcer which had so narrowed the outlet of Pitt's stomach that nothing could get through. He would thus have had pain, vomiting and weight loss; this would be caused by stress, alcohol and diet. Since there is no evidence of jaundice, he probably did not die of hepatic (liver) failure or severe chronic liver disease. His liver function may, nonetheless, have been impaired as a result of his drinking. One other possibility exists, that he had acute or chronic relapsing pancreatitis - i.e. inflammation of the pancreas, as a consequence of his alcohol excess".

character at Catania and looked up to by the inhabitants. I heard a thing of him yesterday by accident which gave me so much pleasure as I cannot refrain from mentioning it to you as it shows so good a heart and disposition so different from my other brother[44]. There was a sergeant of the Guards shot by one of the privates at Taormina when James was there, he was a very good man and it is the more distressing as he has left a widow and children. Colonel Anderson was asking a sergeant of the Guards who acts as clerk in the Adjutant General's Office what had become of the poor woman. He said that there had been a subscription among the officers which gave her enough for the present to make her comfortable but that Mr Stanhope had settled £10 a year on her for life, and paid the first year in advance. Now, though I have had a great many letters from him, he never made the slightest remark on his having done anything of the kind, which in my eyes adds greatly to the merit of the action.

In October 1807 James was sent to Gibraltar with the First Guards under Sir John Moore, in order to provide aid for Portugal against the French, but they arrived too late and could have done little against Junot anyway, and so Moore, and James with him, sailed back to England; Moore arrived just in time for dinner at home on 1 January 1808[45].

There is virtually no information about James for the first eleven months of 1808; Newman[46] says that he served in Gibraltar, Sicily and Sweden, but at least the part about Sweden comes from a very short document in the Stanhope collection[47], somewhat ambitiously called a diary, when in fact it consists of a couple of pages of scribbled notes. The folder in the archive says it is a "Journal of Campaign of 1808-9 kept by Col. Hon. J. H. Stanhope". James was not a Colonel in 1809, which shows that the annotation was made much later.

The journal reads "General Moore went to Stockholm on 12th and returned on 29th June" – a reference to his infamous adventures with the mad king Gustavus IV, who effectively kept Moore under lock and key until he would agree to his lunatic idea of invading Russia together; Moore escaped on one of his permitted outdoor walks and returned to the fleet and England[48]. The keeper of the journal sailed to Portugal with the main part of the army in July 1808, and gives the briefest outline of the Corunna

---

[44] I.e. Philip, who later became the fourth Earl Stanhope.
[45] Cf. Oman, *Sir John Moore*, pp. 440-442.
[46] *Stanhopes*, p. 196.
[47] U1590 C 264/1.
[48] Cf. Oman, *Sir John Moore*, pp. 443-487.

campaign and the retreat. We know that James was definitely not on this campaign; he sailed out to Corunna much later (see below) and reached the city in time for the battle and to witness the death of Sir John Moore and see the dead body of his brother.

The "journal" must in fact have been kept by his brother Charles, who was with Moore in Sweden and on the whole Corunna campaign. The last note is the arrival of the troops in Corunna on 11 January. Like Moore, Charles did not survive the battle.

There is a much shorter version of the notes concerning the Corunna campaign[49], consisting of just half a small page. The notes start on 23rd (December 1808) with the words "Ordered to march at night", and end on 6 January 1809 with the arrival of the troops in Lugo. This time whoever wrote the titles on the folders (probably the 5th Earl Stanhope), realized that it must have been James' brother, as the title is "Extracts apparently from the pocket book of the Hon. Charles B. Stanhope at Corunna 1809" (although there is no reason to suppose that these notes were written at Corunna, as if they had been, they would surely have been updated to include the arrival in Corunna).

Sir John Moore wrote to Lady Hester from Lisbon on 16 October 1808; to the left of his signature at the end of the letter he added the words "Do remember me kindly to James". In November Moore reached Salamanca; he had clearly received there a letter from Lady Hester requesting him to accept James as ADC. He answered Lady Hester as follows on 23 November[50]:

I shall be very glad to receive James, if he wishes to come to me as an extra aide-de-camp, though I already have too many, and am obliged, or shall be, to take a young Fitzclarence. But I have a sincere regard for James, and besides, can refuse you nothing, but to follow your advice. He must get the Commander-in-Chief's leave to come to Spain. He may then join me. He will, however, come too late; I shall already be beaten.

Moore's despondency was a constant part of the whole campaign; he felt enmormous frustration at the attitudes of both his own government and that of Spain and thought that he was just wasting his time and effort in Spain. He was mistaken in this letter. James did, however, reach Corunna in time for the battle. We see him next in Portsmouth on 6 December 1808, waiting

---

[49] U1590 C 261.
[50] Quoted in Hamel, *Lady Hester Lucy Stanhope*, p. 59.

to sail to join Moore. This is further proof that the Corunna diary must have
been by Charles and not by James. He wrote as follows to his mother:

> My dear mother,
> Having heard at your house on Thursday last that you were
> coming to London by dinner time next day, I delayed my departure
> till the latest moment I could in hopes of seeing you – I need not tell
> you [how] disappointed and grieved I felt at being obliged to leave
> England without taking leave of you.
> I am going ADC to Sir John Moore, bettering my situation in
> Holland until I find myself settled. My horses are embarked this
> morning and we expect to sail with the first fair wind. I remain, my
> dearest mother, with the greatest affection, though in great haste,
>   Your most affectionate son,

It is clear from all the sources that James did not take part in the retreat
to Corunna, although his brother Charles did[51]. However, James left
England in early December 1808, and only arrived in Corunna on 14 January
1809. It is generally assumed that he sailed directly from Portsmouth to
Corunna, although this would have been an extraordinarily long voyage,
even if the winds were adverse. The direct route was recently questioned in
a book by Gareth Glover[52]:

---

[51] Cf. Cleveland, *Life and Letters,* p. 73: "Charles Stanhope went with him as Aide-
de-Camp, and James joined him soon afterwards in a similar capacity"; Christopher
Hibbert, *Corunna* (London, 1961) p. 191: "Captain Percy came into the room with
Charles Stanhope's brother James who had arrived from England a few days
before"; Haslip, *Lady Hester Stanhope*, p. 68: James had arrived at Corunna "a few
days previously". Glover (ed.), *A Staff Officer in the Peninsula and at Waterloo –
the Letters of the Honourable Lieutenant Colonel James H. Stanhope, 1st Foot
Guards, 1809-15* (Godmanchester, 2007), p. 3, mistakenly says James was on the
retreat: he "clearly arrived in northern Spain in time to take part in the retreat"
(although Glover rectified the numerous mistakes in this booklet in his later
publication *Eyewitness* in 2010), while Kirsten Ellis, *Star of the Morning: The
Extraordinary Life of Lady Hester Stanhope* (London, 2008), p. 81, is ambiguous
but seems to think that James went with Charles: "[Hester's] brothers would be
leaving for Spain too. The hope that they might be near Moore at least gave her
greater confidence that she would see them all safe again".
[52] Glover, *Eyewitness*, p. 13 and 234. He corrects what he mistakenly affirmed in
Staff Officer, p. 3.

We know that James was at Portsmouth on 6 December 1808, and arrived at La Corunna [sic][53] on 14 January 1809, but he does not say how he actually got there. Initially I thought that he had sailed directly to Corunna; however his later journal mentions being at Lamego in 1808 and again at Torre de Moncorvo in 1809. Given that James was only in Portugal during the short period of Moore's retreat in 1808/9 these facts can only make sense if James landed at Oporto and rode across country towards Zamora in pursuit of Moore's army, and these places were on the direct route from there. Having heard of the retreat he must have ridden through the mountains and joined the army at Corunna from some port on the coast such as Vigo where the fleet of transports was, as he states that he 'landed' at Corunna the day before the battle.

Glover contradicts himself by saying that James arrived in Corunna on 14 January, and on the day before the battle (i.e. 15 January). Other sources (see footnote 47) state that he arrived "a few days before" or "a few days previously".

Glover is also mistaken in saying that James was only in Portugal in 1808/1809, as his own diary (as edited by Glover) states otherwise[54]. It is true, however, that later on in his diary (the entry for 26 February 1813), James says that he had been billeted in Lamego in 1808:

When I entered the convent yard I was astonished at seeing so many people assembled in gay habits, as in celebration of some festival. Presently three young ladies passed whom I thought I recollected and on addressing found I was right as they were the daughters of Senhor Mota, a physician at Lamego at whose house I had been billeted at the end of 1808[55].

---

[53] The historical name in English is Corunna, with no article. In Spanish today, the name is La Coruña, and in Galician A Coruña (Galicia is a bilingual region, where both Galician and Spanish are official). According to a law issued as recently as the 1990s, the name should always be A Coruña, no matter which language is used, although there is firm resistance to this, and the Royal Academy of the Spanish Language states that the name in Spanish is La Coruña, regardless of the fact that it is officially A Coruña (the official name is understood as reserved for official administrative use, but not for linguistic purposes). Politics should not influence linguistics.

[54] Chapter 5 of *Eyewitness* is actually entitled *A Visit to Portugal*.

[55] The story of the three sisters is rather surprising, as James tells in his diary: "On asking them the excuse of the fete, they said it was in honour of some ladies who were going to take the veil. I said I was very glad to be in time to see the ceremony,

If the date is correct (the manuscript reading is correct) then Glover must be right as there was no other occasion "at the end of 1808" when James could have been there. His use of the word "billeted" could suggest that he was travelling with a group of soldiers of a certain size; it would have been strange to employ this term if he was travelling alone.

Another point in favour of Glover's theory is that when James sailed from Portsmouth (shortly after 6 December), the retreat had not even begun; Moore was still in Salamanca with no clear plan and so there would have been no reason at all to land the troops (assuming James was not the only soldier on board) at Corunna, but rather in Portugal.

The matter is actually confirmed by a letter dated 2 February 1809 from James to Lord Lonsdale when he was safely back at Montagu Square in Londond[56], which says

> I should not have neglected any promise of writing to your Lordship, but having failed in my attempt to join the army on their march (altho' for the space of above three weeks travelled more than 600 miles in pursuit of them) I had no means of communicating with England till the 14th, two days only before the action, and then I conceived my information could not be interesting.

While James was travelling from Portsmouth and then from Portugal to Corunna in search of the army, Moore and his troops, with Charles Stanhope among them, were undergoing one of the most arduous episodes in the whole Peninsular War.

---

when they burst into tears saying 'We are the victims'. Soon after I had more opportunity of conversing, I asked if it was possible that they would be going to take such an irrevocable step rather against their will and they said yes, that their father was too poor to support them and they had used every means to alter his determination in vain; that out of respect to him, they had determined so to self-devote themselves. I argued in vain that no-one should take a false oath for a father or anyone". He stayed to see the sisters taken inside the convent and never mentions them again. Their tears at such a huge and unwanted sacrifice are perfectly understandable.

[56] Cumbria Archives in Carlisle, DLONS/L/1/2/63. Glover mentions the letter, but ignores this part of it, which clearly confirms his theory.

CHAPTER TWO

CORUNNA

The Battle of Corunna on 16 January 1809 proved to be a decisive day in the life of James Hamilton Stanhope; within the space of a few hours he went from the euphoria of being officially named ADC to the commander in chief, Sir John Moore, in the last general orders issued before the battle started, to just a few hours later seeing the dead body of his brother Charles, shot through the heart as he led an attack on the village of Elviña, the nerve centre of the action, and seeing how his beloved commander in chief expired in his lodgings in the centre of the city after being wounded by a cannon ball on the battlefield.

The whole campaign has remained in the collective memory of Great Britain for over two hundred years now. Even though James did not take part in the retreat to Corunna, he was present in the battle, and his brother Charles was present throughout; a short account of the campaign will help to put the fateful battle on 16 January 1809 into context. The British expeditionary force sent to Portugal in the summer of 1808 to advance into Spain and collaborate with the Spanish armies to evict the French invader was placed under the command of two ageing and semi-retired officers, Sir Harry Burrard and Sir Hew Dalrymple. Sir John Moore (see Figure 2.1) was sent out from England to serve under them – conscious of the slight to his rank and honour but prepared to serve nevertheless. The British won a resounding victory over the French at Vimeiro, but the terms of surrender agreed to by the commanders and known as the Convention of Cintra were much too lenient (the British had to take the French home with all their weapons and plunder). Burrard, Dalrymple and Arthur Wellesley were ordered home for an official enquiry – the latter was exonerated as he had opposed the Convention while the two former commanders were removed from office and never served again. This left Sir John Moore[1] as senior

---

[1] Moore was an excellent soldier and extremely popular with the rank and line. His career had not been favoured by his open and invective scorning of politicians. Ellis, *Star of the Morning*, p. 81, mistakenly says that he had "distinguished himself in the American War of Independence", which was his first ever posting and in which he

Figure 2.1 – Sir John Moore

went completely unnoticed, as was only to be expected. She also says that he "spoke several European languages", which is a huge exaggeration of his schoolboy French. Linguistic ability was a serious problem throughout the Peninsular War, with the English and Spanish often forced to communicate in broken French, the language of their common enemy.

British officer in Portugal, and Lord Castlereagh appointed him as Commander in Chief. The purpose of the mission was stated again in exceedingly general terms, although no details were given as to how Moore and his army were to fulfil it.

Moore divided his army up into four in the advance from Portugal into Spain, trusting in old maps that showed that the artillery could not travel along the most direct routes. Meanwhile, he gradually received news that put the whole expedition into question; Napoleon himself had come into Spain at the head of two hundred thousand troops (compared to the thirty thousand under Moore's command), and all the Spanish armies had been defeated and dispersed one after the other.

On 24 November Moore wrote to Castlereagh[2]. He was beginning to see the reality of his situation – it had taken him much longer than expected to reach even Salamanca, and he had been there for eleven days when he wrote this letter. He has heard about the complete defeat of the Spanish army under Blake and is not in contact with any Spanish generals. The French have advanced to Burgos and for the first time Moore considers the option of withdrawal. If the French advance he will have to return to Portugal and Baird, who had arrived at Corunna with more troops and was advancing to meet him, would have to turn round and go back. His scathing comments about the nature of the inhabitants of the country he was in should not be taken as a national feeling – on other occasions Moore had much worse to say about his own soldiers and government. The Commander in Chief explains how it is better to show things as they are – a clear trait of his personality and one that was never popular among politicians of any nation:

> My Lord,
> I had the honour upon the 17th instant to receive your Lordship's dispatches of the 2nd, conveyed to me by a King's Messenger.
> My letter from Lisbon of the 27th October would apprise your Lordship, that having concluded every arrangement there, I was about to follow the troops then already upon their march into Spain. As I travelled with my own horses, and was necessarily detained by business at different places upon the road, I did not reach Salamanca until the 13th. On the day following the regiments began to arrive, and continued daily to come in by corps in succession. The three divisions of infantry, which marched under Lieut. Gen. Fraser, Major Generals Paget and Beresford, are now all here; together with one brigade of artillery, which with infinite difficulty followed the road

[2] National Archive WO 1/236 ff. 143-150.

by Abrantes and Castle Branco. One brigade of infantry, which left Lisbon last, is still absent. It is employed in the escort of the ordnance, and the other stores which are forwarding for the service of the army.

The troops have performed their march well, in spite of very bad weather and the worst roads I ever saw. Their appearance now is as good and their fitness for service much better than when they left Lisbon. Their conduct upon the march and since their arrival here has been exemplary. All this does them honour and marks strongly the care and attention of the Generals and Officers who conducted the marches, and who are in the immediate command of the troops.

Lieut-General Hope, with the corps which marched from Badajos in the direction of Madrid, will arrive with the head of that division at Arevalo on 25th; where I have ordered it to halt and to close up. The first of the troops under Sir David Baird from Corunna reached Astorga on 13th; and the whole, including the 7th, 10th and 15th dragoons, will be assembled there about the fifth of December; before which time General Hope's corps will also be collected at Arevalo.

If we are not interrupted, the junction of the army will be effected early in the next month. But the French, after beating the army of Estremadura, are advanced to Burgos. Gen. Blake's army in Biscay has been defeated, dispersed, and its officers and soldiers are flying in every direction; and the armies of Castanos and Palafox, on the Ebro and Aragon, are at too great a distance to render me the smallest assistance. Under such circumstances the junction of this army becomes exceedingly precarious, and requires to be conducted with much circumspection. Should the French advance upon us before it is effected, Sir David Baird must retire upon Corunna, and I shall be forced to fall back upon Portugal or to join General Hope and retire upon Madrid.

The information which your Lordship must already be in possession of renders it perhaps less necessary for me to dwell upon the state of affairs in Spain, so different from that which was to be expected from the reports of the officers employed at the headquarters of the different Spanish armies. They seem all of them to have been most miserably deceived; for until lately, and since the arrival of Mr. Stuart and Lord William Bentinck at Madrid, and of Colonel Graham at the Central Army, no just representation seem ever to have been transmitted. Had the real strength and composition of the Spanish armies been known, the defenceless state of the country and the character of the central government, I conceive that Cadiz, not Corunna, would have been chosen for the disembarkation of the troops from England; and Seville or Cordova, not Salamanca, would have been selected for the proper place for the assembling of this army.

The Spanish government do not seem ever to have contemplated the possibility of a second attack, and are certainly quite unprepared to meet that which is now made upon them. Their armies are inferior even in number to the French. That which Blake commanded, including Romana's corps, did not exceed 37,000. A great proportion of these were peasantry. The armies of Castanos and Palafox united do not now exceed 40,000, and are not, I suspect, of a better description; and until lately they were much weaker.

In the provinces no armed force whatever exists, either for immediate protection, or to reinforce the armies. The French cavalry from Burgos, in small detachments, are over-running the province of Leon, raising contributions, to which the inhabitants submit without the least resistance. The enthusiasm, of which we heard so much, nowhere appears; whatever good will there is (and I believe amongst the lower order there is a great deal) is taken no advantage of.

I am at this moment in no communication with any of the Generals commanding the Spanish armies. I am ignorant of their plans, or of those of the government. General Castanos, with whom, after repeated application, I was desired to communicate, for the purpose of combining the operations of the British army, was deprived of his command at the moment I had begun my correspondence with him. The Marquis of Romana, who is appointed his successor, is still at Santander. Whatever weight the Marquis may have, when he assumes the command, General Castanos had very little; the Generals intrigued against him, and Civil Commissaries sent by the Supreme Junta, without any plan of their own, served no other purpose but to excite dissension and to control his actions. In this state of things it is difficult for me to form any plan for myself, beyond the assembling of the army. I shall then be in a state to undertake something; and if the Spaniards, roused by their misfortunes, assemble round us, and become once more enthusiastic and determined, there may still be hopes of repelling the French. It is my wish to lay before your Lordship, for the information of Government, things exactly as they are; it answers no good purpose to represent them otherwise, for it is thus that we must meet them. I feel no

despondency in myself, and nor do I wish to excite any in others, but
our situation is likely soon to become an arduous one.

Reverses must be expected – and though I am confident this army
will always do its duty, yet ultimate success will depend more upon
the Spaniards themselves and their enthusiastic devotion to their
cause than on the efforts of the British; who, without such aid, are
not sufficiently numerous to resist the armies which will be
immediately opposed to them.

Moore and the army were still in Salamanca on 5 December, a crucial
date in the history of the campaign. In the morning, the Commander in Chief
was planning to withdraw into Portugal and take his army home[3]; later in
the day he received news that changed his mind and kept him waiting in
Salamanca to see how events developed[4].

Five days later Moore heard that Madrid had fallen to Napoleon, but
now resolved on a surprise attack on the French communication lines in the
North; subject to the immediate retreat and evacuation of the army if the
French came after him from Madrid (Napoleon was still not aware of
Moore's presence in the country). On advancing from Salamanca, the
British army was made aware of a letter sent to Marshal Soult[5] in the north,

---

[3] He wrote the following words to Castlereagh in the morning (National Archive
WO 1/236 ff. 149-155): "I feel the weight of responsibility fallen to me; I had
nothing but difficulties to choose; whether I have chosen the least, and that which
will be the least disapproved by His Majesty and my country, I cannot determine:
my wish has been to decide right: I reflected well upon the different duties I had to
discharge; and if I have decided wrong, it can only be because I am not gifted with
that judgement which was imputed to me when I was entrusted with this important
command".
[4] In the afternoon he wrote as follows (National Archive WO 1/236 ff. 155-162):
"Since I had the honour to address my dispatch to you this morning, I find
considerable hopes are entertained from the enthusiastic manner in which the people
of Madrid resist the French. I own I cannot derive much hope from the resistance of
one town against forces so formidable, unless the spark catches and the flame
becomes pretty general; and here the people remain as tranquil as if they were in
profound peace".
[5] Jean-de-Dieu Soult, the Duke of Dalmatia (1769-1851). Known to the British
troops as the Duke of Damnation. In 1837 he was invited to the coronation of Queen
Victoria and met Wellington, who apparently crept up behind him, clapped his hands
on Soult's shoulders and exclaimed "Got you, at last!". According to a legend
created by his enemies he planned on setting himself up as king of Portugal under
the name Nicholas; he is still mistakenly referred to as Nicolas Jean de Dieu Soult
as recently as 2010, in Glover, *Eyewitness*, p. 234, footnote 5. Cf. Nicole Gotteri, *Le*

informing him that the British army was on its way back to Portugal; Moore decided to take advantage of the faulty French reconnaissance and launch a surprise attack on Soult in the north[6].

The cavalry won a clear victory over the French advance post at Sahagún, and the first troops were already advancing for the attack on Soult (which would no longer be a surprise, as the survivors from Sahagún had fled back to their commander) when Moore received intelligence that Napoleon was coming after him in person. The orders were withdrawn and new orders issued taking the army on its fateful journey to Corunna.

The events of the retreat were forever engraved in the memory of those who took part in it. Sergeant Hamilton gives a personal description of the retreat and its effects on the army. Here he is describing the events before the army arrived in Lugo[7].

The road was bestrewed by the bodies of men dead and dying. But the agonies of the women were still more dreadful to behold. Of these, by some strange neglect, or by some mistaken sentiment of humanity, an unusually large proportion had been suffered to accompany the army. Some of these unhappy creatures were taken in labour on the road and amid the storms of sleet and snow gave birth to infants, which with their mothers perished as soon as they had seen the light. The wife of Sergeant Thomas, my pay sergeant of Captain Dalziel's company, was among the unfortunate sufferers. Others, in the unconquerable energy of maternal love, would toil on with one or two children on their backs, till on looking round they perceived that the hapless objects of their attachment were frozen to death. But more frightful even than this was the depth of moral degradation to which these wretched followers of the camp were frequently reduced. Nothing could be more appalling to the heart than to hear

---

Maréchal Soult (Paris, 2000), and Peter Hayworth, *Soult, Napoleon's Maligned Marshal* (London, 1990).

[6] Moore was overjoyed at the opportunity offered – he even talks about a battle with Soult in almost comical terms ("If then Marshal Soult is so good as to approach us, we shall be much obliged to him"). Everything that happened from this moment on suggests that the attack would have been entirely successful, and it was within hours of becoming reality when the final orders for the retreat to Corunna were given. Even so, Moore was aware from the start that the only fruits of victory would have been prestige for the British army and that retreat and embarkation would necessarily have been the final outcome.

[7] Sergeant Anthony Hamilton, *Hamilton's Campaign with Moore and Wellington* (Troy, N.Y., 1847), pp. 47-48.

the dreadful curses and imprecations which burst from the vivid lips
of intoxicated and despairing women as they laid them down to die.
I am well aware that the horrors of this retreat have been again and
again described in terms calculated to freeze the blood of such as
read them; but I have no hesitation in saying that the most harrowing
accounts which have yet been laid before the public fall short of the
reality.

Amidst the horrors of the retreat, there was room for a touch of
humanity, as told by Commissary Schaumann[8].

The road now became more terrible than ever. It was so stormy that
we could hardly stand against the wind and snow, and it was horribly
cold. A division which had been unable to continue on its way had
evidently bivouacked here on the previous night and had left
melancholy traces of its sojourn. To the right, at the summit of the
peak, we saw by the wayside, under the shelter of a ledge of rock, an
overturned cart with the mules lying dead beside it. Under the cart
lay a soldier's wife with two babies in her arms, evidently twins,
which could not have been more than a day or two old. She and a
man, who was probably a canteen attendant, lay frozen to death but
the children were still alive. I halted for a moment to contemplate the
wretched group. A blanket was thrown over the bodies and I had the
pleasure of witnessing the rescue of the infants, who were handed
over to a woman who came along in a bullock cart, to whom a few
officers offered a substantial reward for taking care of them. It was a
most harrowing spectacle. The enemy did not need to inquire the way
we had gone; our remains marked out his route. From the eminence
on which I stood I saw our army winding its way along the serpentine
road, and the motionless blotches of red, left and right, upon the
white snow, indicated the bodies of those whom hunger and cold had
accounted for.

Despite the fact that over five thousand people were lost on the retreat,
succumbing to cold, hunger and exhaustion (and occasionally to the
French), the will to survive took extraordinary forms, as shown in a little

---

[8] August Ludolf Friedrich Schaumann, *On the Road with Wellington – The Diary of
a War Commissary* (London, 1999), pp. 122-123.

book containing one of the best-known and best-loved memoirs of the whole Peninsular War[9]:

> Many trivial things which happened during the retreat to Corunna, and which on any other occasion might have entirely passed from my memory, have been, as it were, branded into my remembrance, and I recollect the most trifling incidents which occurred from day to day during that march. I remember, amongst other matters, that we were joined, if I may so term it, by a young recruit, which when such an addition was anything but wished for during the disasters of the hour. One of the men's wives (who was struggling forward in the ranks with us, presenting a ghastly picture of illness, misery and fatigue), being very large in the family way, towards evening stepped from among the crowd and lay herself down amidst the snow, a little out of the main road. Her husband remained with her, and I heard one or two hasty observations amongst our men that they had taken possession of their last resting place. The enemy were, indeed, not far behind at this time, the night was coming down, and their chance seemed in truth but a bad one. To remain behind the column of march in such weather was to perish and we accordingly soon forgot all about them. To my surprise, however, I, some little time afterwards (being then myself in the rear of our party), again saw the woman. She was hurrying, with her husband, after us, an in her arms she carried the babe she had just given birth to. Her husband and herself, between them, managed to carry that infant to the end of the retreat, where we embarked. God tempers the wind, it is said, to the shorn lamb; and many years afterwards I saw that boy, a strong and healthy lad. The woman's name was M'Guire, a sturdy and hardy Irishwoman, and lucky was it for herself and babe that she was so as that night of cold and sleet was in itself sufficient to try the constitution of most females.

The troops eventually came into Corunna on 11 January, only to find that the ships had been held up by storms further down the coast (a coastline appropriately known locally as Death Coast due to the number of ships that were caught in storms there and sank). The British army had time to rest, recover, eat and more importantly, get new weapons (the rain and cold were fatal for the muskets and rifles of the time), all of which gave them a

---

[9] *The Recollections of Rifleman Harris, Edited and Introduced by Christopher Hibbert* (Moreton-in-Marsh, 1970), pp. 84-85.

significant advantage over the French in the battle five days later. At some time between 11 and 14 or 15, James arrived in Corunna (possibly on board the ships, in which case it would have been on 11 January).

On 16 January, while the sick and wounded were embarking, the last general orders were issued:

> The Commander of the Forces directs that Commanding Officers of Regiments will, as soon as possible after they embark, make themselves acquainted with the names of the ships in which the men of their regiments are embarked, both sick and convalescent: and that they will make out the most correct states of their respective corps: that they will state the number of sick present, also those left at different places: and mention at the back of the return where the men returned on command are employed.
>
> His Majesty has been pleased to appoint Lt. Col. Douglas to be Assist. Qr. Mr. General. Appt. to bear date 5th Decr. 1808.
>
> Hon. Capt. James Stanhope, 1st Guards, is appointed extra Aide-de-Camp to the C. of the Forces.

Shortly afterwards the French columns attacked the British position[10]. William Napier's description of the Battle of Corunna remains unsurpassed even today[11].

> When Laborde's division arrived, the French force was not less than twenty thousand men, and the Duke of Dalmatia made no idle evolutions of display, for distributing his lighter guns along the front of his position, he opened a fire from the heavy battery on his left and instantly descended the mountain with three columns, covered by clouds of skirmishers. The British picquets were driven back in disorder and the village of Elvina was carried by the first French column, which then dividing attempted to turn Baird's right by the valley and to break his front at the same time. The second column made against the English centre, and the third attacked Hope's left at the village of Palavia Abaxo[12]. The weight of Soult's guns overmatched the English six-pounders and the shot swept the position to the

---

[10] Ellis, *Star of the Morning*, p. 83, says that "Moore made a last-ditch stand", whereas his intention was never to fight but rather embark the army and get back to England. He only made a stand because the French attacked.

[11] W. F. P. Napier, *History of the War in the Peninsula and in the South of France from the year 1807 to the year 1814* (New York, 1844), pp. 121-123.

[12] I.e. Palavea de Abaixo.

centre; but Sir John Moore observing that, according to his expectations, the enemy did not show any body of infantry beyond that which moving up the valley outflanked Baird's right, ordered General Paget to carry the whole of the reserve to where the detached regiment was posted, and as he had before arranged with him, to turn the left of the French attack and menace the great battery. Meanwhile, he directed Fraser to support Paget, and then throwing back the fourth regiment, which formed the right of Baird's division, he opened a heavy fire upon the flank of the troops penetrating up the valley, while the fiftieth and forty-second regiments met those breaking through Elvina. The ground about that village being intersected by stone walls and hollow roads, a severe scrambling fight ensued, the French were forced back with great loss, and the fiftieth regiment entering the village with them, after a second struggle drove them beyond it. Seeing this, the general ordered up a battalion of the guards to fill the void in the line made by the advance of those regiments, whereupon the forty-second, with the exception of its grenadiers, mistaking his intention, retired, and at that moment the enemy, being reinforced, renewed the fight beyond the village; the officer commanding the fiftieth was wounded and taken prisoner, and Elvina then became the scene of a second struggle, which being observed by the Commander-in-Chief, he addressed a few animating words to the forty-second and caused it to return to the attack. During this time Paget, with the reserve, had descended into the valley, and the line of skirmishers being thus supported, vigorously checked the advance of the enemy's troops in that quarter, while the fourth regiment galled their flank; at the same time the centre and left of the army also became engaged, Sir David Baird was severely wounded, and a furious action ensued along the line, in the valley and on the hills.

Sir John Moore, while earnestly watching the result of the fight about the village of Elvina, was struck on the left breast by a cannon shot; the shock threw him from his horse with violence, but he rose again in a sitting posture, his countenance unchanged, and his steadfast eye still fixed upon the regiments engaged in his front, no sigh betraying a sensation of pain. In a few moments, when he was satisfied that the troops were gaining ground, his countenance brightened and he suffered himself to be taken to the rear. Then was seen the dreadful nature of his hurt. The shoulder was shattered to pieces, the arm was hanging by a piece of skin, the ribs over the heart were broken and bared of flesh, and the muscles of the breast torn into long strips, which were interlaced by their recoil from the dragging of the shot.

Meanwhile the army was rapidly gaining ground. The reserve overthrowing everything in the valley, obliged La Houssaye's dragoons, who had dismounted, to retire, turned the enemy on that side, and even approached the eminence upon which the great battery was posted; on the left, Colonel Nicholls, at the head of some companies of the fourteenth, carried Palavia Abaxo, which General Foy defended but feebly; in the centre, the obstinate dispute for Elviña had terminated in favour of the British, and when the night set in, their line was considerably advanced beyond the original position of the morning, while the French were falling back in confusion. If at this time Fraser's division had been brought into action along with the reserve, the enemy could hardly have escaped a signal overthrow; for the little ammunition Soult had been able to bring up was nearly exhausted, the river Mero with a full tide was behind him, and the difficult communication by the bridge of El Burgo was alone open for a retreat. On the other hand, to continue the action in the dark was to tempt fortune; the French were still the most numerous, and their ground was strong, moreover the disorder they were in offered such a favourable opportunity to get on board the ships that Sir John Hope, upon whom the command of the army had devolved, satisfied with having repulsed the attack, judged it more prudent to pursue the original plan of embarking during the night. This operation was effected without delay, the arrangements being so complete that neither confusion nor difficulty occurred. The picquets, kindling a number of fires, covered the retreat of the columns, and being themselves withdrawn at daybreak were embarked under the protection of General Hill's brigade, which was posted near the ramparts of the town.

When the morning dawned, the French, observing that the British had abandoned their position, pushed forward some battalions to the heights of St Lucia, and about midday succeeded in establishing a battery, which playing upon the shipping in the harbour caused a great deal of disorder among the transports; several masters cut their cables and four vessels went ashore, but the troops being immediately removed by the men of war's boats, the stranded vessels were burnt and the whole fleet at last got out of harbour. General Hill's brigade then embarked from the citadel, while General Beresford, with a rear guard, kept possession of that work until the 18th, when the wounded being all put on board, his troops likewise embarked; the inhabitants faithfully maintained the town against the French and the fleet sailed for England.

Sir John Moore was hit by a cannon ball early in the action and carried from the battle field in a blanket back to his accommodation in the centre of the city[13]. Meanwhile, Charles Stanhope had been shot in front of the church in Elviña (see Figure 2.2). General George Napier wrote the following account of the event, written for the private instruction of his children and published in 1884[14].

As it would have been very improper to have left the field, and being aware that Colonel Anderson, Sir John's oldest and dearest friend, was with him, I attached myself to General Hope, who was now in fact commander-in-chief. During the battle I had seen your uncle Charles charging the enemy at the head of his regiment, the 50th, with

---

[13] The event is reported in numerous books, some of them more accurate than others. Roger Day, *Decline to Glory, A Reassessment of the Life and Times of Lady Hester Stanhope* (Salzburg, 1997), pp. 93-96, spells the name of the battle "Corruna", says that Sir John Moore was hit by a cannon ball that rebounded off the city walls, when both the French artillery and Moore himself on the battle field were about two miles away from the walls (this would have been a fantastic shot, and the rebound even better), that Moore gave James his blood-stained glove to give to his sister (it was General Paul Anderson who took the glove back and gave it to Hester), that Charles Stanhope was killed during the night by a French sniper (he was killed during the battle in daytime), and that James received the wound in his shoulder blade at Corunna (it was actually four and a half years later at San Sebastian). The book is a mixture of half-truths and the writer's own fantasy. Joan Haslip, *Lady Hester Stanhope* (London, 1934), p. 68, adds a dramatic detail that there was "sleet and hail" on the night Sir John Moore died, whereas the weather had been exceptionally good all day and was the following day too; cf. Charles Steevens, *Reminiscences of my Military Life* (Winchester, 1878) p. 76, "At Corunna, one fine winter afternoon, the 16th of January 1809 ....", and Louis-Florimond Fantin des Odoards, *Journal du Général Fantin des Odoards: Étapes d'un officier de la Grande Armée* (Paris, 2008), p. 147, talking about Corunna on 16 January: "Un beau ciel, un soleil brillant, et tout le luxe du printemps naissant complétaient ce magnifique panorama". Ian Bruce, *The Nun of Lebanon* (London, 1951) p. 52, says that James only found out about Charles' death after Sir John Moore had died (Moore died at night, whereas James had encountered his brother's corpse on the battlefield). Finally, Roger Parkinson, in *Moore of Corunna* (Abingdon, 1976), p. 234, says that Moore's last words ("Stanhope, remember me to your sister") were spoken to Charles, not James, but Charles had been dead for some hours when Moore expired.

[14] George Napier, *Passages in the Early Military Life of General Sir George T. Napier* (London, 1884). pp. 71-72.

Figure 2.2 – The church in Elviña, on whose steps Charles Stanhope was killed

his friend and second-in-command Major Stanhope. They had taken
the village of Elvina, and were driven out again three times, for the
enemy, being able to reinforce their attacking troops after every
repulse, at last overpowered the 50th, which was forced to retreat. At
this period Captain Stanhope, a brother of the major, and myself
were riding toward the 50th in order to make some inquiries
respecting our brothers, and I was just at the rear of the regiment,
when I met some soldiers carrying the body of an officer who was
shot through the heart. I jumped from my horse, removed with
trembling hands the handkerchief which was over the face, and
beheld the pale and ghastly countenance of my valued friend,
Charles Stanhope! I had no time to shed a tear to his memory – his
poor brother was approaching; I quickly remounted my horse, and
meeting him said, "Come along, we must instantly return to General
Hope[15]"; at the same time I seized the bridle of his horse, and turned

---

[15] Major-General Sir J. F. Maurice, the editor of the *Diary of Sir John Moore*
(London, 1904, 2 vols.), Vol. 2, p. 392, blames Hope for Charles' death: "Hope,
though a most competent soldier, was not a Moore; and no man taking up a battle

him round before he had time to recognise the bleeding corpse of his gallant brother. As we went along I told him what had happened, and he bore it as every soldier ought, but could not resist the desire of going to take a last look at poor Charles. To this I could not object, but did not accompany him[16].

Captain John Patterson is one of the very few people who mention the burial of Charles[17]:

Soon after nightfall, and when the clash of arms was no longer heard, an internment of the dead took place, and many a poor fellow, who had a few hours before been full of life and strength, was now deposited in his narrow bed. The remains of Major Stanhope were lowered to the grave by his brother officers and comrades, with their sashes. He had worn this day a suit of new uniform, and a pair of bright silver epaulets, in which, with his military cloak around him[18], upon the same hour as his lamented chief, he was consigned to an honourable tomb.

While we were engaged in the performance of this melancholy duty, the Honourable Captain Stanhope of the Guards, aide de camp to Sir John Moore, rode up, directed by the torch light, to the mournful group. It was the first intimation which he received of his

---

command at such a moment could fully realise the thought of the man he succeeded. So Moore's orders were countermanded. Charles Napier was wounded and made prisoner, and Stanhope killed instead of heading a triumphal march through Elvina".
[16] Day, *Decline*, p. 95, confuses fact and fancy to a degree that is difficult to find in a book that claims not to be a novel. After Moore died (which was late in the evening), he says that James stumbled out of the room only to be told that his brother Charles had been shot by a sniper "during the night", which is of course chronologically impossible. Not only that, but James then returned to the battlefield and was wounded by "spent rounds" in the vertebrae and back "that could not be removed for fear of leaving him paralysed". Quite apart from the fact that James' serious wound was a consequence of the attack on San Sebastian over four years after this date, and the fact that nobody was firing at night, a "spent round" by definition cannot lodge anywhere in the body; it might bruise a soldier, but if it enters the body it is not "spent". Newman, *Stanhopes*, p. 197, says that "James was hit by several spent bullets", and says this after recounting the death of Moore, but once again, the battle finished when darkness fell and Moore died afterwards.
[17] *The Adventures of Captain John Patterson* (London, 1837), pp. 115-116.
[18] Patterson deliberately echoes the words of the poem by Charles Wolfe *The Burial of Sir John Moore at Corunna*, "with his martial cloak around him".

brave relation's fate[19]. Dismounting, and overcome with grief, he took a last farewell, and having obtained his ring, together with a lock of hair, he tore himself away from the heartrending scene.

Moore's friend and companion on the battlefield Paul Anderson wrote the following well-known account of his death:

I met the General, in the evening of the 16th, being brought in a blanket and sashes. He knew me immediately, though it was almost dark, squeezed me by the hand and said, "Anderson, don't leave me". He spoke to the surgeons on their examining his wound, but was in such pain he could say little.

After some time, he seemed very anxious to speak to me and at intervals got out as follows, "Anderson, you know that I have always wished to die this way". He then asked, "Are the French beaten?", which he repeated to everyone he knew as they came in.

"I hope the people of England will be satisfied! I hope my country will do me justice! Anderson, you will see my friends as soon as you ca. Tell them everything. Say to my mother" – here his voice quite failed and he was excessively agitated.

"Hope, Hope, I have much to say to him, but cannot get it out. Are Colonel Graham and all my aides-de-camp well? I have made my will and have remembered my servants. Colborne has my will and all my papers".

Major Colborne came into the room. He spoke most kindly to him and then said to me, "Anderson, remember you go to..... and tell him it is my request, and that I expect he will give Major Colborne a Lieutenant Colonelcy. He has long been with me and I know him most worthy of it".

He then asked Major Colborne if the French were beaten. And on being told they were on every point, he said, "It's a great satisfaction for me to know we have beaten the French. Is Paget in the room?"

On my telling him No, he said, "Remember me to him – it's General Paget I mean – he is a fine fellow. I feel myself so strong, I fear I shall be long dying. It is a great uneasiness, it is great pain, everything François says is right. I have the greatest confidence in him". He thanked the surgeons for their trouble. Captains Percy and Stanhope, two of his aides-de-camp, then came into the room. He

---

[19] This contradicts Napier, who describes how James saw Charles' body coming off the battlefield during the day.

spoke kindly to them both and asked Percy if all his aides-de-camp were well. After some interval he said, "Stanhope, remember me to your sister[20]". He pressed my hand close to his body and in a few minutes died without a struggle.

Moore was buried in Corunna in the early morning of 17 January 1809 (his tomb remains in the city to this day – see Figure 2.3 – and is the scene of annual commemorations every year by the local historical association "The Royal Green Jackets").

James Hamilton Stanhope was one of four officers present at the hurried burial (the others were Paul Anderson, John Colborne and Harry Percy). There were others present too; the chaplain who officiated at the burial was

---

[20] The words are confirmed by James Stanhope in a letter to Lord Lonsdale written in February 1809 (Cumbria Archives in Carlisle (DLONS/L/1/2/63): "A few moments before he expired he said, 'Stanhope, remember me to your sister'". The fact that Moore's last words were for Lady Hester, and her own claim later in life that had he returned from Spain they would have been married, gave rise to the legend of their romance. A local legend in Corunna tells how a mysterious tall woman all dressed in white comes at dead of night on 16 January every year to lay a flower on Sir John's tomb. The woman is course, Lady Hester. However, Moore was of course not aware that these would be his last words when he spoke them. Cf. also William Napier, *Life of Charles Napier* (London, 1857), Vol. I, p. 39: "Sir John Moore was not, as generally believed, affianced to Lady Hester; his attachment to her was strong, his admiration great; but the first was only a sentiment of friendship, enhanced by her realtionship to Mr. Pitt, whose personal esteem he enjoyed in a singular degree. Admiration was a necessary concomitant of acquaintance; it was for such a man impossible not to admire the lofty genius of a woman created to command as well as to attract, but love in the passionate sense was not there. General Anderson, his bosom friend, assured the writer of this biography that the only person Sir John Moore thought of marrying was Mr. Fox's niece, Miss Caroline Fox, a lady who has since displayed a power of mind and enduring fortitude in terrible trials that surpass even the creations of fiction. To her, when in Sicily with her father, Sir John Moore did at one time design to offer marriage, but she was then not eighteen, and after a hard struggle he suppressed his passion with a nobility of sentiment few men can attain to. 'She is', he said to General Anderson, 'so young that her judgment may be overpowered; the disparity of age is not at present very apparent, and my high position here, my reputation as a soldier of service, and my intimacy with her father' – he might have added his great comeliness and winning manners – 'may influence her to an irretrievable error for her own future contentment; my present feelings must, therefore, be suppressed, that she may not have to suppress hers hereafter with loss of happiness'".

Figure 2.3 – Sir John Moore's tomb in La Coruña (the upper cenotaph dates from the 1830s

H. J. Symons (Vicar of St. Martin's, Hereford), who over forty years after the event published the following letter[21]:

> My attention has been called by a friend to an article which appeared in N&Q of June 19, 1852, signed BALLIONENSIS, where your correspondent says, "I believe the clergyman who read the service is now living near Hereford and that he will state that the interment took place in the morning of the day after the battle.
>
> I am the clergyman alluded to, who officiated on that memorable occasion. I was chaplain to the brigade of Guards attached to the army under the command of the late Sir John Moore; and it fell to my lot to attend him in his last moments. During the battle he was conveyed from the field by a sergeant of the 42nd and some soldiers of that regiment and of the Guards, and I followed them into the quarters of the general, on the quay at Corunna, where he was laid

---

[21] "The Burial of Sir John Moore", in *Notes and Queries* No. 151 (London, 1852), p. 274.

on a mattress on the floor; and I remained with him till his death, when I was kneeling by his side. After which, it was the subject of deliberation whether his corpse should be conveyed to England, or be buried on the spot; which was not determined before I left the general's quarters. I determined, therefore, not to embark with the troops, but remained on shore till the morning, when, on going to his quarters, I found that his body had been removed during the night to the quarters of Col. Graham, in the citadel, by the officers of his staff, from whence it was borne by them, assisted by myself, to the grave which had been prepared for it, on one of the bastions of the citadel. It now being daylight, the enemy discovered that the troops had been withdrawn and embarked during the night. A fire was opened by them shortly after upon the ships which were still in the harbour. The funeral service was therefore performed without delay, as we were exposed to the fire of the enemy's guns; and after having shed a tear over the remains of the departed general, whose body was wrapt "with his martial cloak around him", there having been no means to provide a coffin, the earth closed upon him and "we left him alone with his glory".

In my research for another book[22], I discovered that the soldier who held the lantern at the burial (mention of which is made in the poem by Charles Wolfe; "by the struggling moonbeam's misty light, and the lantern dimly burning") was Alexander Rollo, a corporal in the Royal Artillery. His holding the lantern is mentioned on his gravestone at Tynemouth Priory (see Figure 2.4).

Lady Hester's physician, Charles Lewis Meryon, identifies a woman who was also apparently present at the burial of Sir John Moore[23]. When talking of James' generous nature, he tells the following story:

In The Times newspaper, Sep. 10 1863, we also read of him as having rendered pecuniary assistance to an aged woman named Barnes, daughter of T. Gore, a baker in Broad Street, who fell into poverty after having had two husbands and sons in the service. The words are "Her distress attracted the notice of the aides-de-camp (of Sir John Moore) the Hon. Colonel Stanhope and the Hon. Major Murray, who were kind friends to her as long as they lived".

---

[22] Mark Guscin, *Las Coruñas del Mundo* (La Coruña, 2019).
[23] Cf. Meryon, *Additional Memoirs*, p. 297, note 481.

Figure 2.4 – The gravestone of Alexander Rollo, who "held the lantern at the burial
of Sir John Moore"

The newspaper cutting is attached to the original manuscript of the
Additional Memoirs, and we read therein that Barnes' first husband was
killed at the Battle of Trafalgar, after which she was taken prisoner in the
Peninsula and on being freed, she married one Bevan, a soldier in the 42nd
regiment. She was wounded on the retreat to Corunna on 5 January 1809,
and her husband was killed in the battle on 16 January, together with the
Commander in Chief Sir John Moore. Barnes was apparently also present
at Moore's burial in the city.

After the battle, James returned to England with the rest of the army,
bearing the sad news of the deaths of Charles and Sir John Moore. It is often
said that the Battle of Corunna was a battle with no clear victory for either
side, or that both sides achieved what they were looking for; the English to
get back home and the French to see them out of the country. The name of
La Corogne is inscribed on the Arc de Triomphe as a French victory, but

this must be seen as political propaganda and no more. A quick survey of the sources shows us that all the memoirs and diaries written by the British who were in the battle claim victory, although this in itself proves little and to an extent is only to be expected. The matter is clinched by the fact that not one sole French account of the battle claims victory; rather the opposite.

In the early morning of 17 January, Marshal Soult, the Commanding Officer of the French army (Napoleon had given up the hunt in Astorga and gone back to France under a weak pretext, annoyed that Moore had escaped him) wrote to Marshal Ney, saying that the battle had been intense but it had never been his intention to fight one; he just wanted the enemy to show his teeth and says that a greater action would be required to meet his purpose[24]; there is absolutely no claim of victory until a few days later when he realized that the English army had slipped through his fingers, and even so this is an outrageous claim after he had been tricked for the second time in a week (the first was in Lugo) by the simple ruse of lit camp fires and a few men running round making lots of noise to make the French think the whole army was still there.

None of the Frenchmen who wrote about the battle in their memoirs claim a victory for their country. To mention just a few, Pierre le Noble admits that they had not been able to either dislodge the English from their position or to impede the embarkation[25]; General Fantin des Odoards specifically attributes the victory to the English by accusing Soult of launching a half-hearted attack and claiming that the French could have won

---

[24] Jean de Dieu Soult, *Mémoires du Maréchal Soult, Espagne & Portugal, texte établi et présenté par Louis et Antoinette de Saint-Pierre* (Paris, 1955), p. 54: "L'affaire a été chaude, quoique je n'aie eu que le projet de faire una reconnaissance forcée pour le contraindre à montrer toutes ses forces; le résultat m'a persuadé qu'il faudrait en venir à une affaire plus sérieuse pour l'obliger à se rembarquer entièrement ou même à se renfermer dans la Corogne". Soult was a noble enemy; when the city surrendered to him a few days later, one of the first things he did was engrave an inscription on a rock in honour of Moore, with the following words: HIC CECIDIT JOHANNES MOORE, DUX EXERCITUS, IN PUGNA JANUARII XVI 1809 CONTRA GALLOS A DUCE DALMATIAE DUCTOS. The inscription was lost long ago, but a replica now stands on what was the battlefield and is now the University campus.
[25] Pierre le Noble, *Mémoires sur les Opérations Militaires des Français en Galice, en Portugal et dans la Vallée du Tage en 1809* (Paris, 1821), p. 43: "Si le combat eut commencé plus tôt, et si le terrain eut permis à la cavalerie de charger, c'en était fait de cette armée anglaise. L'espoir de s'embarquer en combattant encore quelques instants pour attendre la fin du jour, dut exciter les Anglais à un effort pour conserver leur dernière position".

a great victory (i.e. they did not)[26]. Lieutenant Albert Jean Michel de Rocca clearly attributes the day to the British[27] and General Béochet de Léocour also blames Soult for letting the English get away and never even mentions the Battle of Corunna (presumably because he had nothing good to say about it)[28].

The victory remained in the collective memory of the British for many years, to such an extent that various towns and other features (lakes, mountains, forests and second world war airfields) were named Corunna by the governors of the colonies, many of whom had fought at the battle[29]. There are Corunnas in the United States[30], Canada, Australia, and a street and bay (now reclaimed) in the city of Napier in New Zealand.

It is possible, although not likely, that while in Corunna James met Michael Bruce, who would very soon play a major role in the life of his sister Hester and cause such pain to James. Bruce was born in India in 1790 and educated at Eton and St. John's College, Cambridge. For some unknown reason he left home for Spain in 1808 and got tied up with the British army under Sir John Moore, and was part of the retreat to Corunna[31].

---

[26] Fantin des Odoards, *Journal*, p. 147: "Il paraît qu'au lieu d'une attaque générale, le Maréchal Soult n'en a ordonné que de partielles. Je me permets de croire qu'il a été beaucoup trop circonspect, et que s'il avait lancé à la fois toute son infanterie, moins une réserve, il eût obtenu un éclatant succès".

[27] Albert Jean Michel de Rocca, *Mémoires sur la Guerre des Français en Espagne* (Paris, 1814), p. 75: "Le 16, les Anglais furent forcés de livrer bataille devant La Corogne, avant de se rembarquer; l'affaire fut sanglante et vivement contestée. Les Français gagnèrent d'abord du terrain, mais les Anglais reprirent vers la fin de la journée la forte position dans laquelle ils s'étaient placés pour couvrir l'ancrage de leur flotte, et ils s'embarquèrent la nuit du 16 au 17".

[28] Général Béochet de Léocour, *Souvenirs* (Paris, 1999), pp. 317-319.

[29] Cf. Guscin, *Las Coruñas del Mundo*. Special mention should be made of Corunna, Ontario (founded in the 1830s, although some sources say it was in 1823); the central streets are all named after officers who fought at Corunna (Graham, Murray, Baird, Paget, Hill, Beckwith, Bentinck, Colborne and Fane). Right next to Corunna was Moore Township (named in honour of Sir John Moore); both are now in the municipality of Saint Clair Township. The town's museum is called Moore Museum and the main school Sir John Moore School (there is also a Sir John Moore Church of England Primary School in Appleby Magna in Derbyshire, England, although the name in this case comes from a different Sir John Moore, who had been Mayor of London in the seventeenth century).

[30] The largest of which (Corunna, Michigan) was, curiously enough, not named after the battle, but rather because it was founded by a sheep farmer whose last port of call in Europe had been Corunna.

[31] Cf. Ellis, *Star of the Morning*, p. 99: "He [i.e. Bruce] then retreated alongside Moore's army to Corunna, an experience that made him deeply bitter. He held

He was not a soldier, but was in the city when the battle was fought on 16 January 1809. He did not embark with the troops to sail back home, but with the city of Corunna in French hands after the British left he somehow contrived to find his way to Lisbon, and from there to Andalusia and Gibraltar, where in 1810 he would join Lady Hester's group[32]. There is nothing about him in any of the military sources, and it is highly unlikely, given the chaotic state of events in Corunna and the battle and its aftermath, that James and he met; even if they did, they would not have had anything in common at the time. Yet it was not to be the last time they unwittingly coincided in a foreign city.

The campaign of Corunna was a success within the context of the disaster of the expedition as a whole (which in the end accomplished nothing more than gaining some time for the Spaniards, who did not and indeed could not take advantage of it), as the army was saved from the jaws of disaster, and within a few months most of the soldiers were back in the Peninsula under the command of Arthur Wellesley. For James Stanhope, however, Corunna and 16 January 1809 would remain forever etched into his memory as one of the most painful and excruciating days of his life[33]. Within just a few hours, he lost his beloved elder brother[34], his esteemed commander in chief, and with him, his position as aide-de-camp.

Wellesley – soon to be the Duke of Wellington – personally responsible. Three days before Moore and Charles Stanhope were killed, Bruce had still been at Corunna. Was he present at the battle, or had he managed to avoid it? Had he also met Hester's brothers? Neither he nor James ever mention this detail; it is safe to assume he stayed out of danger's way".

[32] For the story of Bruce and Hester (and his story without her), see Bruce, *The Nun of Lebanon*, and Ian Bruce, *Lavallette Bruce* (London, 1953).

[33] Cf. Haslip, *Lady Hester Stanhope*, p. 71: "… his grief over his brother's death had brought about an underlying melancholy streak in his nature", and George Charles Moore Smith, *The Life of John Colborne, Field-Marshal Lord Seaton* (London, 1903), p. 113, quoting George Napier: "… poor James Stanhope, completely struck down and overwhelmed by the double loss of his brother and his friend". Newman, *Stanhopes*, p. 197, claims that at Corunna James was wounded by several spent bullets, which is recorded nowhere else. Newman also says that James brought back with him Charles' sash and other items from his dead brother's body; these items are still kept at Chevening, which although not open to the public, I saw thanks to the kindness of the Stanhope Trust and its Chairman Colonel Alastair Mathewson.

[34] Hester had a plaque placed in Westminster Abbey in honour of Charles; it can still be seen there, although it is not with the large Stanhope family monument, but rather hanging on a wall. The text reads as follows: "To the memory of the Hon. Charles Banks Stanhope, second son of Charles Earl Stanhope, and nephew of the Right Hon. William Pitt, Major of the 50th Regt. of Foot, who in the act of gallantry, encouraging his men, fell by a musket shot in the Battle of Corunna; this tablet is

Later on 1809, after the death of her brother and her good friend Sir John Moore, Lady Hester retreated into Wales and rented a farmhouse called Glen Irfon. Her intention, according to a letter she wrote on 24 April 1809[35], was to visit the Duke and Duchess of Richmond in Ireland, and James was apparently planning on accompanying her. Hester never made it to Ireland; we are not so sure about James, as he wrote to his mother from Llanthony Abbey in the Black Mountains on 30 June saying that "we" (i.e. presumably James and Hester) had visited Tintern Abbey, Chapstow Castle, the magnificent scenery of the Rye, Raglan Castle, but that "I" (i.e. just James) intended to visit as much of Wales as possible on his way to Holyhead. At the end of the letter he instructs his mother to write to him in Dublin, under cover of the Duke of Richmond. There are, however, no further letters either to or from James for July and August, so we do not know if he went to Dublin or in the end stayed with Hester in Wales.

Hester stayed at Glen Irfon from May to October[36]. A letter written by Hester on 13 September 1809 from Margam gives a general idea about when James was there:

Upon General Clinton's mission being at an end, James came down to me; he spent some time at Glen Irfon, and since then we have been to Swansea. He has just left me to relieve Lord A. Somerset, and I am again become a wanderer.

Hester's reference to Swansea is backed up by a letter James to his friend Richard Heber from Swansea, dated 27 August 1809[37], showing that he was at Glen Irfon before this. The General Clinton referred to by Lady Hester was presumably Sir Henry Clinton (1771-1829), who was present at Corunna. The mission that Hester mentions was no doubt his part in the campaign in favour of Sir John Moore, who had received severe criticism

---

affectionately inscribed by his afflicted sister, who can neither do justice to his virtues, nor sufficiently deplore his loss. Born 3rd June 1785, died 16th January 1809".

[35] Quoted in Cleveland, *Life and Letters*, pp. 86-88.

[36] Cf. Hartwig A. Vogelsberger, *The Unearthly Quest – Lady Hester Stanhope's Legacy* (Salzburg, 1987), p. 56.

[37] Cholmondeley, *Letters*, p. 225. The letter contains James' comments on the Talavera campaign in Spain (27 and 28 July 1809), a costly victory, and Walcheren in Holland, which also started in July, and was a pointless campaign and defeat.

for the retreat to Corunna[38]; Clinton wrote a book to justify Moore's actions[39].

James went on leave and applied for permission, which was granted, to accompany his sister to Sicily and then return to England with her. Events, however, turned out quite differently.

Numerous books have been written about Lady Hester Stanhope, James' half-sister, and all of these books necessarily mention the beginning of her journey in 1810, after which she would never return to England. James was with her on the first stage of the journey, from Portsmouth to Gibraltar, where he left her to rejoin his regiment. Just as Hester did not know she would never return to England[40], neither James nor Hester realized at the time that it would be the last time they would ever see each other.

The party had to wait two weeks for good sailing weather in Portsmouth; James wrote as follows to Richard Heber on 30 January:

I have been boxed up with my sister here in a damp, cold house under the accumulated grievances of cold, disappointment and the Lords Commissioners of the Admiralty. The misconduct of the latter has become more irksome as all our injuries have been accompanied with the highest assurances of regard.

---

[38] In a letter dated 1812 (Cholmondeley, *Letters*, 247-252), James had just been part of the retreat from Burgos under Wellington and has the following to say about Moore: "But allow me to look back to former events and touch on a string you know vibrates more strongly than any other in my heart – I mean the much censured retreat of Sir John Moore. Though I regret the events and much more the innate cause of them, I cannot but feel a satisfaction in perceiving that such things may occur under the command of the greatest general of his day, the favourite of fortune and the unlibelled commander of a large army who besides has the advantage that no perfidious government opposes and no visionary minister clogs him with his aid" (i.e. Sir John Moore did not enjoy these advantages which Wellington did).

[39] *A few remarks explanatory of the motives which guided the operations of the British army during the late short campaign in Spain* (London, 1809). Cf. Brian L. Kieran, *Corunna 1809: Sir John Moore's Battle to Victory and Successful Evacuation* (Milton Keynes, 2011), p. 60: "General Clinton upon his return to England was the first to defend Moore's proceedings, which had prevented Napoleon's total domination of the Peninsula". Haslip, on the other hand (*Lady Hester Stanhope*, p. 74), says that "James had gone on a mission abroad with General Clinton", but provides no further details.

[40] Cf. Cleveland, *Life and Letters*, p. 93: "I do not for a moment believe that she contemplated leaving England for good and all", and Newman, *Stanhopes*, p. 210: "Although, as a precaution, she made her will before departing, the terms of the will made it clear that she had every intention of returning".

They finally sailed on 10 February[41]. They reached Gibraltar almost a
month later, on 9 March. Lady Hester's physician describes the journey
from Portsmouth to Gibraltar as follows[42]:

On the 10th of February, 1810, we embarked at Portsmouth, on board
the Jason frigate, commanded by the Hon. James King, having under
convoy a fleet of transports and merchant vessels bound for
Gibraltar. Our voyage was an alternation of calms and gales. We
were seven days in reaching the Land's End; then, having passed
Cape Finisterre and Cape St. Vincent, we were overtaken, on the 6th
of March, by a violent gale of wind, which dispersed the convoy, and
drove us so far to leeward that we found ourselves on the shoals of
Trafalgar.

It was for some hours uncertain whether we should not have to
encounter the horrors of shipwreck, on that very shore where so
many brave sailors perished after the battle which derives its name
from these shoals: but, on the following morning, by dint of beating
to windward, under a pressure of sail, in a most tremendous sea, we
weathered the land, and gained the Straits of Gibraltar, through
which we ran.

We anchored in the Bay of Tetuan, at the back of the promontory
of Ceuta, facing Gibraltar, on the African coast. Mount Atlas, the
scene of so many of the fables of antiquity, was visible from this
point; but its form was far from corresponding with the shape
pictured by my imagination, presenting rather the appearance of a
chain of mountains than of one single mount.

The wind abated the next day, when we weighed anchor, and
entered the Bay of Gibraltar. As we approached the rock, we were
struck with the grandeur and singularity of its appearance. Lady
Hester and her brother were received at the Convent, the residence
of the lieutenant-governor, Lieut. Gen. Campbell. Mr. Sutton and
myself had apartments assigned to us in a house adjoining the
Convent, where we occasionally partook of the hospitality of
Colonel M'Coomb, of the Corsican Rangers, although we dined and
lived principally at the Governor's palace.

---

[41] Although cf. James' letter to Richard Heber (Cholmondeley, *Letters*, p. 232),
dated 17 March, from Gibraltar: "We were detained at Portsmouth some days after
I wrote last to you and finally weighed the 14th ulto".
[42] Charles Lewis Meryon, *The Travels of Lady Hester Stanhope, forming the
completion of her Memoirs, narrated by her physician* (3 vols. London, 1846), Vol.
1 pp. 2-4.

I visited the fortifications in company with the Lieutenant-Governor and Captain Stanhope. As I had never before sailed to a latitude so southern as Gibraltar, I was much struck with the difference of temperature into which we were now transported. There were flowers in bloom, shrubs in leaf, and other appearances of an early spring; and I hastened, the morning after our arrival, to enjoy the luxury of bathing in the sea. These feelings of pleasure at the change of climate were, however, greatly abated by the attacks to which we were daily and nightly exposed from the musquitoes, which entirely destroyed our rest.

How impartial has Nature been in all her dealings! Go where you will, if you sum up the amount of good and evil, every country will be found to have about an equal portion of both; and, in many cases, where Providence has seemed to be more beneficent than was equitable, a little fly will strike the balance.

The French, about this time, had overrun almost the whole of Spain, and parties of their cavalry had approached within three miles of the fortifications of Gibraltar. Our excursions, therefore, beyond the isthmus were exceedingly limited, and the only neighbouring places I saw were St. Roque and Algeziras. Numbers of Spanish fugitives flocked in every day. Those who bore arms were sent to Cadiz, and the rest remained in security at Ceuta, a possession of the Spanish on the African side of the Straits, ceded about this time to the English.

The Marquis of Sligo and Mr. Bruce, both of whom afterwards joined Lady Hester's party, were also at Gibraltar. These gentlemen, with several other Englishmen and many Spanish noblemen and officers, who, with their families, had taken refuge here, constituted the society at the Lieutenant-Governor's house.

Gibraltar seemed to me to be a place where no one would live but from necessity. Provisions and the necessaries of life of all kinds were exceedingly dear. The meat was poor and lean; vegetables were scarce; and servants, from the plenty of bad wine, were always drunk. Out-door amusements on a rock, where half the accessible places are to be reached by steps only, or where a start of a horse would plunge his rider over a precipice, must be, of course, but few; although, to horsemen, the neutral ground, which is an isthmus of sand joining the rock to Spain, affords an agreeable level for equestrian exercise.

Soon after our arrival at Gibraltar, Captain Stanhope, Lady Hester's brother, received an order to join his regiment, the 1st Foot

Guards, at Cadiz; and Mr. Sutton departed for Minorca, whither his affairs led him. Her ladyship, for whom a garrison town had no charms, was anxious to pursue her voyage.

This account was written some thirty years after the trip, which does not mean it is inaccurate in any way, although the physician's letters from 1810 are in contrast contemporary and show his innocent wonder at being accepted by people such as Hester and James. On 12 March Meryon wrote to his sister Sarah[43], still in amazement at the treatment he was receiving from a noblewoman:

> After a tedious voyage of nearly a month, and the pleasing alternations of calms and gales, we arrived at this place on Friday last. I ought not, however, to call a voyage tedious in which I experienced all the civilities that can make the sea, or any other place, comfortable. I find my situation not merely such as satisfies, but one that gratifies me. For instead of encountering all those haughty condescensions, which are always reminding us of our inferiority whilst they profess to overlook it, and which we feel so sensibly when coming from persons to whom we are superior in everything except in wealth, I find civility that sets me at my ease and a treatment that never humiliates me. Yet with Lady Hester and her brother I could brook a conduct almost the reverse of what they show me; for there is in both such an air of nobility, such a highly cultivated mind, which I am convinced that nothing but high birth and the first society, and that, too, from one's infancy, could give, that on every occasion I am obliged to confess a superiority which they never seem inclined to lay a stress on.

English society has always been divided by class, much more than other Europeans could ever imagine unless they experience it at first hand. The situation was even more evident in the early nineteenth century, and Meryon's surprise at a mere doctor of medicine being accepted so openly by someone of the stature of Lady Hester Stanhope is perfectly understandable for the times. The letter also shows his own pride, most probably in his academic achievements, when he tells his sister that he is superior to the nobility in everything but money.

---

[43] This letter, along with numerous others, is held at the Wellcome Medical Library in London.

In Gibraltar Lady Hester and James lodged at the convent, Meryon in a nearby apartment. From here the Doctor once again wrote to his sister:

Here, then, we are, receiving all the civilities that the chief people of the place can show us, and in most respects so comfortable that I do not regret at all the necessity we were under of disembarking. But Lady Hester, for whom, of course, the splendour of a Governor's table has no new charms, how many soever it may have for me, is anxious to pursue her voyage, and to be freed from the ceremonious attention of the people here, who bore her with civilities, which in her state of health are rather injurious than beneficial. She is, on the whole, much better than when we left England. She rises at about midday, breakfasts in her chamber, and at one or two makes her appearance. At this time I converse with her on her health, if occasion require, or walk with her for half an hour in the convent garden. I then ride, read, or amuse myself as I please, for the rest of the day until dinner-time, and she never puts the least restraint whatever upon my actions or wishes. In fact, her disposition is the most obliging you can possibly conceive, and the familiar and kind manner in which she treats me has the best effect on persons around me, from all of whom, through her, I experience the politest civilities. At about six we meet at the convent to dinner, and the General's table is, of course, made up of the best company in the place.

Meryon himself saw the ingenuousness of his own words in later life; in the 1860s, when he was checking the texts, over the original letter he wrote "Stuff and Nonsense". He then wrote a very similar letter to his mother, informing her that he had been at the site of Nelson's great victory at Trafalgar and that the weather in March was like England in July. Lady Hester and Captain James Stanhope had him on the "footing of a friend rather than a dependent".

James' own account of the journey opens his military journal[44], which for some reason does not include the Battle of Corunna, and which he himself entitled *Private memoranda and Journal from the beginning of 1810 to the 20th[45] of July when I returned to England.* His text reads as follows (see Figure 2.5):

---

[44] U1590 C264/2.
[45] The date is blurred by a stain in the manuscript.

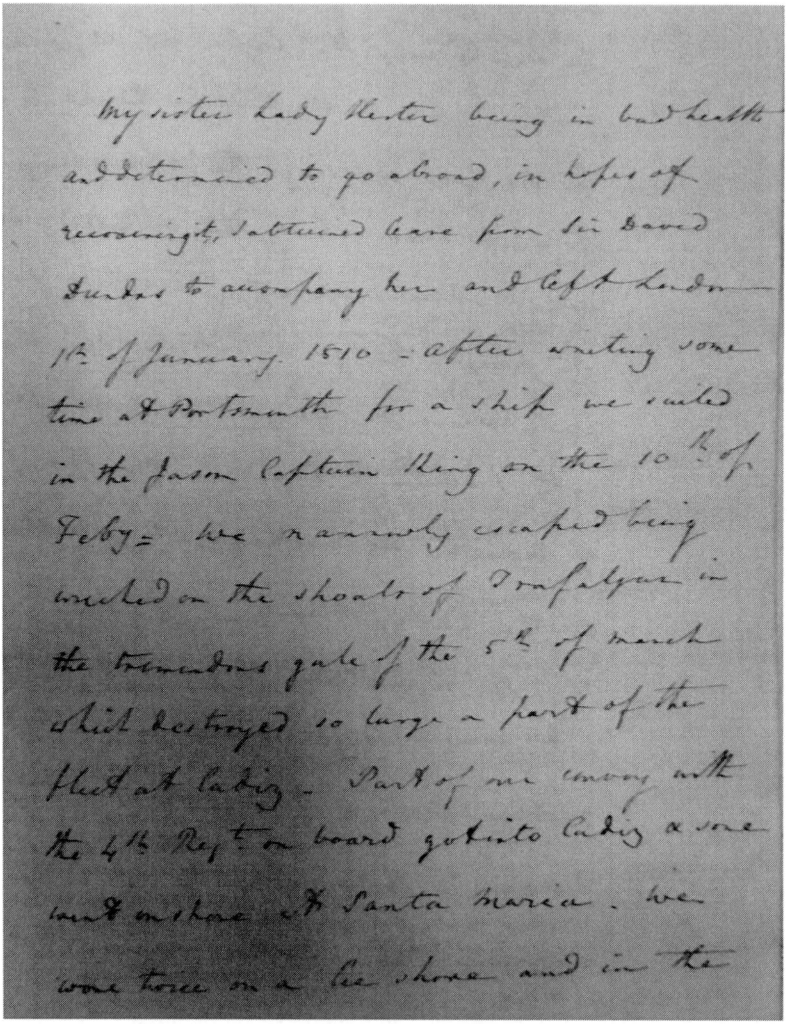

Figure 2.5 – The first page of James Stanhope's diary

My sister Lady Hester being in bad health, and determined to go abroad, in hopes of recovering it, I obtained leave from Sir David Dundas to accompany her and left London 1st January 1810. After waiting some time at Portsmouth for a ship we sailed in the Jason Captain King, on the 10th of February. We narrowly escaped being wrecked on the shoals of Trafalgar in the tremendous gale of the 5th March which destroyed so large a part of the fleet at Cadiz. Part of our convoy with the 4th Regiment on board got into Cadiz and some went ashore at Santa Maria. We were twice on a lee shore and in the middle of the night crossed the shoals in weathering the cape in 13 fathom water, hearing distinctly the sound of the breakers and seeing the glimmering of the white foam which they created. We could not bring up at Gibraltar from the fury of the gale but scudded under Ceuta, where on bringing to we drifted with 3 cables a head. On the 9th of March we anchored at Gibraltar. On the 22nd of March I accompanied Captain Heywood of the Navy with the 4th Regiment, who were destined to garrison Ceuta. During the few days I remained there the same jealousy and suspicions of our intentions prevailed as we have so often witnessed since and it required a good deal of tact and conciliation to get our troops admitted into the Citadel.

Despite Meryon's great admiration for both Hester and her brother, James does not even mention the physician in his account of the trip and stay in Gibraltar.

One small and relatively insignificant incident in the lives of both – James' rejoining his regiment from Gibraltar – shows just how confusing it can be to find the exact details of an event, even when there are numerous sources. Each book gives different reasons for his move, and all of them differ in saying when he made the decision.

The Duchess of Cleveland states the matter succinctly[46]: "Soon after, however, the party separated. Captain Stanhope was summoned to join the Guards at Cadiz … and Lady Hester … accepted the offer of a passage in the *Cerberus* frigate to Malta". Frank Hamel is likewise short and to the point[47]: "James Stanhope left for Cadiz to join his regiment, the 1st Foot Guards".

Ian Bruce says that "James Stanhope was recalled to his regiment at Cadiz"[48]. Newman says that James had obtained six months' leave of absence to go with his sister to Sicily, but then rejoined his regiment at Gibraltar (and not Cadiz)[49], while Joan Haslip provides somewhat confusing details: Lady Hester was "to lose her brother's companionship owing to his regiment being called to Cadiz"[50]. Kirsten Ellis mentions the six months'

---

[46] *Life and Letters*, p. 94.
[47] *Hester Lucy Stanhope*, p. 74.
[48] *Nun of Lebanon*, p. 32.
[49] *Stanhopes*, p. 210.
[50] *Lady Hester Stanhope*, p. 81.

leave and James' intention of going to Sicily with his sister, but says that on 2 April he received an "official letter, which he chose to view as a summons"[51], giving the impression that he had changed his mind and no longer wished to continue the journey with Hester, and that the "official letter", whatever its contents were, was the perfect excuse to leave the group.

Roger Day[52] states that James received orders to report to his regiment for active service, and that before leaving he had a "long, man to man conversation" with Michael Bruce and was convinced of his honour, although it should not be forgotten that there is a great amount of embellishment and fantasy in this book. Charles Roundell[53] tells us that "Lady Hester did not long remain in Wales. She could not rest, and as her brother was about to join his regiment in Spain, she determined to accompany him as far as Gibraltar, and possibly to go on to Sicily, which was then under British protection", i.e. the whole trip had been organized by James, who was only travelling in order to rejoin his regiment. She was accompanying James rather than him going with her.

Brett-James[54] says "But on learning in Gibraltar that his Regiment, the 1st Foot Guards, had been posted to Cadiz, he waited only till his sister had left for Malta and the Levant with Michael Bruce, before presenting himself to Graham at an opportune moment – most of the General's staff were ill – and received the appointment of aide-de-camp".

The simplest way to find out exactly what happened is just to read James Stanhope's own diary:

> 2nd of April heard that the battalion of Guards to which I belonged had arrived at Cadiz. I did not hesitate to sacrifice my private feelings and determined to join it, although I had 6 months' leave. On the 7th my sister sailed for Malta. On the 10th embarked on the Undaunted, Captain Maling for Cadiz, fresh wind, anchored at Algeziras[55], returned to Ceuta, got back strapped, as it is termed, when a vessel passes the narrow strait and gets into the Mediterranean, when from the indraft of water and the funnel through which the wind collected rushes with amazing force, ships frequently are detained during long periods of westerly winds.

---

[51] *Star of the Morning*, p. 101.
[52] *Decline to Glory*, p. 105.
[53] *Lady Hester Stanhope* (London, 1910), p. 19.
[54] Antony Brett-James, *General Graham 1748-1844* (New York, 1959), p. 197.
[55] The correct spelling is Algeciras (although the two forms are phonetically identical in Spanish).

It is clear – he had six months' leave and was planning on travelling with Hester, but when he got to Gibraltar he heard (he makes no mention of any letter or summons) that his battalion was in Cadiz and decided to join them. There is a story that James on leaving took Doctor Meryon's saddle, reported by Joan Haslip[56]:

> Brother and sister bade an affectionate farewell to one another, and Dr. Meryon had to pay for his friendship with the great, by parting with a much-prized saddle which he had had the forethought to buy before leaving Portsmouth. James Stanhope had forgotten to procure one in England, and in his casual, airy way he thought nothing of depriving the doctor of his most treasured possession.

The story can be found nowhere in any of the Doctor's writings (the argument that he would have not written about such a humiliation to himself holds no water, as he frequently includes much worse treatment to his person by Hester herself) or in any of James' letters or diaries. It is never easy to decide whether an event mentioned by just one of Lady Hester's numerous biographers actually happened or not[57]; it could be argued that as the story has no direct bearing on Hester herself, other biographers simply omitted it. Haslip mentions no source, which is only to be expected as the book is not scholarly. She has a tendency to exaggerate (e.g. it is doubtful that the supposed saddle would have been Meryon's "most treasured possession") and provide mistaken data; which makes it all the more difficult to believe the story of the "theft" of the saddle.

According to Meryon[58], when they parted, James gave Hester forty English guineas. When Hester's party was shipwrecked (all of them were in grave danger, although in the end the only casualty was Hester's pet dog, which could not be convinced to leave the sinking ship for the lifeboat), the forty guineas were saved, and Lady Hester later sold them to an Albanian soldier (presumably for local currency and presumably at a loss to Hester).

In 1809, James had taken leave of his brother Charles and Sir John Moore; now in 1810, he took leave of his sister Hester and although they exchanged letters for a while, Hester never returned to England and they never met again.

---

[56] *Lady Hester Stanhope* p. 82.
[57] Day, *Decline to Glory*, also includes the (embellished) story, but this book can hardly be counted as a historical source or serious biography.
[58] *Memoirs* Vol. I, p. 160.

CHAPTER THREE

THE REST OF THE PENINSULAR WAR

When Hester and those travelling with her arrived in Malta, Michael Bruce was her lover. Neither of them ever tried to conceal or justify their relationship. James was against it from the start, and consequently from the time when James saw her off in the vessel to Malta and then rejoined his regiment in Spain, and for the few years that Hester's love affair with Michael Bruce was lived openly and unashamedly, Hester's relationship with James was, to put it mildly, volatile. This is perfectly understandable; she loved James and felt extremely protective of her little brother, but at the same time he was deeply prejudiced against Bruce and her relationship with him. Her mood and comments regarding her brother changed from day to day; in a letter to General Oakes in Malta, dated 13 July 1811, she actually compares James to Michael; "As to my brother, he is rather less wild, but he is not all I could wish"[1]. In August the same year, she again wrote to General Oakes about James, "I can never see him again, nor will I allow him to torment me by letter"[2]. In another letter to Oakes dated 2 May 1812, she says "… my brother James, whose natural levity and wild spirits are always to be suppressed"[3], which coming precisely from her, is so ironic it is almost amusing[4]. On another occasion she compared James and Michael from an academic point of view: "I am sure that my brother James at 16 would have got through more in a day than Bruce would in a week". This was written to Bruce's father[5] and shows that Hester's sharp tongue had no limits.

Hester was equally spiteful about her doctor; despite everything he did for her throughout her life, every time he left her or gave his wife priority

---

[1] Quoted in Hamel, *Hester Lucy Stanhope*, p. 103.
[2] Bruce, *Nun of Lebanon*, p. 122.
[3] Bruce, *Nun of Lebanon*, p. 134.
[4] Although cf. Newman, *Stanhopes*, p. 198: "James, quick to take offence at slights, imagined or otherwise, and of high mercurial spirits, was however the only one who had kept on close terms with his father and grandmother after the final breach between them and Mahon".
[5] Bruce, *Nun of Lebanon*, p. 150.

over her, she said the cruellest possible things about him[6]. At other times, however, she was very kind about him[7], especially when he was doing something for her. In other words, Hester was excessive and impulsive in both her praise and her criticism, and usually the same people received both from her at different times in their lives. Her comments about James have to be seen in the same light as those made about Meryon; it all depended on the moment and whether what the person in question had done or was doing was to Hester's liking or not.

This said, James' reaction to Hester's relationship with Bruce does seem somewhat excessive, even if he already held the religious beliefs he lived by later on. Even assuming he was moved by the family honour, his father already enjoyed a deserved reputation for being eccentric and his disdain of what people thought about him, and Hester was now doing the same. London society had long been used to Hester's devilish tongue and scandalous actions in person, and what she now did many miles away from home was most probably of little concern to anyone except gossips; nobody judged the sober fourth Earl or his brother by what she did so far away. Of Lady Hester's biographers, the Duchess of Cleveland ignores James' reaction (which is only to be expected as she could never bring herself to mention her aunt's scandalous love affair anyway), Hamel diplomatically states that "James Stanhope had shown her little sympathy"[8] while Haslip is of the opinion that "there is very little excuse for Major Stanhope's cruel condemnation of his sister's conduct"[9].

As so often happens when someone criticizes others for their relationships, James was at the same time doing something similar; he was enjoying the

---

[6] E.g. in a letter to Lord Hardwicke shortly before she died, and just after Meryon had left her for the last time: "Should you see the Doctor in England recollect that his only good quality in my sight is, I believe, being very honest in money matters. No other do I grant him; without judgment, without heart, he goes through the world like many others, blundering his way, and often, from his want of accuracy, doing mischief every time he opens his mouth". Quoted in Mark Guscin, *A Very Good Sort of Man: A Life of Doctor Charles Lewis Meryon (1783-1977), Physician to Lady Hester Stanhope* (Brighton 2017), p. 192.

[7] E.g. precisely when he was on his way out to see her again, in a letter from 1827: "My kind friend and former physician, Dr Meryon, has blasted his own prospects in life by giving up everything in Europe to join me in this country, without consulting anyone", quoted in Guscin, *Good Sort of Man*, p. 193.

[8] *Hester Lucy Stanhope*, p. 98.

[9] *Lady Hester Stanhope*, p. 102. On p. 202 she states, however, also in reference to James, that "no brother could have been more affectionate and more loyal".

company of a female, as can be seen in a letter he wrote to Richard Heber on 22 April 1810[10]:

After I wrote last, we remained till the 7th when we obtained a passage on board the Cerberus, but finding that my battalion was at Cadiz I was (most unwillingly) obliged to abandon my Mediterranean prospects and witness her sailing alone. I think she is ere this arrived at her journey's end as the same strong western blast that has detained us till this time must have expedited her.

The last fortnight has been passed by me in the society of a most agreeable, well informed and (what is more surprising) a very modest Spanish female who with her brother-in-law General Mendoza are also passengers to Cadiz with my old friend Malling. The wind being foul we have passed from Gibraltar to Algeciras, Tarifa, Ceuta, Tetuan and finally Tangier so you can conceive what with society on board and riding and shooting on shore the time has passed rapidly and pleasingly away.

General Graham in the handsomest manner has appointed me as his extra ADC. He could not do more as I am still on Sir D. D's staff. Fine work here. The only good news is the occupation of Ceuta by our troops, the 4th Regiment occupies the citadel and as there are no other troops in it with them, I conceive our interests are well secured in that quarter.

In July James was "taken ill of a fever which confined me three weeks to my bed", and soon after, as he narrates in his diary, the Spanish lady he had met earlier left, much to his dismay and sorrow:

My friend Doña Juana leaves Cadiz for Ceuta, and I deeply regretted her absence, for though I have since seen many classes of Spanish society in different parts of Spain, I have never met anyone who surpassed her in the characteristic charms and qualities of the Spanish women, who only require a better education and more regard to bienseance to be the most delightful creatures in the world; for in point of natural unsophisticated talents, of unforced and inoffensive gaiety of heart, of total absence of mean, selfish, envious feelings, for warmth of heart, for elevation and magnanimity of mind, for fortitude under distress, humiliation and danger, for keen feelings of pity and tenderness for others with the most heroic self-

---

[10] Cholmondeley, *Letters*, p. 235.

devotion in their own persons, for the liveliest passions of love and hate, which climate, education and example can give, the Spanish woman is not to be surpassed[11].

While in Cádiz, James attended the proceedings of the Spanish Cortes, and made abundant notes. No doubt his time with Juana had helped him improve his language skills; in a letter to Alexander Murray (the family lawyer) dated 15 August 1810, he says "I find Spanish very easy and can now speak it with fluency". James sometimes wrote in Spanish in his diary[12].

In October he left Cádiz for Lisbon, where Lord Wellington was, behind the newly created and very well known Lines of Torres Vedras. He reached Lisbon on 1 November, and joined General Hill the next day. James was deeply impressed by the defensive lines set up by Wellington: "It is impossible to give an accurate idea of this wonderful line of defence without entering into long military details". He stayed at Wellington's headquarters, but did very little except attend a ball in the palace of Mafra. He was not impressed with Lisbon: "I then returned to Lisbon, the mosaics in the church of St Roque are the things best worth seeing and least seen in this most filthy and stupid town". He was back in Cádiz on 29 November 1810. James had rejoined his regiment in April, visited Portugal and from a military point of view done nothing else in 1810, just like so many thousands of other soldiers in the Peninsula in this year and all the others. Most of their time was spent doing very little, with two, maybe three actions per year. In 1811 and 1812 he saw more action; as this is just one chapter in James' life it is impossible to describe each campaign and battle in detail. I have provided sufficient information to put his own role in context and some interesting anecdotes from his diary; for anyone with an interest, the literature on the Peninsular War is immense, from histories of all six years to detailed analyses of each battle, biographies of the main officers and numerous memoirs written by both officers and men from the rank and file.

At this point in James' diary there is an insert of eight pages, in his own hand, containing a military analysis of the Spanish defences at Cádiz. James

---

[11] As Glover, *Eyewitness*, p. 236, footnote 62, says, "It would seem he was smitten!". Nothing is said about how serious/intimate the relationship was, and it is doubtful that even if it was intimate, it would surely not have reached the same level of notoriety and disdain for what others might think as Hester's relationship with Michael Bruce.

[12] Considering that James had only been in the country a few months his Spanish was excellent, although there are of course some mistakes.

was involved in the Battle of Barrosa[13] in March 1811. This battle was an unsuccessful attempt under General Graham (who politely yielded command to the Spanish, a decision he heartily regretted) to break the French siege of Cádiz; a single British division defeated two French divisions and captured a regimental eagle, but did not follow up on the victory and the positions at the end of the battle remained the same as when they started[14].

The Spanish troops had basically refused to fight. Brett-James describes what happened as follows[15]:

> Incredible as it may seem, less than three miles away they had done nothing to assist their allies. Having drawn up his divisions to defend the bridge at the mouth of the Sancti Petri river, La Peña waited for news. When the five Spanish battalions straggled down off the Cerro del Puerco and told of the French attack, he assumed that Graham must inevitably be defeated if he stopped to fight. When he learned that Graham had in fact turned round and attacked Marshal Victor, he still refused to move to his aid.
>
> …
>
> At no time did La Peña even send a staff officer to discover the situation or to inquire from Graham whether help could be given. Safely ensconced with ten thousand troops in his almost impregnable situation, he inexplicably left his allies to extricate themselves from a most dangerous predicament.

James was extremely critical of the Spanish in his diary after the battle, both the army and the civilians in Cádiz:

> The most important feature of this action is the non-cooperation of the Spaniards, which led to the decision which General Graham

---

[13] Also known as the Battle of Chiclana and the Battle of Cerro del Puerco, especially in Spanish. The names of various battles in the Peninsular War are sometimes different, e.g. the Battle of Corunna is known in Spanish as the Batalla de Elviña (Elviña was the village at the heart of the battlefield). The name of the battle is sometimes spelled Barossa.

[14] This led Marshal Victor and the French to claim victory; strangely enough, in exactly the same situation in Corunna, where at the end of the fighting both armies held the same positions as when they started, although the French attacked the English and were not able to move them, the French also – and mistakenly, as shown above – claimed victory *a posteriori*.

[15] Brett-James, *General Graham*, p. 214.

assumed of withdrawing from any further operations. A Spanish general officer (I believe Cruz) was close by me when the cannonade began and I begged him to go and report to La Peña the situation that we were in; he went but nobody returned, the Spanish general crossed the bridge at Sancti Petri and then enquired of everyone going to the rear the fate of our division. Had the Spaniards moved towards Chiclana (and they were upon the chord) the utter ruin of the French corps was certain, or of General Whittington had chosen to move his cavalry rapidly round their left to have profited by the victory, which our two squadrons of Germans, bravely as they conducted themselves, were not in numbers to effect, much more advantage might have been reaped.

...

General La Peña in his own pamphlet stated that being so near the seat of government, he would have sent to them for ulterior orders. But if the misconduct of the Spanish general was flagrant in the action, tenfold more disgusting was the ingratitude and vanity of the whole population of Cádiz. La Peña was declared by a court of enquiry to have deserved well of his country and received the order of Charles 3rd as a reward for having abandoned his allies and lost the brightest moment which had occurred of striking a severe blow, and the British troops who had toiled and fought, had bled and conquered for them, were assailed with every species of illiberal abuse which jealousy and hatred and consciousness of their own misconduct could produce.

The Spanish Cortes, possibly aware that the popular reaction was unfair to their allies, and not wishing to offend them further, thanked Graham for his victory and offered him the title of Duke and Grandee of Spain. Graham initially accepted, but mistakenly believing that La Peña was also to receive an award, eventually refused, which did little to improve relations with the Spanish.

Other battles were fought in the Peninsula, such as Albuera and Fuentes de Oñoro, both in May 1811, although James was not involved in either. In fact, we know almost nothing of his life in Cádiz until July 1811, when General Graham was called to Portugal to be Wellington's second in command. James, quite naturally, accompanied him; they sailed from Cadiz and anchored in the Tagus on 9 July. Included in the diary is a flyer, announcing the performance of a play on 16 January 1811; James was not in Lisbon on this date and most probably kept this as a souvenir. The English translation of the Portuguese text leaves much to be desired (it is somewhat reminiscent of automatic translation in the twenty-first century) (see Figure 3.1). He also reports in his journal one of the numerous examples of deceit and fraud from the time:

> At the time I arrived the Portuguese government a trick perfectly in character and indeed I hardly ever found people more consistent in all the weak and bad and base of human nature than the gentry and nobility of Portugal. The Prince of Wales had just sent a present of some salt fish to be distributed gratis among the poor sufferers from the French inroad. The Portuguese government lodged it in their magazines and opened an office where licences for receiving this present were issued at two dollars each and numbers paid the money, hoping to receive a valuable compensation of food. When they produced their tickets at the magazines, they received about one dollar's worth of fish.

On 26 August 1811 James wrote to his mother from Fuentes de Guinaldo (now known as Fuenteguinaldo, a municipality in Salamanca); Wellington had advanced in a first and unsuccessful attempt to besiege Ciudad Rodrigo. In this letter we once again see James' great concern for anyone he knew who fell on hard times; in this case the family nurse, Nash. It would not be the last time in his life that people who knew of his generosity took advantage of him. Lady Hester also felt sorry for her.

James told his mother that "I have received long letters from both Lucy and Griselda about poor Nash – any arrangement which clearly conduced to her comfort must of course meet my approbation", while Lady Hester, in a letter written from Rhodes on 2 January 1812, says "To be ignorant about poor dear Grandmama, and not to know what is become of poor Nash, and if I have the means to assist her, is really very painful to me". In her biography of her aunt, the Duchess of Cleveland adds the following in reference to Nash[16]: "The old nurse at Chevening. My father always spoke of her with much affection, and paid her pension till, as he computed, she must have been more than 100 years old. He then made enquiries, and found she had been long dead and fraudulently represented".

James agreed to let Griselda pay Nash 10 guineas, even though he had paid her 20 guineas per year thinking it was enough. He added 20 pounds for 1811 and agreed to pay more if needed. He adds in his letter "I feel and nature tells me warmly too, that half my fortune would not clear away the

---

[16] Cleveland, *Life and Letters*, p.118.

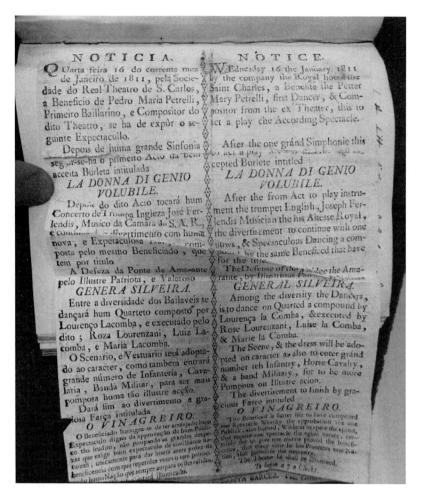

Figure 3.1 – One of James' souvenirs from Portugal

vast debt of gratitude I owe to the best of women". We know little about Nash, but whoever kept on collecting these pensions long after she had died is certainly not deserving of James' praise.

James was present at the siege and taking of Ciudad Rodrigo in January 1812, when Wellington's Anglo-Portuguese Army defeated the city's French garrison under General Jean Léonard Barrié. After two breaches were blasted in the walls by British heavy artillery, the fortress was successfully stormed on the evening of 19 January 1812. After breaking into the city, the

British troops went on a rampage for several hours before order was restored. Strategically, the fall of the fortress opened the northern gateway into French-dominated Spain from British-held Portugal.

James tells an amusing anecdote of how they captured the French general's cook:

> We got the governor's cook in a droll way, when the assault was given the governor was just going to supper, but ran out to the breach, and there being two chimneys the cook betook him to his natural hiding place; but soon came our officers, who took the governor (who had returned to his house) and ate his supper, then the house became filled with soldiers who wanted both fires and on the other being lighted down came Clement. The general heard of it, sent for him, gave him handsome wages and has had him ever since.

Meanwhile, Hester was still living her adventure and romance with Michael Bruce. James' attitude to everything was no secret, as can be seen in a letter from Crauford Bruce (Michael's father) to his son, dated 22 January 1812[17]:

> Captain Stanhope on the first learning of the situation she [i.e. Lady Hester] had placed herself in wrote to her a severe and threatening letter denouncing vengeance on you, that one or other of you must fall; it was what might be expected and was natural on the first emotions of his feelings ... Captain Stanhope has I doubt not on cool reflection seen the impropriety of his intrusive address to her.

From Ciudad Rodrigo Wellington moved on Badajoz, and finally took the city in April 1812 (it was the third time the British had made the attempt). The siege was one of the bloodiest in the Napoleonic Wars and was considered a costly victory by the British, with some 4,800 allied soldiers killed or wounded in a few short hours of intense fighting. The troops broke into houses and stores and consumed vast quantities of alcohol; many of them then went on a rampage, threatening their officers and ignoring their commands to desist. The men were only brought back into order three days later. James' final comments about the storming of Badajoz show Wellington's great frustration at the troops' appalling behaviour:

---

[17] Quoted in Newman, *Stanhopes*, p. 198.

"Lord Wellington fulminates orders and has hardly thanked the troops, so angry is he at the pillage of the poor Spaniards"[18].

James was also involved (although not present) in Hill's successful attack on the Bridge of Almaraz[19], on 18 and 19 May 1812. He has the following to say in his diary:

> On the 12th Sir Rowland Hill began is movement from Mérida to try to get possession of Almaraz. In order to support the movement the 6th division was moved to Alegrete and Arronches and General Graham moved to Portalegre. On the 21st information being received of Douet's being in motion the general sent me to communicate with General Hill.

On his way back he almost lost his horse:

> Next day rode to Albuquerque (having my answer from General Hill that all was successfully concluded) 11 leagues, towards night my horse being tired I laid my sword and sabretasche across the horse and walked before him. An eagle passed close over our heads, frightened the horse, which went off kicking at a gallop and left me in the middle of the plains of Extremadura. I ran as long as I could, picking up sword, cloak etc. as they successively came off. I met a peasant whom I promised a doubloon to if he could catch him, as he had gone off towards Valverde; after some time he came back with him. I was most uncivilly treated at Albuquerque for the first time in Spain, because the landlord found me cleaning my horse.

The reference to James' being treated uncivilly is curious. Cleaning a horse is something that presumably people did in Spain at the time too, and even if they did not, it would be no reason to treat someone poorly, but just to be surprised. The landlord possibly thought that as James was cleaning

---

[18] Charles Esdaile, *The Peninsular War: A New History* (New York, 2003), p. 470, says that the attacks on Ciudad Rodrigo, Badajoz and San Sebastián should be acknowledged as war crimes.
[19] Cf. Joanna Hill, *Wellington's Right Hand: Rowland, Viscount Hill* (Brimscombe Port, 2011), p. 97: "The success at Almaraz, although not a full-scale battle, was, on the other hand, greeted with great enthusiasm in London. After years of disappointments and many retreats, people sensed that the British were now finally gaining the upper hand".

his own horse and had no servant to do it for him, he cannot have been a real officer or nobleman.

In May and June the army started its advance on Salamanca. If James had been unsparing in his criticism of the Spanish army and civilians after Barrosa, he is full of praise for the people of Salamanca:

> When Marmont was in our front, of course the troops were kept together, there was no wood or water on the hill and every inhabitant of Salamanca, with every horse, mule and ass in the town turned out to bring us all we wanted, the higher classes bringing cakes, sweet things and liquers. Marmont retreated on the morning of the 28th, he meant to have fought on the 29th. It was mentioned by Lord Wellington that as an action might be fought a hospital would be wanted. Every class of inhabitant brought their beds and in 24 hours a hospital for 3,000 men was complete in everything.

In July 1812 General Graham resolved to return to England as he was suffering from problems with his eyes, and the doctors warned him that unless he followed a given treatment, which was not available in Spain, he could go blind. James Stanhope took Graham's letter to Wellington, and informed the Duke that he would like to accompany his general. He wrote in his journal:

> Lord Wellington does not in common express himself warmly, but he did so in this instance, and he said more than I think he ever did before of regret and approbation. I said that if his Lordship did not imagine anything would happen, I should like, as a mark of respect, to attend my General home.

Wellington agreed and told him that if he decided to come back to Spain, he would be looked after. James of course missed the Battle of Salamanca, which as he explains in his diary was frustrating:

> I had not been long in England when an account arrived of the Battle of Salamanca (22 July 1812). It is needless to describe the vexation I felt at having through my own fault been absent; I determined on returning immediately. Sir Edward Paget, who was appointed 2nd in command in the room of Sir Thomas Graham offered to take me out with him and we sailed from Portsmouth on the 25th of August in the Rota frigate, Captain Somerville.

James had been in England for under two months before arriving back in Lisbon on 20 April. A letter dated 21 August explains his plans[20]:

> I am on the eve of again returning to Portugal and I trust the shortness of my residence in England will plead my excuse in not personally stating to you what I am now obliged to do by letter. There is an old servant who lived many years with Lord Stanhope and afterwards with my sister Lady Hester, who is now under the pressure of both age and want.

The servant in question was male (i.e. it was not nurse Nash); James asks the unnamed addressee to find him a simple position to work in. He reached Salamanca on 2 October and walked over the battlefield, remarking that Marmont had "manoeuvred until he outmanoeuvred himself".

After Salamanca Wellington went to Madrid and then marched north to lay siege to the fortress of Burgos. On 11 October James reached Wellington's headquarters near Burgos. He visited the trenches and wrote down his impressions; the same description would not have seemed out of place as a picture of the horrors of the First World War:

> I visited the tranches, they are the very devil, for if one is not drowned or choked in mud in the first bayou, one is nearly sure of being shot in the first line if above 5 feet high. I never saw anything like it, if you held up a cap you had two or three balls through it at once.

Wellington however, had miscalculated the enemy's strength, and on 21 October he had to abandon the Siege of Burgos and retreat, much to James' dismay. He wrote to Richard Heber, and showed no qualms about criticizing Wellington[21]:

> When we parted in London I certainly did not expect to be cantoned in the middle of Portugal this winter. I had hopes of sharing in future victories and that expectation certainly occasioned my short stay at home; although I have been disappointed and only arrived in time to witness a bright display of unprofitable gallantry and a repetition of the melancholy scenes unavoidable in every retreat but more prominent in a British one. I by no means regret the determination I

---

[20] U1590 C 271/1. The letter is addressed "Dear Sir" and written from 2 Little Stanhope Street.
[21] Cholmondeley, *Letters*, pp. 247-252.

have taken as the lesson of the last month is worth an age of pursuit. When one looks back on the campaign, one seeks anxiously for the reason why the tables were so rapidly turned and how it happened that we could hardly keep face before a French army which three weeks before was considered *hors de combat* for the year.

I think the prime cause and keystone of our reverses was Lord Wellington's entry of Madrid, abandoning thereby the pursuit of an army which he could have been [right] to bring to action, and secondly, when he remained at Madrid for some time returning to the chase of an enemy he had released from his fangs – of all this I know nothing but from reports, but Burgos I saw, but a rational prospect of success I never could see[22].

James was deeply critical of the Spanish army, but at the same time equally critical of his own army's action regarding the country:

We have also seen that regular Spanish soldiers who for two years have been organising in the Galicias cannot stand against French conscripts who had been 20 days from Bayonne though they have British soldiers by their side as an example.

...

Against this we have our great disadvantage that for the third time we have abandoned the Spaniards and we shall never be considered otherwise than as birds of passage and we cannot expect Vivas from the heart whatever the tongue may utter. It really makes one's heart bleed to think of the poor people of Madrid and Salamanca whom we have left to be tenfold worse plundered and more oppressed in proportion to their attachment to us. I cannot blame the Spaniard for being weary of the war, when sacrifices are so recompensed, and when zeal and kindness so repaid, it must be more than human constancy that does not pray for a cessation of such friendship. I well know that the retreat was necessary and though it justifies our conduct, it cannot remove one's feelings for the poor wretches who are paying for their attachment to us.

---

[22] In an earlier letter (17 March 1810) James had even stated that "Sir John Moore fought for England and Wellesley for himself" (Cholmondeley, *Letters*, p. 234), although as he spent more time with the Duke his opinion became much more favourable.

James was aware that he generally wrote at length and in great detail, as he signs off "If this letter does not put you to sleep, there is no faith in any soporifics".

The army abandoned Madrid too, and retreated first to Salamanca then to Ciudad Rodrigo, near the Portuguese frontier, to avoid encirclement by French armies from the north-east and south-east. Wellington spent the winter reorganizing and reinforcing his forces. By contrast, Napoleon recalled to France numerous soldiers to reconstruct his main army after his disastrous invasion of Russia. On 20 May 1813 Wellington marched 121,000 troops from northern Portugal across the mountains of northern Spain and the Esla River to outflank Marshal Jourdan's army of 68,000, strung out between the Douro and the Tagus. The French retreated to Burgos, with Wellington's forces marching hard to cut them off from the road to France. Wellington himself commanded the small central force in a strategic feint, while Sir Thomas Graham conducted the bulk of the army around the French right flank over landscape considered impassable.

It was a total victory for the English army. The French literally abandoned everything and fled, which led to further scenes of disorder as the English once again forgot all about discipline and plundered what the French had left behind. Wellington's comments were scathing: "We have in the service the scum of the earth as common soldiers", and again "The 18th Hussars are a disgrace to the name of soldier, in action as well as elsewhere; and I propose to draft their horses from them and send the men to England if I cannot get the better of them in any other manner".

James tells the following story in his diary:

I took a gallop to the right and seeing an officer getting out of his carriage, put a pistol to his breast and ordered him to surrender, which he did, dropping his hands. As I was getting my horse over a ditch which was between, he ran off, mounted a horse which an orderly was holding and galloped away. I pursued and hollered till some dragoons joined me, the French officer rallied some of his men and charged us, fired his pistol in my face, but they got the worst of it, but the blackguard escaped.

He seems to be deeply offended at the French officer's lack of honour in surrendering and then making the most of the situation to fight back and run away. After the battle, James was appointed Assistant Quarter Master General, and went with the army to San Sebastián. At dawn on 25 July an attack was launched, which was supposedly to be preceded by the explosion of a mine, after which the plan was for the troops to assault the breaches.

The mine, however, exploded too early, when it was still dark; the troops attacked anyway but had no support from the artillery as it was too dark to see. The troops assaulting the walls were exposed to fire for three hundred yards across the tidal flats. Although they reached the top of the breaches, the supports were again slow and they were beaten back with great loss of life. When this became evident, Graham sent James Stanhope to call off the attack, but as he stood up to wave to the soldiers and signal them to come back, he was hit by a bullet that lodged in his shoulder blade[23]. He narrates the happenings in his diary:

On the 25th a little before daylight, the Royals supported by General Hay's brigade, stormed. It was a fine thing to see the countenances of the men by the light of the burning houses. The French opened a murderous fire though they were rather confused at first by the explosion of the mine. The French showered shells on us, one of them stuck under the fascine Lord March, Fletcher and I were sitting on, it broke the small bone of his leg and gave us a good hoist. Meanwhile the Royals reached the top of the breach and found that by taking away the rubbish the French had made a fall of 15 feet. They were so mowed down with the enemy's fire that they rushed back into the trenches; others were pressing on and there was a great crowd. I stood up to wave them back saying the retreat was ordered, when I received a ball which broke my shoulder blade and lodged in my back. I was helped out of the trenches and was obliged to return to England and so ended my Spanish campaign.

James never went back to Spain after this. Back in England, he wrote to his friend Richard Heber in August 1813[24]:

Although you may regret that the papers are not black letter and printed by Aldus, yet I know you still condescend to read them; you may therefore have seen that I was wounded and that I arrived in the

---

[23] Presumably James was facing away from the French soldier who shot him, as it does not seem that the bullet entered through his chest or shoulder. He must have ridden or run to where his own troops were and tried to signal to them to withdraw, and on so doing he was facing the British soldiers while his back was exposed to the enemy fire. Charles Oman, *A History of the Peninsular War* Vol. 6 (Oxford: Oxford University Press, 1922) pp. 557-586, gives a detailed account of the first siege of San Sebastián but makes no mention of either James Stanhope or the incident in which he was wounded.

[24] Cholmondeley, *Letters*, pp. 256-257.

Parthian at Portsmouth. I meant to have proceeded to town, where I should have met you probably before now, but Lord Buckingham dissuaded me from jumbling myself and brought me over here with him where I have his own surgeon to attend me, and every comfort. I am going on exceedingly well, but the ball remains in my back under the shoulder blade where it will probably reside all my life without molestation. I shall not be any further service this campaign. Have very little pain and sound slumber of 10 hours.

He wrote again in September, this time from St. James' Place in London[25]:

I cannot tell you how I am as who shall decide when doctors disagree. How I feel I am, which is as if I had a decayed tooth in my back; but I must have patience. All the surgeons previous to my coming to town thought that the ball would remain quiet and that the wound would heal. Here they foretell bone coming out, some say the ball, some say by one aperture formed by the ball and others by one which is to be formed by them.

As happens with so many other periods in James' life, there is nothing to tell us or even suggest what he did from his return to England after being wounded until December 1813, when he felt well enough to accompany General Graham to Holland[26]. He wrote to his mother from Williamstadt (Willemstadt) on 26 December[27]:

Had we been favoured by the winds instead of being so long detained by them, we should probably have taken Bergen op Zoom. (But the enemy threw in considerable reinforcements).
    The people here are very willing and well disposed but not very energetic. The country is plentiful but the roads execrable and the inhabitants should be web footed to live in such a bog. The houses are not warm as many of the chimneys have been stopped to avoid paying taxes for them.

---

[25] Cholmondeley, *Letters*, p. 257.

[26] Brett-James, *Graham*, p. 288, says that James was "now largely recovered from the wounds he had received at San Sebastián", which makes it sound like he was cured. It is true that James had moments when the wound troubled him less, but he never actually recovered.

[27] U1590 C 270.

My shoulder aches as usual but I think I sleep better considerably than I did in England – I have got a gig which carries my baggage and which I can go in if I am ill and I have ordered a famous fur pelisse from the Hague so shall be very comfortable.

There was of course no cut and paste before the advent of digital technology, but James came quite close to it if we compare this last paragraph in the letter to his mother to what he wrote to Richard Heber a few days later, on 1 January:

My shoulder aches still but I ride 30 miles a day without fatigue and sleep certainly much better, but still it remains to be tried how I stand winter operations. I have sent to the Hague for a warm fur pelisse.

He wrote to his mother again from Calmhout (Kalmthout) on 14 January 1814[28]:

The intensity of the cold, which has nearly frozen up the Scheldt and of course renders night work and all military operations difficult and dangerous to the troops – although we have not attempted any considerable operation, we have derived no small advantage from the trip, as from being within 1200 yards of the works of Antwerp we have pretty well ascertained the strength of it.

I have had a good deal of fatigue but am not the worse for it. I have had three severe falls on the ice which has hurt one of my knees, but which [will] be well in a few days – one occurred during the fire which gave rise to a report that I was wounded.

I think I shall go to the Hague in a day or two, to see the lions and amuse myself.

He wrote again on 6 February:

I have not written to you since the middle of last month as either my person has been so employed in our operations or my mind so painfully affected with the sad accounts of poor Lucy's health that I have not been able to write – I got very bad accounts yesterday, as late as the 23rd, which make me very low.

We have failed in burning (the enemy's) fleet … but as they fired 2000 shells at it cannot be in a very good state.

---

[28] U1590 C 270.

The attack on Bergen op Zoom took place on 8 March 1814, by the British force led by Thomas Graham, 1st Baron Lynedoch, on the French garrison under Guilin Laurent Bizanet and Jean-Jacques Ambert. The initial British assault force seized part of the defences, but a well-managed French counterattack compelled much of the assault force to surrender. James noted it down in his diary as follows:

Thus failed the attack on Bergen op Zoom; the attempt was justified by circumstances, the idea was bold and the combinations perfect as the success of throwing into the place a superior body of men to the garrison demonstrated and the failure was caused by events which General Graham could neither foresee or avert[29].

On the evening of the 9th Colonel James came out with proposals for an exchange of prisoners, in consequence of which I was sent in next morning with a flag of truce and full powers to sign articles for that purpose. As the French had appointed two officers, when I arrived Colonel Jones was added. Knowing the ulterior destination of most of the troops taken to be America, I proposed that they should not serve against France or her allies 'in Europe' till regularly exchanged. Some manoeuvring was necessary to conceal my reasons and the governor not thinking of trans-Atlantic allies signed it as I wished, our prisoners marched out the same evening. By this he gave us back 1,500 men without exchange although the enemy had a strong interest in getting us out as we should be so many more mouths to feed, it does not diminish the merit of the governor in his treatment of the prisoners. He would examine no letters or papers which I had collected, would set no watch on my actions or confine my steps, as he said he knew 'I should neither act, say nor collect anything unworthy of a British officer'. He was an old officer, had served 34 years and had been taken in his youth by us. He said he never was more kindly treated at home than he was by us and was happy in being able to repay it. I dined with him and his family, at dinner he gave the health of General Graham, 'who must be a brave and able man to have made such an attempt which had so nearly

---

[29] It is all too easy to all into the trap of "We would have won if….", just as many people today try to justify defeats in football (the other team *only* won because they scored more goals). No matter what the reason, despite the brilliant start, in the end the attack was a failure.

succeeded' for at one time he did not know who were masters of the town[30].

James was sent back to England to report to the Prince Regent:

On the 11th I left headquarters with the evil tidings and reached land on the 13th. I waited on Lord Bathurst and was taken to Carlton House where I had an audience with the Prince and explained to him in great detail all that had passed and concluded by expressing my hopes that H.R.H. would not conceive that General Graham had squandered the lives of his men in any rash and impracticable undertaking, but that his reasons for trying it were good, his combinations succeeded and he was not to blame for the failure.

The prince 'By God, so far from blame, I don't think Graham ever deserved more credit for any victory he has ever gained than in the combinations which ended in this failure'.

I then retired and Lord Bathurst remained with the prince; when the former came out, he said he was desired to inform me that 'I might consider myself as a lieutenant colonel but that as no rank had ever been given for bad news he could not set the precedent by giving it once, but I should have it the first opportunity'.

I begged Lord Bathurst to express my gratitude to H.R.H. but to say that being at the top of the list of the Guards I was so near a lieutenant colonel that the brevet rank was comparatively of little importance except as a public testimony of His R. H.'s approbation of General Graham's conduct 'and as such I should accept it, as the greatest gift he could bestow, but to be so considered it must be done at once'.

I repeated the same sentiments to the Duke of York next day and it was settled that in consideration of General Graham's merit in the plan, it should be treated as a victory and all persons mentioned were promoted and I among the others. Since I have been in England.

---

[30] Yet another example of the gentlemanly spirit which prevailed at the times, even in war. Cf. the capture of the French general Charles Lefebvre-Desnouettes, captured on the retreat to Corunna in 1808. Moore washed the French general's wounds himself, had dinner with him and asked him if he needed anything. The Frenchman looked down at his side, meaning that he had no sword; Moore immediately offered him his own. He had wondered if it would be correct to obtain a written promise not to escape from Lefebvre-Desnouettes, but Colborne advised him it would be most offensive (Oman, *Sir John Moore*, pp. 566-567).

Thus ends this part of James' diary. Philip Stanhope (Mahon, James' brother) summarizes the events in Holland in a letter to Lovell Benjamin Badcock dated 2 April 1814 (see Figure 3.2)[31]:

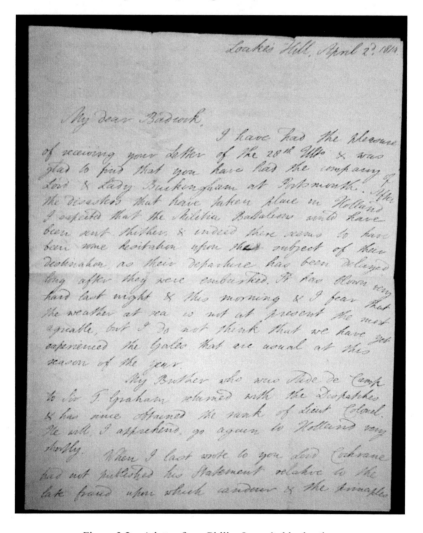

Figure 3.2 – A letter from Philip, James' elder brother

---

[31] The letter is held in a private collection.

My brother, who was Aide de Camp to Sir T. Graham, returned with the dispatches and has since obtained the rank of Lieutenant Colonel. He will, I apprehend, go again to Holland very shortly.

While James was in Spain and Holland and 1813 and 1814, his sister Hester was still travelling around the Middle East, although in October 1813 she had insisted on Michael Bruce's leaving her and going home. He does not seem to have opposed the idea; they quite simply seem to have tired of each other, and he had less and less reason to form part of Hester's more and more grandiose plans. After he left, Hester professed her deep love for him in several letters, even signing off one of them with a dramatic flourish, calling herself the "Nun of Lebanon" (although she did not keep her vow of chastity). In November both Lady Hester and her physician, Dr Meryon, were struck down with plague, which at the time was rampant in the area[32]; despite being seriously ill and close to death, both of them survived.

When Bruce left, he made first for Constantinople, from where he wrote to James – this was the first contact they had had since they met in Gibraltar in 1810, before Bruce and Hester became lovers. The letter reads as follows[33]:

Constantinople, British Palace, Jan 25th 1814

Dear Sir,
I intended to have written to you by the last Vienna Post, but I was really so weak that I had hardly strength to direct a pen. I succeeded with considerable difficulty in writing a few lines to my father and I begged him to communicate to you the accounts which I had just received of Lady Hester's dangerous illness and recovery. As I know that you will be anxious to have the details, I send enclosed Dr Meryon's last letter to Mr. Barker our consul at Aleppo, which that gentleman had the goodness to forward to me. Although I am afraid that you do not entertain a very favourable impression yet I hope that you will do me the justice to believe that no man can entertain a warmer attachment or a higher admiration for the dearest and first of created beings. You may then form some conception of

---

[32] Nobody at this time yet knew how people became infected with the plague (i.e. from fleas on rats). Meryon came close to realizing when he saw that in Latakia, so far free of the plague, he noticed that there was a great number of cats, and hence few rats, although he took the connection no further.
[33] Quote in Bruce, *Nun*, pp. 238-239.

what has been the state of my feelings but upon this subject I shall say no more.

I suppose that before this letter reaches you you will already have been made acquainted with the reasons which have determined my return. I have afforded the greatest violence to my own feelings and it was only in obedience to Lady Hester's positive command that I at last consented. I shall remain here until I receive accounts of her recovery; if she should unfortunately have a relapse I shall then return to Syria. I am aware how unacceptable all congratulations that come from me will prove to you; but I cannot refrain from giving some expression to my feelings upon your late wounds and escape. Yours are indeed honourable wounds and who would not be proud to wear them.

I have heard with sincere pleasure from various quarters of your rising reputation and I hope that the day is not distant when you will be one of the brightest ornaments of your profession. You will observe by the date of Dr Meryon's letter that it is now some time since the last reports of your sister's health. I am waiting as you may well conceive with the greatest anxiety but I have no reason to complain because no ship or courier has come from that quarter. The moment I receive any accounts I shall not delay the earliest opportunity of communicating them to you. I will now put an end to this letter – and I may perhaps both surprise and displease you, but it is the expression of my feelings in subscribing myself your most sincere friend.

Mic. Bruce

James was in London when he received the letter, in April 1814, and promptly sent his servant to Crauford Bruce asking if there was any news (i.e. about Hester). No answer survives, but later in the month James received a card of invitation from the Bruces – he answered by saying that because of the poor publicity of Michael's affair with Hester, he could neither visit the Bruces nor answer Michael's letter. Crauford Bruce's reply to this is carefully crafted to say only good things about Hester and expresses his veneration for her "most superior abilities, genius and understanding, for the independence of her character, and possessing a mind that will not brook control but is equal to guide an Empire".

James answered on the same day, 29 April, another carefully written letter which says only good things about Michael:

My dear Sir,

I cannot refrain from returning you my sincere thanks for your letter, which indeed I expected from a person of so much acknowledged feeling and honour. So far from having any objection to you communicating my feelings to your son, I am particularly anxious for you to do so, and to express to him how high an opinion I preserve of him and how fond a recollection I bear of our former friendship. God grant that the time may come when I may enjoy it once more, improved, enriched and mellowed by time.

Permit me also to thank you for the flattering manner in which you have been pleased to express yourself about me. Next to the humble self feeling of having done my duty, the most valuable reward is meriting the approbation and esteem of men like you.

I remain my dear Sir, with every feeling of respect and esteem

Your very sincere friend

J. H. Stanhope

Bruce's letter to James from Constantinople is diplomatic and respectful, calling on what they hold in common (their regard for Lady Hester) rather than on their disagreements. His comments about his love and concern for Lady Hester do however ring hollow when we take into account the amount of women he seduced from the moment he left the supposedly "first and dearest of created beings". It would seem that James' doubts about Bruce's character were justified to an extent. Indeed, Michael Bruce's adventures after leaving Latakia would seem to suggest that he forgot all about Hester the minute she was out of his sight. As soon as he reached Constantinople he became involved with a woman called Theophanie Ascalon, who wrote to him when he was in Paris, complaining that he had abandoned her (and indeed he had, but she had no idea what kind of man she was dealing with). In June 1814 he arrived in Vienna, where he seduced another woman whose name we do not know, but who also wrote to him with the same complaint. He spent the summer at his home, and in October 1814 returned to Paris, where he enjoyed the physical favours of Caroline Lamb (who had also been Byron's lover), the Duchess of Leu, and what was probably his most dangerous love affair, with Aglaé, the wife of Marshal Ney, Napoleon's most daring marshal, one of the few who survived the disastrous expedition to Moscow in 1812 and was subsequently known as the "bravest of the brave". After Napoleon's defeat at Waterloo, the restored monarchy had Ney shot in December 1815 (Ney himself gave the orders to the firing squad). Bruce's affair with Aglaé started before the Marshal's execution and continued after it; she was smitten, and wrote him several passionate letters from her exile in Italy begging him to join her and her child.

No matter what one might think about Michael Bruce's behaviour, it is true that it was Hester who had decided he should leave her and return to England after his family had financed all her adventures. He had at least some right to find comfort in the arms of other women, however numerous they may have been. What does strike us as surprising is that in his diary, which he kept throughout his travels, he hardly ever mentions Lady Hester at all.

Hester wrote to her estranged lover Michael Bruce on 7 September 1814, a letter which is full of praise for her brother James. She opens by saying that "James is now the Duke of York's A. de C. and everything in the eyes of the world that *even* I can wish him". Hester knew that James was back in England (and presumably that he had been wounded too, although she makes no mention of it), as she goes on to tell Bruce:

> I have written all to James as he is likely to remain in England till I send for him to meet me[34].
> …
> Cultivate the society and friendship of those in England worth knowing. James being there and in such an elevated situation for his age and more admired and well spoken of than you can imagine will be a great advantage to you, and my not being there will do away all awkwardness in the world. James will I am sure act most kindly by you and as a true friend upon all occasions.

---

[34] Lady Hester had several plans to either get James to take her back home, or to meet in the south of France, none of which ever came to fruition.

CHAPTER FOUR

THE PENINSULAR WAR POEMS

No mention is made in any book concerning either James, his sister Hester or indeed of the Stanhope family in general, of James Hamilton Stanhope's poetry and other literary works. It is true that his poetry is not of the best quality (his vocabulary is overly archaic, and he has little sense of rhythm in his verse), but it is written from the heart and teaches us a lot about what kind of person he was.

He wrote a lengthy poem about the Peninsular War, which is to be found in an elegantly bound blue leather notebook with a gilt design, and the words MSS VERSES BY THE HON. COL. J. H. STANHOPE embossed in golden letters on the spine[1]. There are two complete versions of the poem, both copies by James Stanhope himself; the first is written directly into the notebook, while the second was copied onto sheets and paper that were then cut to size and glued onto the pages of the notebook. There is also a partial third version, consisting only of the lines concerning Charles; this part seems to have been written before the rest of the poem and sent to the Countess Stanhope[2].

The first version of the poem, written directly into the notebook, is followed by "Translations of some of the 'Romances Moriscos' 1813, Winter Quarters, Mangualde" (Mangualde is a city in Portugal). These translations from the Spanish are also written on separate pieces of paper and glued into the notebook. The translations are extremely free (so much

---

[1] U1590 C265/1. The front inside cover bears the name and coat of arms of James Banks Stanhope (James' son).
[2] These verses were included in a letter from James to his mother, which from the content and expression of grief seems to have been written soon after Corunna (U1590 C270). The letter is not dated, just headed "6 o'clock", and reads "Dear mother, I send you the lines. To anyone who loved Charles and can appreciate my feelings you are at liberty to show them but I beg you will never let them be copied as I do not mean to get the name of a poetaster. The news is too bad. We may almost say with Richard, 'Let no man talk of comfort more'. Ever affectionately, JS". This letter is followed by the lines of the poem from "Immortal chief! Let Britain's conquering band" to "What are thy prospects, life, thy joys to me?".

so that we are entitled to wonder whether this is poetic licence or simply that James' Spanish was not so fluent as to be able to translate poetry, which is exceedingly difficult even when you master both languages; I have often come up against this difficulty in my thirty-plus years as a professional translator.

The second version of the Peninsular War poem then follows, after which are three other poetic works by James; the first is untitled, while the other two are called "On the destruction of Burton Pynsent" (the house where his sister Hester had lived for a time), and "On the anniversary of Mr. Pitt's birthday in 1814" (Pitt the Younger was James' uncle, whose dying words were addressed to him).

The second version of the Peninsular War poem seems to be the later one; it was copied from the first, and certain changes and additions were made. One line is also missing, which shows that this version was indeed copied from the first, as the remaining verse thus stands alone with no rhyming line; this of course was a mistake typical of copyists and not a modification or improvement. The last verses are also lost in the later copy, and so in the edition given below, which follows the second version as a rule, the ending comes from the first version. I have included any significant differences in footnotes.

The poem basically consists of rhyming couplets, although occasionally the rhyme covers three lines (e.g. verses 482, 483 and 484); in these cases Stanhope marked the three lines (possibly to go back later and reduce them to two, as in the rest of the poem). The rhyme is constant, but no attention at all is given to syllabic rhythm; the quality of the verse suffers from this and we would be hard pushed to praise Stanhope's work as good poetry. Its interest lies rather in the fact that to my knowledge, it is the only poem about an episode in the Peninsular War written by someone who was actually there and took part in it.

The poem is presented as a dialogue between Stanhope (presumably James himself) and an anonymous friend. Stanhope himself provides an introduction to the work, with some general headings for the different sections of the verses. The friend opens, welcoming Stanhope home from Spain; Stanhope replies by expressing his love of Spain and the Spaniards, but criticizes their monarchs Charles IV and Ferdinand VII. He goes on to talk about the British expeditionary force (which was eventually placed under the command of Sir John Moore) and how it was betrayed; "By friends deceived, by foes encompassed round". Nevertheless, Moore accomplished his purpose of drawing off the French forces against himself, giving the rest of Spain time to breathe and reorganize.

The poem then described Moore's heroic death (of which Stanhope was a personal witness), and also laments the death of his brother Charles Stanhope (who was shot through the heart on the steps of the church in the village of Elviña while leading his troops forward). This was James Stanhope's first battle, and he lost both his brother (who he describes in the poem as "Youth's earliest friend, companion of the heart") and his commander in chief; it was a deeply traumatic day for him.

In verses 208 ff. the friend asks how then Stanhope can praise Spain, if indeed only the British army fought while the Spaniards did nothing to help their allies. Stanhope has to agree with him, but instead of justifying what Spain did (or rather did not do), he in turn criticizes the British government for the useless expedition to Wagram in 1809; the troops would have achieved much more in Spain.

The friend bids him stop criticizing England and focus on Spain, which has no leader worthy of the name. Stanhope tells the friend that the Spanish army was deceived by the French, and its best troops sent to Scandinavia by the French. The friend insists, saying that Spain showed no gratitude to England for all the efforts made by the latter on her behalf; "No grateful thanks from Spanish bosoms flow, vain in their sunshine, sullen in their woe".

Once again Stanhope defends and justifies Spain and its inhabitants; if they look on past glories and take pride in them, Englishmen do no less. He ends the poem with an admonition that wealth and commerce is all vain and meaningless if it is not backed up by freedom.

In the following edition the two versions are abbreviated as V1 and V2. V3 contains the lines about the death of James' brother Charles in Corunna, as sent to his mother shortly after the event.

Argument
The real state of Spain inquired into - feelings and character of the Spanish peasant described. Their first successes and regret at their not having attacked the French behind the Ebro before reinforced and united. General actions after they were so – Spanish defeats, English retreat – character of Sir J. Moore. Apostrophe to his and my brother's memory – character of the supreme junta – impolicy of British Government supporting them against the people. Causes why no great leader has appeared in Spain – in difference between this and other revolutions – their gratitude proved, their pride extenuated. Character of Guerrillas – little hope from the exertion of the Cortes during war – their utility in peace. Reflections derived from the Spanish war – conclusion.

Spain – begun in winter of 1811, finished in winter of 1812

Friend
Welcome once more from famed Iberia's strand
To enjoy the blessings of thy native land
Canst thou describe yet free from factions far
This strange camelion[3] of a Spanish war?
For here alas, contending passions throng
Events not reason hurry us along;
Some blindly censure in one sweeping clause
Her manners, people, government and laws;
Some in the spirit of her own romance
Foretell her triumphs in the heart of France
Make guideless hordes, unarmed, unclothed, cursed
Rout hosts inured to blood[4], by science led
And tell of prowess and of zeal unknown
When Cortes won or Carlos left a throne.
Stanhope:
No easy task, for who with steadfast eye,
Shall falsehoods, mists and prejudice defy
Each nice distinction make and bounds decide
When overstrained virtues are to vice allied
Yet to attempt the sketch, a pleasing toil
For well I love the tillers of her soil.
Who long had felt their wrongs, and patient borne[5],
with panting bosoms and with silent scorn,
insatiate vice in regal pomp arrayed
their rights forgotten and their power decayed;
yet as the child maternal love once blest
still fondly clasps his stepdame's barren breast.
So did their loyal bosoms check the groan
Despise the monarch but revere the throne[6]
Till France by fraud her guileful path prepared
Their bulwarks purchased and their frontier bared;
Though treason then spread forth its fatal net,
And weakness wooed the Gallic bayonet,
Though he, their shepherd who the flock should guide,

---

[3] An old spelling of "chameleon".
[4] V1 reads "inured to war".
[5] V1 They long had felt their wrongs, but patient borne.
[6] V1 They scorned their monarch but revered the throne.

Himself betrayed them and his oaths belied[7],
Though feudal chiefs could every tie forego
In acts as abject as their souls were low,
By all abandoned yet unawed by fear
Dauntless stood forth the hardy mountaineer
And couched in Freedom's cause the patriot spear[8]
His was the zeal which armed one father's hands
With giant's force to burst oppression's bands
which arts and gold and regal power withstood,
redeemed our rights and sealed them with their blood,
Here might the Swiss recall the brow of toil
And kindred breast which loves the parent soil
Oppressed with vain remorse might idly trace
Their ancient virtues brightening in his face[9],
E're yet the French which Gallia's friendship poured
Unnerved Helvetia's arm and rusted deep her sword
Here glowed the spark which unsupported braved
Ten thousand banners where the crescent waved
Which 'fanned by conquest's wing' still fiercer spread
And whelmed the Moslem pride in the ocean's bed.
Religion's rays their kindling powers combine
Pealed every choir and trembled every shrine
And love combined to fan the powerful flame
In matchless charms, Spain's dark-eyed daughters came
Theirs is the frank resolve, the lofty mind
With gentle mien, tenderness refined[10],
Theirs is the form where unspoiled nature shone
Which framed by love seemed fit for love alone.
Yet could that fairy form high might disclose,
When loud and stern the song of war arose[11],
The eye which lately swam with fond desire
Disclaimed the joy and gleamed with patriot fire[12]
Theirs was each toil, each danger and each care
The sick to comfort or the war to share
Who would not fight for freedom led by ye?

---

[7] V1 Betrayed them barely and his oaths belied.
[8] These three lines are bracketed in V1, but not in V2.
[9] V1 Their ancient virtues dignify their race.
[10] V1 With all a woman's tenderness refined.
[11] V1 When stern and fierce the sounds of war arose.
[12] V1 Gleamed bright with zeal and sparked with patriot fire.

Beneath your glance, who struggle to be free?
Bright fell the gleam on Tajo's golden tide[13]
Where her rich flood reflects Aranjuez's pride
Till on Morena's cliffs[14] it blazed amain
Throned mid the clouds the beacon star of Spain
The bannered bird which towering to the sky[15]
Braved the rude storm of northern chivalry
His sickening eye reverts from freedom's light
Covers his dark wing and trembles at the sight.
For mid the Mancha's cliffs he kenned afar
The mustering banners of a nation's war
No silken tissues waving to the sky
In idle pomp and gilded panoply
But valor, faith and constancy were there
These are the nation's arms and these her banners were.
Why pauses Spain? Whilst yet the wreath is new,
Thy rustic hands from Gallic veterans drew
Whilst still in flight the unsceptred monarch hears
Thy shouts of triumph pealing in his ears
Whilst curdling still remains thy foeman's blood
Whilst yet the Ebro rolls in Spanish flood
Why pauses Spain? March o'er the invaders' land
Fresh legions form and darken all the strand
From every realm their iron bands unite
And he the ruthless spoiler rules their might
Oh then whilst yet the precious hour remains
To crush thy flying foe and burst thy chains
Thy energies unfold, stretch forth thine hand
To seize the mountain passes of the land
Alas not so! Their mighty powers unite
Shall untaught valor dare them to the fight
Oppose the meteor terror of their course
And meet a giant with a pygmy's force?
As mid thy cliffs when wintry floods of rain
Pour their wild waters headlong to the plain
Then sink thy oaks and scathed pines, a prey
In hideous ruin rolled and rapid borne away,
Till in the windings of the oozy vale

---

[13] V1 The patriot fire gleamed first on Tajo's tide.
[14] Explanatory note in V1: Battle of Baylen.
[15] V1 The bannered bird which soaring to the sky.

Its furious rage and baneful efforts fail
Drinks every plant its devious current laves
Each creature round some trifling portion craves
O'er all the land it spreads its useless spoil
And lends its wave to irrigate your soil
This shall thy foe concentred in his views
Diverge advancing and diverging lose,
The parching fever shall their veins invade
And agues shake the miserable shade
Famine's dire curse shall smite the band forlorn[16]
And dark despair hang o'er each rising morn
Each wandering wretch, no friendly succour near,
Shall rue the vengeance of the mountain spear
Whilst formed amid her cliffs, regenerate Spain,
Shall glut with gore the furrows of her plain
But mark, the mighty victor moves his band
Lets loose his rage and bares his crimson hand
Round his dread car ambition's slaves appear
Fraud in his van and famine in his rear
Iberia's sons desert the unequal field
Resign the sword and cast away the shield[17]
Whilst fate's dark clarion rends the lurid air
With yells of rout and havoc and despair
Far from their track remorse and pity driven
Bear on their wings the sighs of Spain to heaven[18]
Amid such scenes of ruin and defeat
Britannia's sons unwilling sought retreat
By friends deceived, by foes encompassed round
But their resource the able chieftain found,
Yet as he tracked the snowclad dreary way
He lured the bloodhounds from their destined prey
Foiled by his skill their armies toiled in vain
And spared awhile Iberia breathed again;
But Moore the great, the patriot and the brave
Fell in that cause so well he fought to save
Immortal chief! Let Britain's conquering band
The impression cherish of thy powerful hand

---

[16] V1 Famine's gaunt hand shall smite the band forlorn.
[17] V1 Drop their blunt sword and throw away the shield.
[18] V1 Bear on their wings Iberia's woes and heaven.

Paint the high zeal thy early breast imbued[19]
Which owned no passion but thy country's good
Which knew no barrier to her mighty claim
Which loved no object equal to her fame
That independence which no court could pall
No interest dazzle and no faction thrall
The native talents of thy vigorous mind
By thought matured by elegance refined
Thy generous soul affection's gentle seat
Honour's pure fount and mercy's loved retreat
Be theirs to banish base detraction's gloom,
And guard untouched the trophies of thy tomb!
Mine be the task an humbler wreath to entwine
And gem with friendship's tears[20] thy hallowed shrine[21]
Whilst aching memory oft recalls the day
When all serene the expiring hero lay
E'en at that aweful hour each breast must own
As pausing on[22] the infinite unknown
(not as when age lets forth[23] the flitting breath
And preparation smooths the path of death
But when stern fate outstrips the wings of time
And clips the budding hopes which deck our prime)
The unaltered eye no sign of pain expressed
No groan issued from that mangled breast
But calm as erst upon[24] the mountain's side
He ruled the battle and its rage defied
His anxious thoughts for Britain's weal provide
Yet mid the pressure of his army's care
Affection's ties the fleeting moments share -
His gentle spirit for himself resigned
Mourned for each friend he left to weep behind
So all around some soothing accents flow
(oh precious balm true friends alone can know)
Then as an infant on its mother's breast
With a fond smile reclined his head to rest!

---

[19] V1 Let them relate the zeal thy breast imbued.
[20] V3 tear
[21] V1 And deck with humble tears thy hallowed shrine.
[22] V3 o'er
[23] V3 slip
[24] V3 when on

Was not his fall enough for fate to claim,
Renowned for valor and mature in fame
Without that blow which o'er my leader's bier
In bitter streams drew forth the brother's tear.
Beloved shade, nor could thy joyous bloom
Nor ripening virtues save thee from the tomb
Nor all thy country's hopes nor friendship's wail
Check the cold shadow of oblivion's veil?
Yet that untimely shroud its solace bore
And hid the fall of him whom we deplore.
Then at thy loss shall egoist love repine
When mercy's gift and virtue's crown entwine?
The worth which in this vale of tears below[25]
Puts forth reluctant shoots which tardy grow
Chilled by malignant breath and hatred rude
False smile of friends and dark ingratitude
Shall freely flourish in a purer air
Expand in endless light and bloom unfading there
Ah no! Too true these bursting teardrops tell
'Tis hard to bid one loved so dear farewell
Youth's earliest friend, companion of the heart
Who guessed each thought and bore a kindred part
In all I wept at and in all enjoyed
The widowed soul hangs over the dreary void
In hopeless agony[26], unshared by thee
What are thy prospects, life, thy joys to me?
Friend
Enough of woe, I grant thy feelings true;
But how can Spaniards then be praised by you?
When thus confusion stalked amid their bands
And steel gleamed forth alone in British hands
With folded arms in sluggard pomp they lay
Nor made one effort to retrieve the day.
Stanhope
Too true alas! How ebbed Iberia's zeal
Not bowed alone beneath the Gallic steel
Not sunk by treachery's unsupported art
A deadlier venom rankled at the heart.

---

[25] This was changed in V2 to "this misty vale below" and then back to the original text.
[26] V3 comfortless despair

Some hoary dotards who usurped the throne
Feared in the people's power to lose their own
No acts they framed to exalt the public good
No laws they sanctioned and no rights renewed
No care employed to discipline their arms
To find some chief whom martial genius warms,
Who might collect, inspire, reform and train
And rise perhaps the Washington of Spain.
Yet Britain's chiefs in folly's wildest hour
Forgot the people's claims and backed their power
Nor saw amid self-willed deception's air
Or what her means or what her vices were,
Nor looked at Spain but through their fancy's prism
Which shed o'er all the glow of patriotism.
Couldst thou fair island justly famed afar
As first in arts in commerce and in war
But chief, that Freedom wooed thy stormy spring
Dwells in thy breast or nestles 'neath thy wing
That unbribed justice hears the weak implore
And spreads her guardian aegis o'er the poor
Bids the poor slave from Africa's sultry sands
Move his free limbs and wave the unfettered hands
Couldst thou in Freedom's cause thy aid decree
Nor give the Spanish kind what keeps thy peasant free?
Woe to their rashness who with viewless aim
In mad delusion played Napoleon's game
Who tardy roused by Austria's cannon roar
Began to plan when action's hour was o'er
Fond to attempt what hardly could succeed
Slow to advance and slower to recede
Slow to advance when speed alone could gain
And doubtful victory paused o'er Wagram's plain
Slow to recede when useless valor lay
To pale inglorious pestilence the prey
And all the bravest hearts of Britain's land
Were left to perish on the Belgic strand
Oh had thy sons, thus doomed to fall in vain
Been timely sent to wage the fight of Spain
Then had we reaped from Talavera's field
More precious fruits than barren laurels yield
Then were ambition's wrongs by vengeance laved

And Freedom's cause secured and Europe saved.
Friend
Nay cease this keen recriminating strain
And turn from English politics to Spain
Oft as I have studied History's fairest theme
When states their long-lost liberty redeem
In every age some brighter star appears
Who guides the powerful and the timid cheers
And some great leader seems designed by fate
To raise, redeem or to usurp a state[27];
But still in Spain the scene which talent draws
Has formed no leader to uphold her cause.
Stanhope
Who marvels that in Charles' later day
To unblushing[28] vice and perfidy the prey
Each honest talent cramped, each virtue bound
Iberia's genius cowered upon the ground?
What matters now a revolution's name
The effect continues as the cause is the same
For all the leaders who her cause[29] oppress
Prove the old actors in a patriot dress
Why then this struggle with the rest compare
Which if we study, no resemblance bear.
Ours was the voice of an enlightened state
By cautious wisdom formed and long debate
A generous impulse given to freedom's end
Which well we knew to prize and well defend[30]
And cautious William ably could unite
His own ambition with the people's right
Our cause supported and assumed the sway
And learnt at once to govern and obey
Or when America to madness driven
Boldly usurped what wisdom should have given
Nursed in the bosom of the western spring
Where murky damps the wild savannahs fling
Her infant freedom rose in stern array

---

[27] Lines 269 and 270 are not in V1.
[28] V1 hardened.
[29] V1 has "arms" for "cause"; so does V2, but crossed out and replaced by "cause".
[30] V2 adds two lines here: No tractors paved the conquest of the land, Nor legions backed what perfidy had planned, but then crosses them out.

And led by genius conquered by delay
The orient beams which gild their mountain strand
Dispelled no shadows of the invader's land
But long she gazed upon the waves serene
E'er the dark sails of England's wrath were seen
But Spain in peace possessed, to fiends a prey,
Who gaily march when rapine leads the way
Each just suspicion lulled to lazy rest
With fondness clasped the invaders to her breast
Saw from each mountain hold and stern profile
The western sun gleam back from Gallic steel
And marked unmoved the warders of her land
Removed to guard the Scandinavian strand
Yet thus betrayed, disarmed, forlorn
She held submission and the foe in scorn
And shed a blaze of fame on ages yet unborn.
Friend
Well though you thus may gild their weakness o'er
A darker passion o'er their friends deplore
For all the wealth that bounteous England spread
The arms she squandered and the blood she shed
No grateful thanks from Spanish bosoms flow
Vain in their sunshine, sullen in their woe.
Stanhope
Ungenerous thought! And is it thus we view
The general feeling in the intriguing few
Who strut the fleeting pageant of an hour
Nor own the assistance which supports their power.
Scared from the Court amid her mountains wild
Still in each cot, the angel visions smiled
The grateful tear from manly eyelids hung
And praise flowed faltering from the infant's tongue
Why does your matron trim her evening fire
Why clasp you babes their long lamented sire
Who faint and weary mid Galicia's snow
In dark despair reclined his aching brow
Whilst memory's pangs within his bosom burn
And joys long past which never would return
Him did the grateful peasant dare to save
And blest with little yet that little gave
Nor toil nor danger could his zeal allay

His guide by night his faithful guard by day
Till safe from savage foe and war's alarms
He gave him safely to his comrade's arms
It's thus that heartfelt gratitude should shine
And scorn the fulsome vote and studied line.
Friend
Should every virtue in their breasts entwine
What present chance what future hopes are thine
What arm can this presumptuous nation save
Who boast their vigour o'er the yawning grave,
The distant danger trace with nicest art
Nor see the dagger pointing at their heart
Stanhope
As midst the tempests howl a fearless crew,
So storms long past revert a cheerful view,
When spent its rage, soft slept the raging main
And gave them safely to their homes again.
So does Iberia mid the hideous blast
Still fondly gaze on ancient glories past
Nor heeds whilst thus the flattering dreams prevail
Her yawning timbers and her tattered sail.
Such pride, what breast has never learnt to feel
Ne'er beat responsive to his country's weal
Can virtue's hand a nobler passion crown
Than fond remembrance of our old renown?
What British youth in history's fairy way,
But dwells with rapture on one Alfred's sway
Our early empire 'stablished on the main
The deathless laurels of our Henry's reign?
Shall Spain alone be then forbid to feel
Her proud resistance to the Roman steel
To guard in thought Numantia's stubborn gate
Or mourn her heroes at Saguntum's fate
(Whose moss-grown ruins yet alive to fame[31]
Still guard the ancient splendour of her name,
And like immortal Zaragoza's wall
Prostrate on earth are nobler from their fall).
To watch in fancy mid the mental night

---

[31] There is a footnote in V1 here, reading "Murviedro which made a glorious defence".

The last faint vestige of the Christian light
Or joyful hale in triumph's proudest mood
Midst ages spent in battles and in blood
Each shrine recovered and the Moor subdued.
When acts like these are borne sublime to heaven
One note of pride may peal and be forgiven
Too true their haughty mood repels the friend
And mars the object which themselves intend
But still this failing when the foe draws near
Which now is pride is perseverance here
For force ne'er bent their stubborn people's will
Who e'en when routed were unconquered still.
For mark that motley band in loose array
Who scorn to crouch beneath the oppressor's sway
Well skilled to rally and when fit to yield
And shun the fortunes of a marshalled field
Here's the brave band Guipuscoa's wilds send forth
The dark-browed, belted warriors of the North
And they the gallant sons of rich Navarre[32]
The dauntless wagers of the frontier war
Clothed in each trapping of the modern Hun
Which force had conquered or which craft had won
And there with souls of fire unconquered yet
The enduring, firm, impetuous Miquelet[33].
Freedom's fond hopes in some beguile the toil
The thirst of vengeance or the love of spoil
Blightly they rove around each well-known hill
Which echoed once their joyous sequadille[34]
Or sweetly woke when balmy evening fell
Where the rude cork tree stretches o'er the dell
The gay guitar whose wildest nearness met
The tabor, pipe or lively castanet.
The graceful dance the village maidens trace
Which livens each eye and animates each face,
Or late carousing where the moonbeams shine
Quaff the rich produce of their native vine

---

[32] V1 "gay Navarre".
[33] The Miguelete (or Miquelet in the Valencian language), is a tower in the Cathedral of Valencia, not in Navarre.
[34] A lively dance.

Or wildly carol some romantic strain[35]
Tolosa's fight and Roncesvalles' plain
Or what of beauty's power and valor's steel
Tradition's voice and Moorish tales reveal
Unchanged by war, their hardy life's the same
But vengeance points them to a nobler game
The spear in woodland chase employed no more
Now gladly quivers in their foeman's gore
And each fusee[36] the quarry left at rest
Now wings its bullet at a fiercer breast
Friend
But should their bands with British shill combine
And victory's rays with cloudless lustre shine
Should Wellesley's mighty hand the prostrate shield
For none but him the various mass could wield
Could make conflicting elements agree
And weave himself the web of victory[37]
What change to Spain would triumph's progress bring
But rule despotic or a dotard king?[38]
Lost Lusitania's ancient fame could hear
Reserve her feeble arm, point her blunted spear[39]
For when at length to bless the patriot's prayer
Their Cortes met, were Freedom's champions there?
Though some directed by historic light
Renewed the basis of the people's right
Yet seemed forgotten mid discussion's jar
How blunt the sword; how slack[40] the nerves of war
Whilst Spain's opinion once their firmest stay
Like the faint sunshine of a winter's day
Poured down one quivering glance then melted slow away.
Stanhope
Yet as that sun shall in a milder hour
O'er earth's wide span exert his genial power

---

[35] This verse is missing from V2 and so is supplied from V1. This shows that V2 is a later copy of V1 and not vice versa, because as V2 stands, there would be nothing to rhyme with "plain" in the following verse.
[36] Fusee is an old word for rifle.
[37] V1 And weave from nought the web of victory.
[38] V1 But wild rebellion or a dotard king?
[39] These two lines are only found in V2.
[40] V1 reads "weak" for "slack".

Call animation from the rugged clay
Shed balmy fragrance on the leafless spray
With life impregnate the neglected seed
And deck[41] with waving gold the enamelled mead,
So may their light in peaceful days burst forth
And wake to life her long-neglected worth
Expand the secret germ of mental ore
And rouse the native[42] virtues of her shore.
Whilst smiling peace shall visit every glade
And arts bud forth beneath the olive's shade
Not yet alas! Awhile foredoomed to know
Just retribution for Columbia's woe
In either world to pour her children's gore
And feel the havoc she let loose before
And mark the cloud of guilt her avarice spread
Roll in deep thunders o'er her prostrate head
Yet shall not vengeance cease her iron reign
Shall millions weep and valor bleed in vain
Midst conscious fears and hopes in visions fair
Conquest's paired scales still hang sublime in air
And round their verge a mingled throng appears
Of orphan's, parent's, widow's bitter tears,
Of shades which sink in virtue's modest bloom
Of honour's bedding o'er an early tomb
The flowery wreath which Hope had twined so gay
E'er death's cold hand had torn the sweets away
The mocking dream which expectation wove
The faint expiring glance of absent love
And flitting mates of proud triumphal show
And dismal shades of past and forms of future woe[43]
Yet we will hope that the all righteous power
Who smiling hallowed freedom's natal hour
Bore her triumphant through the rifted flood
On bare Thermopylae 'gainst Persia stood
Will still protect her in her hour of age
And wrest her children from the tyrant's rage
But if on Heaven's blest aid in vain we call
And naught below can check Iberia's fall

---

[41] V1 reads "paint" for "deck".
[42] V1 reads "slumbering" for "native".
[43] This and the following ten verses are only found in V2.

Looks

The glorious cause shall History's pages keep
When all their faults in dark[44] oblivion sleep
Still o'er the mournful page shall future ages weep
But we who view the dark ensanguined scene
An aweful[45] lesson for ourselves may glean
"'Ere Spain was goaded by a foreign sway
The internal freedom of the state gave way".
In open war our fear may threat in vain
For force can keep what force attempts to gain
The tide of triumph may by shoals be crossed
The sword may conquer what the sword has lost
But should we lose that heavenly beacon's light
Which on the throne reflects the people's right
Which when the waning orbs of Europe set
But purer[46] shone a beacon unclouded yet
Midst stern revolt and war's unnumbered woes
Bore her triumphant through a world of foes
The cheering star of ocean's troubled wave
To guide the helpless and the weak to save
Tho every breeze should Europe's tributes bring
Through all thy courts should peals of conquest ring
Tho commerce earned and plenty bless thy shore
Nor they nor peace can bless if freedom be no more[47]

James Stanhope expressed a wish for some of his poetry to be included in a possible (auto)biography. The style of his verse is the same in every poem he ever wrote, be it on the battles of the Peninsular War or a passionate love poem to his beloved Lady Frederica; an archaic vocabulary and noble air, an attempt to make his work sound like it comes from another age. There is little to commend it as art (unlike, for example, the translated and original poetry by his sister's physician, Charles Lewis Meryon, which was clever, metrical and at times moving); his work's only interest lies in the fact that here was a soldier who wrote a kind of verse, an eye-witness of the events he describes.

Another poem from the time of the Peninsular War written by James was to celebrate the memory of his uncle, William Pitt the Younger; it is similar in style to the poem on Spain. There are two copies of the poem;

---

[44] V1 reads "deep" for "dark".
[45] V1 reads "A useful" for "An aweful".
[46] V1 reads "Still brighter" for "But purer".
[47] The last five verses are missing from V2 and supplied from V1.

U1590 C-264/1 (V2) is the later version, as it has parts of 1590 C-265/4 (V1) crossed out and replaced, and also verses that are not in the earlier one. The later version also says at the start *Written on the 28th of May 1814*, which was Pitt's birthday. It is therefore meant as a kind of commemoration.

> Ye friends of Pitt on whose persuasive tongue
> Wisdom and wit and strong conviction hung
> Have ye forgot ere shrouded in his grave
> The words prophetic which his spirit gave
> "England firm standing with her flag unfurled
> By her example shall redeem the world".
> Dark was that hour, when o'er each prostrate land
> Waved the stern vengeance of the victor's hand
> Which buried Europe in sepulchral gloom
> and stretched the narrow limits of the tomb
> far from his track fair freedom forced to roam
> Found in Brittania's arms a welcome home
> Beneath her shield reposed her languid form[48]
> Till bold from danger, stronger from the storm
> On Lusitanian cliffs she took her stand
> And placed her holy[49] cause in Wellesley's conquering hand
> Then o'er the north with radiant wings she flew
> Expiring nations fresh existence drew
> Concord and hope bade warring nations cease
> Their civil feuds and joined their hands in peace
> Oh sacred bonds in which entwined we see
> by mercy's hand a crown of victory
> of brighter hues than ever labouring thought[50]
> Or patriot prayer or youthful fancy wrought
> And when once more is sheathed the ensanguined[51] blade
> Before whose edge ambition shrank dismayed
> When freedom smiles upon the closing scene
> And olives deck the plains where Mars has been
> With mad ambition's victim to declare

---

[48] These last four lines in V1 read "And burst the narrow bounds of Nature's tomb, forced from her home amid his wild carrouses, The outcast freedom found a refuge, Beneath Brittania's aegis rose her form".

[49] V1 does not have the word "holy".

[50] V1 has "A purer wreath than ever labouring thought".

[51] V1 has "avenging".

"The avenging hand of Providence is there".[52]
But next to Him who o'er this changful ball
Decrees the rise of empires and the fall
Be his the need, whose grim unnerving hand
Maintained the freedom of his native land
Whose might mind the steadiest[53] barrier stood
Against invasion's desolating flood.
Midst civil rage and war's unnumbered woes
Bore her triumphant through a world of foes
The beacon star of Europe's stormy wave
To raise the sinking and the wandering save
Which when the waning orbs in darkness set
But brighter shone and beams unclouded yet[54]
Oh had he seen by Europe's patriot band
The work completed which his wisdom planned
Then had we proved by loud and heartfelt cheers[55]
That love, alas now clouded by our tears
For well it glads the conquering veteran's eye
To see unhurt the victor chief pass by
Yet still in silence, by our hearts approved
Drink to the memory of the man we loved[56]

With this particular poem there could be some very interesting debates about the borderline between influence and plagiary. There is a poem by Reginald Heber called *Europe: Lines on the Present War*[57], published in 1809, i.e. before James wrote his poem, so there is no doubt about who influenced who.

Reginald Heber (1783 – 1826) was Bishop of Calcutta in the latter years of his life; he was the cousin of Richard Heber (1774 – 1833), a great book collector and tireless letter writer. One of his many correspondents was indeed James Stanhope.

---

[52] Footnote in original by Stanhope – "Alluding to what Bonaparte said of Moreau's death".
[53] VI has "firmest", which was also in V but crossed out and replaced by "steadiest".
[54] The six lines from "Midst civil rage" to "unclouded yet" are only in V2.
[55] V1 has "Then had we marched with fond and grateful cheers".
[56] These two lines in V1 read "But fill in silence by each heart approved, Here's to the memory of the man we loved!"
[57] There are numerous print on demand versions available on Internet. The poem was reproduced in Glover (ed.), *Staff Officer*, pp. 33-41.

The style of Heber's poem is very similar to those of James; the same poetic adjectives are used throughout (e.g. tardy, ensanguined[58]), and England is constantly referred to as Albion in both poems. Perhaps the clinching point lies in James' lines in the poem on Pitt:

> But next to Him who o'er this changeful ball
> Decrees the rise of empires and the fall

Which are almost a direct copy of Heber's own verses:

> Who, Lord of Nature, o'er this changeful ball
> Decree the rise of empires, and the fall.

Heber too has nothing but praise for Pitt:

> And thou, blest star of Europe's darkest hour,
> Whose words were wisdom and whose counsels power.

Not only was James Stanhope an aspiring poet, but he also had a fair hand at sketching. There is a book of sketches in the Stanhope manuscript collection[59], which contains twenty excellent landscapes and ten full-body profiles of different people. The landscape sketches evidence depth and feeling (see Figures 4.1, 4.2, 4.3 and 4.4), while the figures show a wide range of walks of life, each one with a few words that must have meant something to James (and possibly to others) at the time; most of the words for the drawings are in French, which could mean that the sketches date from his time in France and especially in Paris in 1815 and 1816.

The first sketch is a soldier under the words "Calicots de service"; calicot is a kind of material (known as calico in English) and is presumably a reference to the soldier's uniform (see Figure 4.5). An elegant elderly lady walking her dog is the next sketch, under the word "Thuilleries" (i.e. Tuileries) (see Figure 4.6), followed on the next page by a soldier, entitled

---

[58] The fact that in the later version of James' verses on Pitt "ensanguined" replaced "avenging", which was crossed out, could suggest that he read Heber's poem between writing his own first version and copying out the second version; he was drawn by the use of the word.

[59] U1590 C267. The manuscript catalogue attributes the sketch book to Frederica, but many of the scenes are from Spain and Portugal, drawn from memory according to the notes on the back; the handwriting of these notes is clearly James' and not Frederica's, and Frederica never visited either country in her short life while James spent time in both during the Peninsular War.

"English gravity" (see Figure 4.7). An older woman goes under the title of "English fashions, Boulevarts" (an unusual spelling mistake given that James' French was excellent) (see Figure 4.8), while a bespectacled Frenchman gestures with one hand while holding a scroll behind his back with the other, under the enigmatic title "Messieurs, dans le fond des deserts" (see Figure 4.9).

The next drawing is suggestively entitled "Tart woman in front of my door", and shows a woman with a strange headdress holding a basket. Just like in any other cartoon, her words are contained in a bubble in the best Franglais (see Figure 4.10): "I have un jeu, achetez priez, Lizanne[60] de Dieu".

The next sketch shows a thin man with a ponytail and the inscription "Le duc et voltique", and "Oui, merci, la duchesse est importante" (see Figure 4.11).

The sketches and drawings suggest that James was a better artist than he was a poet; they show he had a delicate appreciation of nature and a subtle sense of humour (even though the references are now lost on us).

---

[60] The reading "Lizanne" is not clear as the text is smudged. Lizanne is a name and Lizanne de Dieu (or whatever the correct reading may be) was possibly someone known to James in Paris.

Figure 4.1

Figure 4.2

Figure 4.3

Figure 4.4

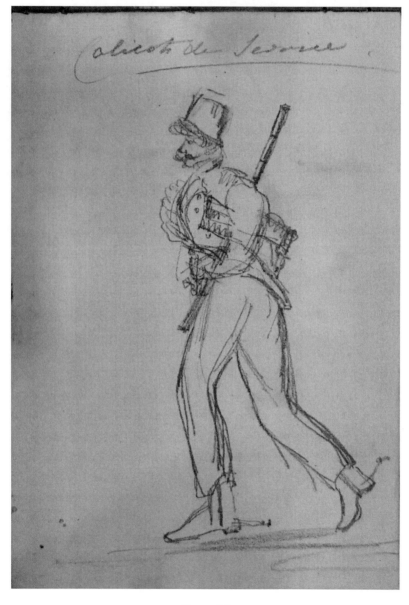

Figure 4.5

Figure 4.6

Figure 4.7

Figure 4.8

Figure 4.9

Figure 4.10

Figure 4.11

CHAPTER FIVE

WATERLOO

With his work at Bergen op Zoom in 1814, James no doubt that his part in the war against Napoleon had come to an end. The Emperor had surrendered and was a prisoner of the British. When he escaped and returned to France, however, in a chain of events that led to the final battle at Waterloo in 1815, James was once more involved. He wrote an account of his part in the campaign in his diary, which given the importance thereof in the history of Europe, I have chosen to give in full.

Journal of the Campaign of 1815, written the same year at Paris.

The return of Bonaparte broke upon the world like a hurricane, no one who did not witness the mute consternation of London at that period could believe it. No one who did will ever forget the impression. For the first time I went abroad with rather a heavy heart, it seemed as if all was to begin again and that all our former toils and blood and triumphs had been in vain.

However, I was not slow in getting off; on the 7th of April I left Dover and after a 38-hour passage in a crowded packet with all the passengers but myself wretchedly sick, arrived safely at Ostend. I set off immediately on my landing for Brussels where I arrived the following morning. I expressed my wish to the Duke to be placed again in the Quarter Master General's Department and he promised not to forget me, but seeing no immediate probability of a vacancy and having completed my equipment and bought a pair of Belgian coach horses and a farm one to carry my baggage, I left Brussels and joined the 3rd Battalion of the 1st Guards at Enghien on the 19th.

From this time till the opening of the campaign, I passed a very quiet but not disagreeable time, in the solitude of the farmhouse where I was quartered and the society of Brussels where I generally went twice a week. The army was gradually reinforcing and at the end was formed into 6 divisions of infantry and 2 corps. The 1st under the Prince of Orange with its right at Enghien and its left at Nivelles with its headquarters at Braine le Comte; the 2nd under Lord Hill on the Dender with his headquarters at Grammont, the cavalry occupying his front and right. The 5th Division was at Brussels; one brigade only of the 6th had arrived, the rest was in cantonments. We had about 30,000 British infantry, 7,000 British and old Hanoverian cavalry, about 3,000 more of New Hanoverian and Belgian. We had nearly Hanoverian infantry, about 20,000 Belgian and Dutch, including the Corps of Prince Frederick, and near 8,000 Brunswickers; in all about 80,000 men with about 100 pieces of British artillery and perhaps 30 others. I am not sure I am accurate in this statement but the correct states have been published.

Every exertion was now made to restore the works which the folly of Joseph 2nd had ordered to be dismantled, and they soon became a l'abri d'un coup de main. No communication was allowed between the outposts but no hostilities were committed. We were in constant expectation of hearing the advance of the larger allied armies, but Austria had detached a great part of her force into Italy and the Russians had not approached the Rhine. The Prussians had an army of 120,000 men along the Meuse under Blucher, whose headquarters were at Liege. General Seidlitz had the Prussian advance at Charleroi and to him principally was entrusted the charge of sending intelligence of the enemy's movements.

On the 9th of June it was known that the corps from Metz was in movement towards the Sambre and that the remaining corps were collecting near Maubeuge. On the 13th we heard of Bonaparte's arrival on the frontier and on the 15th the enemy drove in the Prussian outposts, who retreated to concentrate. The Prince of Orange on the 15th rode round the outposts and found the French withdrawn from our front and returned into Brussels to communicate that and the Prussian retreat to the Duke and at ½ past 5 p.m. on the 15th he received the first intelligence of the real intentions of the enemy. At 7 the orders were issued for the army to be ready at a moment's notice, but no order for movement was issued till night. When the Duke conceived that the enemy's movement on our left was a feigned one and that by a flank march Bonaparte would attempt to turn our right flank and gain Brussels by the Ath road, or whether he imagined the French were not sufficiently prepared to commence the campaign so early; but it is certain that the Duke never had the army so little in hand as on the 16th[1].

---

[1] Footnote by James: The Duke afterwards explained in a conversation where I was present his motives, which were as follows and nearly in his own words. "It is impossible to be everywhere. I knew my army was a more manoeuvring one than the Prussian. I left mine so placed that I could collect them on any point of the main road to Brussels. This was of the greatest consequence, for I knew I could get to the assistance of the Prussians but I could not so well trust on their being in time to assist me". Another unlucky circumstance was that part of Lord Hill's Corps had been moved several miles to the front for a field day and had consequently so many more miles to march. On such small circumstances sometimes hang great events.

The Duchess of Richmond gave a ball the evening of the 15th but I thought it imprudent to be absent, besides which I was very unwell with an abscess beginning to form in my back with every appearance of my old wound breaking out again[2]. The Duke was at the ball and conversed I am told with as much indifference as if the eventful moment had not been at hand. At 3 he was on horseback and in the morning a general movement took place. The Prince of Orange concentrated all he could at 4 Bras, consisting of Netherlands troops and Brunswickers. The 5th Division moved at night from Brussels and arrived at 4 Bras about 3 o'clock. The 1st Division moved at daylight to Braine le Comte where we were halted for some hours and then moved on to Nivelles. The 2nd was ordered also to move on Braine le Comte from Ath and the cavalry were to halt between it and Steenkirk and feed and then move on again in the evening. We had hardly taken up our ground in the rear of Nivelles at 4 o'clock which had been pointed out for the night when we received the order to move on with all speed as there was a severe action in which the Belgians had suffered considerably. We soon perceived the truth of this, for soon after passing Nivelles we met a good many wounded men going to the rear with ten times their number to take care of them, which did not strike me as a good specimen of the first trial of our allies.

A little farther on I met Colonel Dick of the 79th who was also wounded and who told they had been rode in upon by the French cavalry and suffered dreadfully. As far as I can recollect of the ground it was like this: the wood being so thick that it was impossible to see what we were about or where the enemy was in force (see Fig. 5.1).

We had hardly arrived opposite the wood when Colonel Abercrombie, Quarter Master General of the 1st Corps, rode up to us in great haste and said 'The French are close to you, a battalion must go into the wood and happen what will you must maintain it'. The 2nd Battalion wheeled into line, entered the wood and in an instant were engaged and we followed also in line. We soon drove the enemy from the wood, but not without confusion from all the companies getting mixed in the wood. We suffered severely from the fire of the enemy's grape and round shot from a battery on the hill and still more from partial and I think imprudent attempts to attack it. We should have contented ourselves with maintaining the wood and covering our men. It was an unpleasant sort of battle, for we were very much in air and only supported by one battalion and if the French had moved a strong

---

[2] James left a visiting card inserted in his diary at this point, bearing the name Comte John d'Oultremont, Grand Maréchal de la Cour de S. M. le Roi des Belges. It should be noted that this is the correct term; the monarch is not the King/Queen of Belgium, but rather of the Belgians.

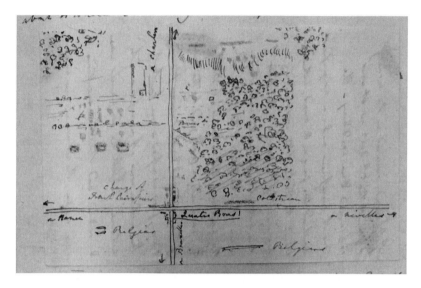

Figure 5.1 – Map from James' diary

column round our right we should have been very uncomfortably situated. The enemy's cavalry behaved with great gallantry, some cuirassiers made a splendid charge up the road at two guns where the Duke was standing at the X-ways and in spite of the grape and the fire of half a battalion of infantry which were lining the bank, whom they probably had not seen, they came close up to the guns, but the fire then was so deadly that they rode into a courtyard of a farm close by where most of them were bayoneted.

In reconsidering this battle there is certainly much truth in Ney's account of it, for our cavalry did not arrive till night having marched 25, 30 and some nearly 40 miles. Till very late we had no support and had the French carried the wood or been able to send a strong column round it, our communication with Nivelles and the advance of our supports would have been cut off. Two divisions of the French army, of the Guard, were neutralised completely by having first been sent from Ney to assist Bonaparte arriving near Fleurus when the action was decided and returning too late to cooperate in Ney's final attempt on our position.

If Ney had had this addition, he would have outnumbered us so much as to have obliged us to get behind the defile of Genappe; which without cavalry would have been perilous in the extreme. But the great fault which Ney committed was not engaging us the next morning as early as possible so as to impede our retreat, which Bonaparte with the victorious army should have been gaining on our right and moving towards our communications. The

Prussians sent no report of their defeat and retreat, at least none arrived and it was only by a personal reconnaissance next morning, the Duke ascertained they were gone. Soon afterwards the report arrived, but during this interval we were in a most critical position, but Ney's inactivity let us depart in quiet. Our brigade suffered a heavy loss, nearly 500 men killed and wounded; I had to deplore many of my best friends, poor Lord Hay, General Maitland's A.D.C., than whom a finer creature could not be seen, Gore, whose education and acquirements were beyond what is commonly found, and enhanced the esteem his amiable qualities inspired. Poor Miller was a great loss to the service as his whole heart and mind were concentrated in the pursuit of his profession. I met a wounded person in a blanket, on asking the men who it was, he knew my voice and calling me to him, embraced me and bade me an affectionate farewell; passing the colours of the battalion afterwards which were in the rear of the wood, he desired that he might be carried under them and laid hold of them, he felt for the last time. He had been terribly wounded by the lancers and died some days afterwards.

The morning of the 17th summoned us from our clammy beds to perform the last sad offices to Gore and Hay who were buried under a hollow oak on the skirt of the wood. There is nothing more awfully impressive than this sublime service, affecting at all times, a moment when the bearers feel the decisive hour is not yet come, when the enemy is still marshalled before their eyes and when perhaps before one night has passed, they may themselves require the aid, their affection and piety are now bestowing on their friends.

I took advantage of the pause before we moved to ride over the remainder of the field of battle. The highlanders were cut up from having been too slow in throwing themselves into squares. As I passed the spot where a heap of French cuirassiers were laying, a figure covered and clotted with blood so that his face was indistinguishable rose up from the heap and with a swift but staggering pace went across the country towards the Guards. I returned and sent 2 drummers after him, but he was too far and the retreat commenced. I never knew who he was or heard of him more, but it was like an apparition, so rising from the mound of the dead.

About 9 o'clock the Duke began to retire, everything by that time having joined, which he required[3], for Lord Hill was to cover the retreat of the wounded and stores from Nivelles. Whilst the infantry was moving off towards the defile, the Duke kept looking anxiously towards the front and

---

[3] Glover, *Eyewitness*, p. 174, omits the commas from this sentence, rendering it exceedingly difficult to understand.

about 10 he said 'Well there is the last of the infantry gone and I don't care now'. Here Ney lost his best chance! We continued our retreat without interruption to the heights of Mont St Jean in front of the village, having the 3rd Division on our left, the 6th on its left, Hougoumont like a bastion on the front of our right. Lord Hill's Corps at Braine la Leude en potence to the right and the corps of Prince Frederick with the 4th Division watching the great road by Hal.

In the afternoon we heard a cannonade against the cavalry covering our retreat and found afterwards that the Life Guards had distinguished themselves against some of the heavy cavalry which had been too much for our hussars, some of whom came in upon us, rather in too quick time.

Towards the evening we saw the enemy's columns arriving on the opposite hill; they sent some troops forward as if with the intention of occupying the wood of Hougoumont, and some cavalry trotted towards the hill to see what was behind it. This obliged us to show some guns (all the columns being concealed behind the hill). After a few shot the enemy desisted and both armies lay on their arms all night and such a night was hardly ever passed before; for the ground was of such a spongy nature that it soon became a bog and torrents of rain fell without intermission till the morning, the wind driving it along with prodigious force and peals of thunder filling up the intervals of the lightnings. We could get no wood that would burn and we were all miserable enough, but the thoughts of the morrow superseded all others. As for myself I had been getting worse every day, could eat nothing, was wretched in spirits at the idea of being obliged to give it up, for my back was now so swelled I could not button my coat and this completely overcame me. All my friends and the surgeons had urged me to go to Brussels from the 16th when we marched; I agreed that a board should inspect the wound on the morning of the 18th and determined to go to Brussels that night if the French did not attack. Some of my men got me a little dry wood and some straw and I bought a bottle of champagne from a sutler; I sent my servant (a sort of half Frenchman I had hired as a cook) to get a leg of mutton dressed; he was mounted on my horse and I saw him no more for 3 days. When we arrived on the position the day before, it did not appear so strong as a more accurate observation proved it to be. It was the best sort for English troops, a steep glacis on the French side and a moderate slope on ours, so that all movements might take place without being exposed to the observation or fire of the enemy. The army was in columns at ¼ distance in two lines with cavalry in reserve and powerful batteries of artillery were placed just within the ridge of the hill.

At about 10 o'clock it became evident they meant to attack; the Duke had informed Blucher of his belief of it the night before and at ten, he saw part of the Prussian army filing over a small stream towards Lavre from the left of our position[4]; we as regimental officers hoped for their assistance, but did not know of it till we saw them.

The hills on which we had seen but small bodies the night before was now black with clustered troops and large masses of infantry and heavy columns began to move slowly over the plain, sometimes concealed by the undulations of the ground and then showing themselves again with increased magnitude and splendour, for gleams of the sun came out and their lancers' pennons waved gaily in the wind; a column of infantry was directed against Hougoumont and another against La Hay Sainte. During all this our army was invisible behind the hill and the enemy could see nothing but a few horsemen and spectators amid untrodden and waving grain. It is impossible for a regimental officer to describe a battle, I will only attempt to sketch what I saw.

When the enemy's column was considered within range our artillery crowned the crest of the hill. The first shot, the signal of such slaughter, was fired from our front, it fell short; the second plunged into the middle of the column and in an instant a blaze burst from the range of the hill, which roared from 100 mouths. Not many minutes elapsed before some round shot coming about us warned us of the French artillery being in position. The men were ordered to lie down, first being formed in echelon of squares, a field officer having the command of each face (I had the right). We heard the action raging hotly at Hougoumont, and soon after the roll of musketry from the left announced the main attack on our centre at La Haye Sainte. A number of staff officers were soon killed and wounded who were at first alone exposed to the cannonade. General Cooke lost his arm, shells began to fall in our squares, and though many men were blown up and horribly mangled I never saw such steadiness. As the poor wounded wretches remained in the square it was a horrid sight in cold blood. Soon after a cry of cavalry was heard on the crest of the hill and we saw the artillerymen run from their guns and seek protection in our squares. The men stood up; we advanced a few yards and saw a mass of cuirassiers close to us with thousands of forked pennons waving behind them in all their vanity of colours. From the rain there was no dust and it was a most beautiful sight. The square on the left of the 3rd Division opened their fire and soon from every square issued a steady, well directed and destructive fire. For four hours the cavalry never left our front, sometimes retiring a little under the

---

[4] Glover, *Eyewitness*, p. 176, transcribes the word "but" here, which cannot be correct because it makes no sense. The word in the manuscript does seem to start with the letters b and u, but the third letter is blotted, and not crossed as all of James' t's are. I think he made a mistake and so I have omitted the word.

hill to get into order and then charging afresh with all the fury of despair; it is not possible to exaggerate their bravery. They repeatedly rode in upon and got temporary possession of our guns; the instant our fire drove them back, our brave artillerymen returned and poured fresh volleys of grape into their dense masses till successive charges drove them back into our squares. Thus continued our part of the battle and except a momentary impetuosity on first beating off the cavalry, when our men shouted and wished to charge, they were as cool as if in the park. The French cavalry at length sent skirmishers close up to us to fire pistols into our squares to tease us into a volley at these small game, whilst we saw their great masses below waiting to charge; but we were as cool as they were and allowed only a few of our good shots to pick these fellows off. When we drove the cavalry from the guns many came up to us and shook their sabres at us in rage and some smashed their swords on the guns they had so often ineffectively taken. The Duke frequently rode by us, Lord Anglesey rode up to us and said 'Well done men, by God we stand on you. If I could only get my fellows to do the same but by God they won't budge; but I'll try again', and he rode and charged ineffectually at the head of a regiment of light cavalry on our left. The heavy cavalry did wonders, but our light cavalry, partly from their being brought up in small isolated attacks instead of a great mass, in this part of the battle, near us did very little. When the skirmishers were teasing us, Horace Seymour rode up in a great hurry and said 'God damn you; don't you see there are French. Why don't you fire at them?', at which Lord Saltoun, who had returned from Hougoumont, almost all his men being killed and wounded, answered very coolly 'Why damn you; don't you think we know better when to fire than you do?' and away went our advisor. By this time grape began to thin our ranks and the French infantry approached; they ought to have been there three hours before, for by this time we had finished their cavalry. Their first attack we beat off with fire; Maitland, who commanded the division on Cooke's wound, one of the bravest, ablest and best informed of our generals, as he is one of the kindest and best of men, began to fear we might lose the artillery in case of a reverse, and sent me to find the artillery horses which had departed during our conflict with the cavalry. I passed the cavalry dismounted in a hollow in the rear; nothing could exceed the confusion towards the village of St Jean. During the action with the cavalry, numbers of Belgians had left their places and the whole road was choked with their cavalry of all sorts, wounded on horseback and in blankets, artillery wagons passing and returning. I met the Prince of Orange wounded, Fitzroy Somerset, Elley, and as I was returning not having found the horses, I met poor Stables of my own battalion, who had been wounded in my absence with a grape shot through the body. By his looks I saw it was all over, I helped him to an artillery wagon near; he died at a cottage next morning and a sergeant who attended him saw him decently buried.

I hastened back to my battalion, but they had advanced. The first regiment I came up to was the 52nd, who were on the flank of the grand attack of the Imperial Guard, who advanced beautifully with their officers in their front waving their swords and hats and cheering them on with 'Vive Napoleon'.

A shout burst from the English line and such a shout of victory never can be forgotten when the fire poured in on them on all sides, stopped them as if turned into stone. The front sections fell like cards; they began to show timidity toward the rear and the English line shouted and moved on. Some cavalry (I believe the old Heavy Germans of Bock's in Spain now turned into light cavalry) swept round the flank of the 52nd and the confusion from that moment and rout were complete. Pausing on top of the next hill for the first time, saw that it was not all owing to us. I had heard some time an additional firing ion the front on our left, but amid such thunder had thought little about it. It was now getting dusk, but the last gleam showed me a sight all description cannot give an idea of. The plain now dimly seen was dark with a mass of mingled combatants and indistinct from the firing which was still partially kept up on the left towards La Belle Alliance, from the wind setting that way and the ground being wet the smoke of the battle hung low on the ground. Through this at speed came gun after gun and squadron after squadron, who with their lances waving seemed as if they were charging on a cloud. To witness such a glorious soul-transporting sight, to feel that I had been able to go through the battle and to be grateful at having survived it, was the work of a moment; but the last feeling of that day. I was then with the Coldstream and perfectly exhausted had dismounted from my horse and laid down upon the ground and in a moment was asleep. The Guards were ordered on and when they came to their final bivouac for the night, one of my friends (I believe Major Bowles) missed me and recollected he had seen me lay down. He sent back and after a considerable search I was found still asleep among the dead and the dying, the plunderers and the plundered. If they had not remembered me, some kindly hand would have spared me the trouble of awaking again. I remained with the Coldstream all night and next morning rejoined my battalion, which was about a mile in front to the left, close to La Belle Alliance.

In the morning of the 19th I prepared to go to Brussels when Sir John Byng, now commanding 1st Corps, urged me so strongly to take if but for a day the duty of Quarter Master General as Abercrombie QMG of the 1st Corps and Bradford of the 1st Division were both wounded, that I determined at all risks to attempt it; but it was an arduous undertaking for anyone from the ranks with no knowledge of previous arrangements without sufficient horses and with no maps; in my state of health to take such a responsibility, as the charge of the 1st Corps then amounting to I suppose to 15,000 men. At Nivelles the same evening I begged him to write to get someone else, but the orders arrived in the middle of the night and it was impossible. The exertion and fatigue began to absorb the abscess, my appetite returned and I was evidently better. In three days I no longer thought of leaving the army and I was rejoiced in being joined by my servant and favourite mare. He had been taken but had escaped in the confusion of the retreat. But I must add a very few thoughts on the general character of this great battle.

On the whole it has been perhaps the severest ever fought by British troops, for although our infantry has often been exposed to more unequal numbers and as destructive a fire, it was never called on to resist the united efforts of such a tremendous cannonade and such a cloud of cavalry at a moment when our artillerymen were driven from their guns and our cavalry were unable to make head against the stream. The contracted limits of the position made the slaughter immense as the cannonade was concentrated, but it was fortunate, for the Dutch and Belgians soon began to disappear and their gaps would have been fatal to us in a more extended position. When the battle began we had two or three squares between us and the 3rd Division, before it ended the redcoats were the nearest battalion. The Prince of Orange[5], who has been since praised into believing his countrymen to be heroes, wrote the next morning most anxiously to the Duke, 'To know how he could explain or pass over the conduct of the Netherland troops', and the Duke answered, 'I shall praise generally and not detail, so nobody will know anything about them'. We appear to have had the least share as all nations equally claim the victory and even the French scarce allow a defeat.

My unbiased opinion is this, as to the real proportion of the victory due to the Prussian and English armies; without the Prussians we should have held our position, we should have made our first advance so as the occupy the field of battle and with that perhaps 100 cannon and many thousand prisoners would have been the trophies of the English victory. The French would have been secure behind the defile of Genappe; our loss was so immense, the little dependence to our Netherland friends so plain, that it would have admitted of a doubt whether we or the enemy had retreated next

---

[5] Footnote by James: Some time afterwards the Prince of Orange asked General Alava at his father's table what the Spaniards would have done in such a battle, unawed by the presence, that gallantest and [most] honest of men answered, "Like Your Highness's troops, but I think they would have come back again!".

day. To the Prussians[6] therefore is due the great results of the victory, the sanguinary, unrelenting and unceasing pursuit and the total dispersion of the army. So complete was it that our march to Paris was as if through a friend's country, not one man of all that mighty army was to be seen. It seemed by the suddenness of their appearance at Ligny and 4 Bras that the earth had disgorged a host to lay it waste and that they had again crept into her womb, so utter the solitude we witnessed. Beyond the limit where the dead marked the pursuit, no trace remained of that boasting and nearly triumphant army.

As is usual with the unfortunate, Bonaparte has been much blamed for his management of this campaign, and Ney and Grouchy have largely shared in it. I will not enter at length into this question but simply state:

1st that Ney was most to blame at 4 Bras or whoever directed the Guard backward and forward without use. That in answer to the attack made on Bonaparte for not having retired before he was entombed by the Prussians round his flank on the 18th; it must be recollected he was an Emperor as well as a general, and that if he had retreated, the prestige was gone and his empire must have passed away; and he has been blamed for detaching Grouchy and the latter has been more censured for not having come to his assistance. I will relate the opinions of the Duke of Wellington as I heard him express them on these points for I believe them to be the truth. At a dinner at Grassini's at Paris a Frenchman asked if he might speak frankly to the Duke about the battle, who answered yes, and in answer to several questions said 'It is very easy to fight a battle when it's over. How could Grouchy come to his assistance? He had a superior army in his front, which it was necessary to keep in check; and if he had at last wished to detach, there was no time. I saw the Prussians within four miles of us filing over a stream at 10 in the morning. The impediments were so great that they did not reach us till 7. How then could any detachment of Grouchy who had three times the distance to come, have arrived in time?' He was asked what he should have done if he had been Bonaparte, he said 'I think I should have respected the English infantry more after what I must have heard of them in Spain and that I should not have taken the bull by the horns; I should have turned a flank, the right flank. I should have kept the English army occupied by a demonstration to attack or perhaps by slight attacks, whilst I was in fact moving the main body by Hal on Brussels; but if I had determined on attacking as Bonaparte did, nobody could do more'.

The French lost much by the destruction of their cavalry against our squares so early, but it was not Bonaparte's fault for he sent frequently to

---

[6] Footnote by James: The Duke was very anxious for the arrival of the Prussians and said "He never in his life looked so often at his watch".

recall them, but once on the plateau they could not be made to retire. The rain was much in our favour for from there being no dust we saw every movement plain and would fire without risk to each other. Nothing daunts the soldier more so much as a charge of cavalry preceded by a cloud of dust, which concealing the force magnifies the peril. Many days passed before we knew who had fallen; I had to deplore many of my oldest friends. The country had to mourn Picton, the most intrepid and the sternest soldier we had; for De Lancey, who had but one thought, his profession. Few had studied so deeply in theory and fewer still illustrated it so bravely, skilfully and frequently by practice. Frederick Ponsonby, who is physically immortal, was saved to us; his friends, which includes all who know him, could scarcely have rejoiced over a battle in which their favourite had fallen. I escaped entirely untouched, one of the 4 out of 14 field officers who marched on the 16th, all the rest being killed or wounded.

19th moved on Nivelles, 20th on Binche, passed field of Malplaquet. The Duke passed the corps, who cheered him, and such a cheer in such a spot it brought tears into my eyes, and entered Bavay on the 21st.

22nd Headquarters at Le Cateau, we at Gommegnies. I saved a poor woman's cow, whose approaching fate she was lamenting in a most simple and affecting manner.

23rd we halted, went over to headquarters; the Duke put me in orders as Quarter Master General. I congratulated him on his victory and escape; he said with much feeling in his tone, 'Indeed it was wonderful; the finger of God was certainly on me that day'. Cambrai was taken by escalade.

24th Bousies, 25th Premont. 26th 1st Division ordered to Caulaincourt, passed the magnificent canal of St Quentin. At Caulaincourt I found fresh orders for the Guards to attack Peronne, where the Duke already was. He had summoned it and the governor refused to surrender. The chief engineer insisted on the ditch being shallow as he saw reeds. I examined several peasants and reported to the Duke there was 10 feet of water. Fascines were made, the attack ordered and the engineer warned us against the bridge, which was mined. We moved on, in went the fascines, and after them an engineer, who sank like a float with a bite. There was no entrance that way, but the light infantry drove the enemy from the suburb and crossed the bridge which was not mined; a gun was brought up and we blew open the gate. The Duke was on the bridge close by me when we were covered with a shower of grape but escaped. Lord Saltoun was knocked over by one which lodged in his purse. I went in to try to negotiate; on seeing my handkerchief they ceased firing at me and I went in alone. Terms were soon settled; in the meantime some Belgian cavalry cut the ropes of the drawbridge and came in with every appearance of violence. On trying to get them out according to the terms of the capitulation, they tried to cut me down and the French governor was obliged to draw in my defence; I never could find out the men though I reported it.

24th Billancourt 26th Conchy 29th Choisy 30th La Chapelle 1st of July Le Bourget in front of Montmartre, the army took up a position. I went down to Aubervilliers with the 1st Division to relieve the Prussian Corps of Bulow, whose Quarter Master General did not like my visiting the outposts in a red coat and with a white feather, and wanted me to change clothes; loopholed and fortified entrance of Le Bourget; heard of Blucher's crossing the Seine[7]. On the 2nd the convention was signed.

On the 4th we occupied St Denis, 5th Montmartre, and on the 7th the whole army was encamped in the Bois de Boulogne. Much has been said of this convention, it was certainly a purely military one; it was very advantageous to both parties. Blucher, against the Duke's advice, had hurried on to be the first in Paris and would have been attacked next morning by nearly 70,000 men who were in Paris, and he had not above 40,000. The Duke meant to have moved the English army right to support him, and we probably should have arrived in time, but it was foolish to risk anything when the game was our own, and if we had waited a few days in position together we might [have] taken Paris without terms and annihilated the army of the Loire. The French saved their capital and we put an end to the possible intrigues of fortune; and thus ended with a pacific march and a coup de plume our shortest and most glorious campaign[8].

I have provided James' text of the campaign with no interruptions. The following letters are contemporary and provide further details of the campaign and his part in it.

2 May 1815, to his mother, from Hoves, near Enghien
Does not your Ladyship imagine I have great reason to complain when I have not received <u>one</u> line from you since I have left England though I have written 2 letters containing at least 4 each?

I am quartered in a very pretty and comfortable farm, among fresh eggs, pigs, poultry and cows before the house, nightingales in every bush behind it, not a bad cuisine and establishment inside, no aches or cares to molest me, but no letter from you to delight me.

---

[7] In Glover, *Eyewitness*, p. 187, this paragraph is mistakenly included in a letter from James to his mother, while the previous line of the diary is included in a letter to Lady Mansfield.
[8] Glover, *Eyewitness*, pp. 192-193, includes this paragraph in a letter from James to Lady Spencer.

As yet no arrangement has been made towards placing me on the staff …. There are so many candidates with superior claims that I am not very sanguine about it.

The misfortune is that when there is a subject we have no time and when we have time there is no subject.

He wrote again to his mother, also from Hoves, on 14 May 1815:

I received you first letter on the same I day I complained of not having heard from you, and this morning your other two arrived safe.

I have been wandering about a great deal seeing neighbouring towns, ancient fields of battle,

Strained my ankle slightly from my horse falling on me but cela se passe en deux jours.

Adios querida madre[9]

P.S. Give my best love to Nash when you see her.

Hoves, 14 June 1815:

My dear mother,

I have not written to you for a considerable time from the same cause which produced your silence: for your first reason, that of having been unwell, is not a good one, as that is of all others the time I should be the most anxious to receive your letters; and in the full belief of this I am now writing, as I am sorry to say there is every appearance of my wound healing out again – a tumour is formed and the surgeons think that matter is collecting. All that now I feel is nothing but that sort of weaning ache I have so often complained of.

It may be a long time before it lays me up and if I can only stand the beginning of the campaign, shall be contented, for I cannot bear the idea of losing what promises to be the most brilliant war of modern times, but of course against a severe illness it would be useless to struggle, and you need not therefore be apprehensive of my doing anything impudent – but of course I shall stick to the army as long as I can hold on and if I am then obliged to go to Brussels to be confined, I shall not at any rate feel a satisfaction in recollecting that it is not my fault or an illness of my own creation – I have only felt it these past four days, so it is not impossible it may yet absorb.

---

[9] James enjoyed including sentences in French and Spanish in his letters.

There is every probability of the campaign commencing in a very few days – as I believe everything is nearly up – allow me to hint to you not to direct your letters to any particular place, but generally 1st Guards ....

Remember me oft to Sir J B[10] and the ladies, and tell him "my tale of woe" as I have not time to write this post. I am rejoiced to hear he is better. Tell him I heard from Hester as late as the 12th of March, still from Syria, quite well.

Like the good and dutiful son he was, he wrote a scribbled note to his mother on 19 June 1815, the day after the battle, just to let her know he was safe; the writing is very untidy, this is a hurried note (see Figure 5.2).

I have only time to tell you that I am safe, not having 30 left out of 400, in the two actions. I have never gained such a unity as yesterday. My old wound is very troublesome but I want [to] go on as I am acting as QMG for the present, Bradford being wounded. Write to Griselda and tell her with my love I am well and to General Grenville and all friends. God bless you.

He wrote again from Conchy on 28 June 1815, informing the Countess that his wound was getting better and that they were on their way to Paris. He comments on the battle was as follows: "Pour moi je suis satisfait with Waterloo, for no earthly consideration, no wealth or honours would I exchange for the delight of having witnessed such a day. I am confirmed on the staff as Assistant Quarter Master General".

James was not knighted for his services at Waterloo, despite his hopes. As often happens when one is frustrated in such a desire, they say it means nothing to them (a feeling which is generally contradicted by the tone and content of the rest of what they put to paper). He wrote as follows to Lady Mansfield[11] on 24 September[12]:

You must have been a good deal surprised at seeing my name not included in the Companions of the Bath, as I was informed of my being one last year and as at any rate I have not less claim now. I am

[10] I.e. Sir Joseph Banks, the famous botanist, who was to play a significant role in James' life.
[11] His future mother-in-law. James started writing regularly to both Lord and Lady Mansfield at this time.
[12] Glover, *Eyewitness*, p. 199, justifies James' omission: "… but he [James] seems to have forgotten that he served at the battle as a regimental officer, not on the staff".

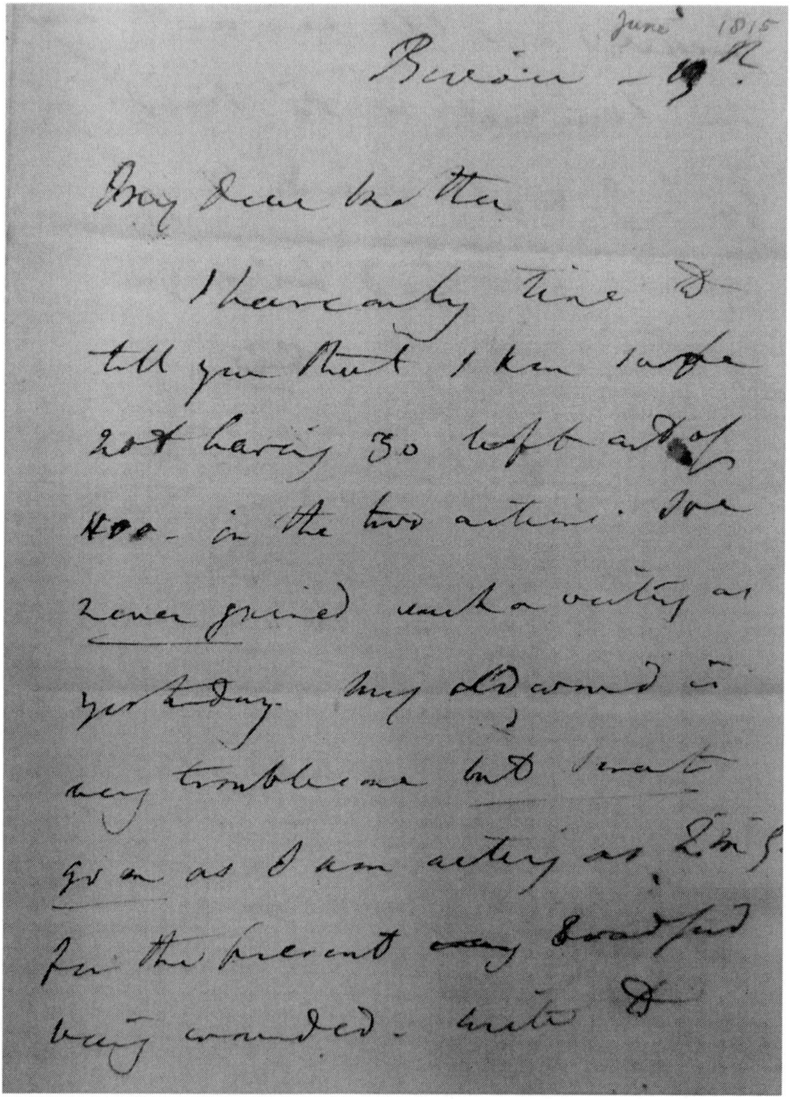

June 1815

[illegible] – 19th

My dear Mother

I have only time to
tell you that I am safe
not having 30 left out of
400 – in the two actions. We
never gained such a victory as
yesterday. My old wound is
very troublesome but I want to
go on as I am acting as 2nd [illegible]
for the present [illegible]
being wounded. Write to

Figure 5.2 – James' note to his mother the day after the battle

quite amazed and very angry, especially when I find my brother
A.D.C. Barclay, who never saw a shot fired till the 18th, among them,
and Colquitt, a junior officer in my own regiment because he
commanded the battalion, which had the circumstance been known
I ought to have commanded. As for the honour, I think nothing of it,
but I consider the omission as a positive disgrace. The moment I saw
I was not included I went to the Duke's and saw him, and stated the
case both as to San Sebastian and Waterloo. He desired me to write
it down and he would see what could be done ... If I got it, the whole
pleasure (if there were any in receiving it) vanishes by being obliged
to extort what ought to have been spontaneously given ... My being
placed on the Staff was in the same manner extorted by circumstance
and had there been an officer to do the duty, I might have still been
with my company. That however, flatters my friends, as I owe no
thanks or gratitude for that, except to Byng, who desired me to fulfil
the duties of the department. I beg you will keep all this quite secret
out of Scone[13].

James remained in France for quite some time after Waterloo, mainly in
Paris. His letters help us trace his movements and understand what he did
before coming home. He wrote to his mother from Paris on 11 October
1815:

The hopes I expressed in my last letter[14] of seeing you in England
this autumn no longer appear likely to be realized, as the delays that
have taken place in the signature of the treaty and the many points
which on it still remain unsettled, have kept and will keep the troops
here a long time.
    The opposing parties cordially join in abuse of us and the
gratitude they should feel to the Duke for having saved Paris and the
esteem they should entertain for an army which has been guilty of
hardly an instance of want of discipline are forgotten in their rage at
the cleaning out of the Louvre.
        ...
    The Louvre has lost all its charms and though it is an act of justice
it really makes me melancholy to look at its bare walls and deserted

---

[13] Glover (*Eyewitness*, p. 199) mistakenly adds the word "and" in square brackets
between "secret" and "out", making it mean that Lady Mansfield was not to mention
it anywhere, neither at Scone, whereas what James means is that she can of course
tell her family (at Scone), but nobody else.
[14] The letter he refers to is not in the collection.

pedestals. In two months I hardly missed a day and the absence of
such amusement is not easily compensated. I am learning to paint in
body colours and am getting on tolerably.

He was still in Paris on 12 November 1815, when he told his mother "If
I do not write often it is from having nothing worth telling you, for I never
repeat scandal and politics would bore you as much as they would perplex
me to explain".

It was mentioned above that James coincided with Michael Bruce in
Corunna (although at the time they would have had no reason to become
acquainted). In Paris in December 2015 they coincided for a second time,
and this time Bruce's activities secured him a name and made him well-
known all over the country and all over England too. On the eve of the
execution of Count Lavalette (under similar charges to those levelled
against Marshal Ney), the Count's wife and daughter visited him in prison.
He changed clothes with his wife and managed to escape dressed in her
garments (his wife, who remained behind in the cell, was later released,
although the harsh time she spent in prison affected her sanity for several
years). Bruce and two other English officers helped Lavalette escape from
Paris, and were consequently sentenced to three months in prison[15]. The trial

---

[15] The Duchess of Cleveland says that Michael Bruce was "one of the three knights
errant that effected Lavalette's escape from prison on the night before his intended
execution; a clever, ambitious man, familiar with every kind of travel and adventure,
and both able and willing (as the event proved) to be of the greatest use to Lady
Hester". As a member of the family with an interest in upholding her aunt's name,
the Duchess never once mentions the fact that Hester and Bruce were lovers,
although knowing that they were, she has nothing to say against Bruce. He did not
actually help in the escape from prison, only in getting the escaped prisoner out of
Paris and France. Joan Haslip says of Bruce's helping Lavalette, "It was an act of
knight errantry, worthy of Lady Hester Stanhope's lover, and it was the one dramatic
hour of a useless, lazy life". In his biography of another of the helpers of Lavalette,
Sir Robert Wilson, Michael Glover describes Bruce as "the wastrel son of a banker"
(*A Very Slippery Fellow: The Life of Sir Robert Wilson 1777-1849*, Oxford, 1978,
p. 151). The diary of Lady Charlotte Bury (*The Diary of a Lady-in-Waiting*, London,
1908, pp. 75-76), says the following: "If ever there was a person to whom the Scotch
proverb of 'Great cry and little wool' is applicable, it was so to Mr. Bruce. He began
his career as a spoilt child, he pursued it as a spoilt youth, and after having become
an Eastern dandy, returned to enact the part of a hero in a Parisian melodrama.
Having reached London, with all his honours fresh upon his head, he turned the
heads of several elderly ladies, and ended his public career by marrying a widowed
lady with several children. Mr. Bruce would have been a very harmless and rather
ornamental member of society in his youth had not an overweening vanity rendered
him the dupe of flattery and froth". Count Lavalette himself says that Bruce left them

did not take place until April 1816, and the term in prison was from that date, meaning a total of six months.

Hester wrote to Bruce on 5 March 1816, before she knew anything of Count Lavalette and Bruce's arrest and imprisonment. What she says suggests that James and Bruce had already met, in which case it must have been in Paris before December 1815 (Bruce had gone back to Paris from England in October 1814). Hester says:

> James contradicts all said about your manner. He says you are most reserved, and that is what I wish, what in these times is quite, is absolutely necessary. He does you justice in all things, may you ever remain the best and dearest of friends and mutually serve each other through life, may he be the representation of my affection without my faults, without that violence of feelings which so torments myself as well as others at times I fear ......

Also before Hester was aware of what had happened to Michael in Paris, she was seriously considering asking James to either come and take her back to England, or at least to ask him to go to the south of France, where she too would go to see him. In one of her numerous letters to General Oakes, the Governor of Malta, dated 25 April 1815, she writes "I have at last decided upon sending for James to take me away from this country"[16], while on 22 April 1816 she wrote to the Marquis of Buckingham as follows; "Once only will I go to France, to see you and James, but only that once". In the same letter she also writes "You and James must let me know if you can come and meet me in Provence, for to Paris I will not go"[17]. In the end she never acted upon either plan, and remained in the Lebanon.

When Hester did find out about Bruce and his adventures in Paris, she wrote to James from Mar Elias as follows on 15 April 1816:

> Dearest James,
> I have just heard of the sad scrape poor dear Bruce has got into, it goes to my heart, that is all I can say. Convey to him, if you can, all I feel for his situation, I believe that is all it would be proper to ask of an Officer and if I have asked anything contrary to your duty,

---

in order to spend some time with Ney's widow, his lover; cf. Le Comte de Lavalette, *Mémoires et Souvenirs* (Paris, 1994) p. 428: "Moi, me dit Bruce, je vais passer trois jours à la campagne de la princesse de la Moskowa, car vous n'avez plus besoin de moi. Mes voeux vous accompagneront, et j'aurai de vos nouvelles par mes amis".

[16] Quoted in Cleveland, *Life and Letters*, p. 176.
[17] Quoted in Cleveland, *Life and Letters*, pp. 185-186.

I am aware you know too well to comply with it. Can you wish me
in France? Am I not better here? For I feel for all unhappy people,
be they who they may, and I feel I should have too much to feel there.
I have never yet said anything to you of the distress the death of a
Frenchman in this country has caused me. I feared you would
reproach me for liking them much too well, and I did not wish to
have any fresh disputes with you, but as the account of the exertions
I have made to avenge his death will probably reach you sooner or
later, I might as well tell you the truth, that I have acted in this affair
as I have ever done in those which interest me deeply. I thought this
man one of the cleverest I ever knew, as well as one of the best
principled, and that is enough. Let dear Lord Sligo know that you
have heard from me again, and that his friend Sir _____ Chatterton,
or some such name, and Mr. Leslie are coming into this part of the
world.

Adieu dearest James, my heart is very heavy, but in sorrow, as in
joy, it has always turned to you.

James was still in Paris on 16 January 1816 (the seventh anniversary of
the Battle of Corunna, although he makes no mention of this), when he
wrote to his mother, "I was much concerned to find by a long letter I
received from Griselda that their affairs are so seriously involved. There is
nothing definitely settled about myself. I never was better".

While in Paris James made the acquaintance of Lady Frances Shelley[18],
who left her impressions and anecdotes about these times in her diary[19]. She
often met James: "On the day after the opera, some officers called, and we

---

[18] Frances was born on 16 June 1787 at Preston. She was a good friend of the Duke
of Wellington - information in her diary and other sources indicates that she and the
Duke enjoyed conversation and riding together as she was a notable horsewoman.
After the Battle of Waterloo, the Shelleys planned a trip to Paris. During their time
in the city, the Duke allowed them to use his boxes at the theatres in Paris, and
escorted Lady Shelley on horseback to various military reviews. She dined with him
regularly as Sir John, Frances' husband, was often out if not ill with gout. Wellington
introduced her to various personages. She attended the Allied Review of Troops in
July in a glass coach with outriders and footmen provided by the Duke. Gossip about
their relationship was, of course, rife. The Duke simultaneously entertained more
than one mistress, about whom Lady Shelley was aware but somehow managed not
to meet. Her diary does not read like one would expect a record of a passionate affair
but as a more platonic, intimate friendship. She also wrote of her husband with great
affection. She died in 1873. Adapted from https://englishhistoryauthors.blogspot.
com/2019/06/the-duke-of-wellingtons-female-circle.
[19] *The Diary of Lady Frances Shelley*, 2 vols. (London, 1912-1913).

took Colonel Stanhope to see Lady Kinnaird, who has been in Paris since November, and is, consequently, very entertaining". On another day she writes:

On the following day we went in the Duke's carriage to Versailles. We had a relay of horses. I never was more deeply touched than when I stood upon that balcony upon which the Queen and all the Royal Family appeared on the night before they were seized. From there one sees the road by which the mob arrived on that tremendous day. I shall not easily forget the impression of that moment.

The orangery is magnificent, but I regret to say that our aides-de-camp sacked the place in our service! Our party consisted of Lord and Lady Kinnaird, Colonel Stanhope, Lord March, Mr. S. Bathurst, and General Maitland. In the evening we dined with the Duke, went on to the Feydeau, and then to Madame Crauford's.
…
Talleyrand gave me his box at the Français; so we went there before going to Lady Castlereagh's very pleasant ball. Colonel Stanhope, the life and soul of every party, surpassed himself in fun and mirth; and we danced until the small hours of the morning.
…
Yesterday we went, with Madame de Peysac, Colonel Stanhope and Sir. D. Packe, to Bagatelle … We sat for an hour upon a grassy bank, while Colonel Stanhope recited some of the finest passages from 'Childe Harolde'. He also repeated some fine lines, written by an unhappy youth on the fly-leaf of 'The Pleasures of Memory'. This young man's idea was that, were it not for the dread that memory would survive the grave, Death would be happiness. It would relieve us from the torment which memory produces. When I heard that the young poet, after writing these lines, immediately committed suicide, I shuddered.

What an extraordinary person is Stanhope! If you happen to be in a frivolous mood, he will say foolish things, and will inspire folly in others. If you are in a serious vein, his conversation becomes interesting, and in the highest degree instructive. If you feel sentimental, his wonderful memory will supply poetical images from the finest passages in poetry. In coming home from Montmorency a few days ago, I asked him to tell me a story. He rolled them out, one after the other, always using the most appropriate expression, and with a precision in detail which made each story appear credible. Without being handsome, Colonel Stanhope is not bad-looking – but he is never two days alike. He is a charming companion; obliging, good-tempered, full of wit; and yet it would be quite impossible to fall in love with him. This makes his companionship especially delightful.

This is a fascinating portrait of James. He was the "life and soul of every party", a fantastic story teller, loved reading poetry and was "not bad-looking". He was a "charming companion; obliging, good-tempered, full of wit", and yet at the same time it was "quite impossible to fall in love with him". Lady Shelley offers no explanation for this somewhat enigmatic comment, unless it is that "he is never two days alike", possibly a reference to a moody, changing personality, something Hester referred to earlier on when talking about their uncle Pitt, saying "James often used to look very black".

What Lady Shelley has to say about the poet who committed suicide is eerily prophetic of what would happen to James ten years later. She makes reference to the poem *The Pleasures of Memory* by Samuel Rogers, who died in 1855. Apparently a youthful poet (who remained anonymous), wrote on a flyer (possibly attached to a book containing the poem that James had, or it might have been a well-known event at the time) claiming that death is a pleasure as it relieves us from the torment of remembering things (although he had the doubt that memory might somehow survive death). The youth took his own life shortly afterwards. Lady Shelley presumably wrote her diary soon after the events described, as she makes no mention of James' death and speaks of him as very much alive.

James wrote home again from Cambrai on 12 March 1816, expecting to be home shortly. He expects to be put on a lower income, but he was "about to revisit England, there is something in those two last words which compensates for a great deal, and I trust in a short time to see you in all the good health and with all the happiness I desire you".

However, he was still in Cambrai on 24 April. He tells his mother that he hasn't written recently because "I have been wandering about a great deal". He revisited the battlefield at Waterloo and Quatre Bras.

We do not know the exact date when James returned to England; the last letter we have while he was still in France is dated 24 April, while the first letter we have written in England is dated 17 October. I would imagine the date of return was closer to April than to October, otherwise there would surely have been more letters to England (although it is also possible that any such letters could have been lost)[20].

---

[20] Glover, *Eyewitness* p. 202, suggests that before writing the letter dated 17 October, James had spent a "considerable period" with the Mansfields at Scone in Scotland.

CHAPTER SIX

JAMES AND FREDDY

David William Murray (see Figure 6.1) was born in Paris in 1777 to David Murray, then 7th Viscount Stormont, and Louisa, daughter of Charles Cathcart, 9th Lord Cathcart. In 1792 his father succeeded to his uncle William Murray's creation of the Mansfield earldom; Murray himself succeeded in 1796, inheriting Kenwood House in Camden, London (see Figures 6.2, 6.3, 6.4 and 6.5). The family also had homes in Scotland and Ireland. On 16 September 1797 he married Frederica Markham (1774 – 24 November 1837). There is a portrait at Kenwood which is reputedly of the Countess (see Figure 6.6). Frederica was one of the seven daughters of William Markham, Archbishop of York, and his wife, the former Sarah Goddard.

David and Frederica had nine children, the eldest of whom was Lady Frederica Louisa Murray (1800–1823), who married James Hamilton Stanhope in 1820[1]. James' friendship with the Mansfields (the family was generally known by the title rather than their natural surname) dates from at least 1814 (when his earliest surviving letters to them were written, but in order to write to them he must have known them beforehand); he wrote numerous letters to Lord and Lady Mansfield, although in these early missives there is no mention of their daughter. In later correspondence James and Freddy claim to have met and if "fallen in love" is too ambitious an expression, to have "noticed each other" as early as 1815, when Frederica was just fifteen years old and James twenty-seven. Frederica had a remarkable memory for dates, and in a letter to James dated 22 March 1821

---

[1] The others were Lady Elizabeth Anne Murray (1803-1880), unmarried, Lady Caroline Murray (1805-1873), who became Lady of the Bedchamber to Princess Mary, Duchess of Gloucester and Edinburgh, William David (1806–1898), who succeeded as 4th Earl of Mansfield, Lady Georgina Catherine Murray (1807-1871), the Honourable Charles John Murray (1810-1851), the Honourable David Henry Murray (1811-1862), a captain in the Scots Fusilier Guards, Lady Cecilia Sarah Murray (1814–1830), and Lady Emily Murray (1816-1902), who married Francis Seymour, later 5th Marquess of Hertford.

says "I want to speak to you today for it is the day on which I first spoke to you six years ago, and as such is a remarkable one in my mental almanach".

Figure 6.1 – David Murray, the third Earl Mansfield and Frederica's father

Figure 6.2 – Kenwood House, front view

Figure 6.3 – Kenwood House, back view

Figure 6.4 – Kenwood House, interior

Figure 6.5 – Kenwood House, interior

Figure 6.6 – Portrait at Kenwood House, reputedly of Frederica's mother

James had written to Lady Mansfield about his wound in December 1814, when he was in England (and refers to previous correspondence):

After I wrote last, I was in such pain with the abscess as to be obliged to take large doses of opium, which took away alike the pain and the memory of what passed for some days. On the 6th however, the abscess was opened and above a quart of what Crambo[2] should say on the half of it we wipe at best, was discharged, since which I am greatly improved. I have now my natural sleep again and a very good appetite, and though rather pulled down, am not much the worse for my trials. As yet we can find no trace of the ball, but I have little doubt this will all finish by its being extracted. The person who attends me is Mr James Moore, a brother of Sir John's, who is a particularly able surgeon and amiable man, and who treats me like a friend. He keeps the new wound open and will so until the ball is found.

...

I have not written these few days past, having been affected with a severe headache proceeding from too great an appetite and no exercise, but I drove out in my mother's carriage and today I have taken a walk, which set me quite to right again. Moore despairs of finding the ball, he probed this morning for the last time (a joyful hearing to me) and explored about 3 inches deep without finding anything. He thinks the wound is going to heal, which I anxiously hope may be the case, as the ceremony of keeping it open is so painful that I should be glad to get rid of the whole concern at any rate. In the meantime I am stronger and better and sleep well.

...

On Monday night I was whilst in bed attacked with a violent pain in my chest and shortness of breathing, that I was obliged to sit up all night and really believed I had a bad chance for the angelic music as I thought the ball must have worked through my ribs but Moore dispelled my fears, it proceeded from the severity of his bandages round my body (for I have been swaddled like an Iroquois child) and that it was the beginning of an inflammation there, in consequence of which he poured a whole shop into me and has curtailed me of meat, wine, porter and all my good things. I am pretty nearly well of that, got to fish today and shall start with fresh vigour on my old diet

---

[2] Glover, *Eyewitness*, p. 245 (footnote 5), suggests that this was a nickname for Colonel Colin Campbell.

tomorrow. I have the most immoderate appetite and begin to fear I shall get too fat. I have great hopes of getting rid of Moore in a day or two as the wound is healing fast but I am to stay a week in or about London to see if the abscess reforms and then I shall be liberated.

When James joined the Waterloo campaign he continued writing to the Mansfields; on 2 May he wrote to Earl Mansfield describing the preparations for the inevitable battle, and to Lady Mansfield three days later. She seems to have written to him too, as on 14 May he says "Your account of the wood is rather triste" (a reference to some clearing work in the woods around their house, Kenwood). He wrote to her again on 21 May and 28 May, and again on 14 June:

I yesterday received your letter ended on the 7th and am more than commonly thankful for the amusement it afforded me as it found me for a wonder much dejected. When you desired me in your last 'not to presume on being free from aches', you as little thought as I did of the approach of another attack. Three days I first felt the old symptoms, about the same as when I sent for Doctor Macfarlane at Scone and on sending for surgeon yesterday, he confirmed that a tumour is formed and an abscess probably is forming.

This letter shows that James had indeed been the guest of the Mansfields at Scone in Scotland, most probably after he came back from France in 1814. Other letters to the Mansfields followed on 19 June 1815, 2 July, 12 July, 6 August, 24 August, 30 August, 24 September and 1 October. Taking into account what James and Frederica later claimed about the origins of their relationship, it seems that the frequent lengthy letters to the Mansfields were written with a view to the future. Frederica is mentioned in just one of the letters, the one written to his future mother-in-law on 24 August, in which James signs off "Affectionately remember me to Mansfield, F, and all".

Towards the end of 1816 Charles, James' father, fell ill and eventually died on 15 December. Philip was in Vienna, Hester in the Lebanon; only James was anywhere near Chevening (no mention is made anywhere of Lucy or Griselda in relation to their father's illness and death). James wrote to Philip on 17 October:

I have just returned from Chevening. I had long heard that my father was ill, but it did not seem to be dangerous. The bad accounts we heard yesterday pronounced his illness to be so. I wrote two letters

entreating earnestly to see him. He sent me his blessing but declined
it. I therefore came away. He has no idea of being in danger and
expects soon to be well. His legs are much swelled and now his
stomach.

James quoted his second written appeal to his father in a letter to Lady
Mansfield (who was in Paris):

Though my last entreaties were in vain I could not leave England,
your son, the only son in England at home is near you once more. I
can add but little to the contents of my last letters but that my most
earnest and anxious wishes have been, are and will be to receive from
yourself the blessing you sent and to offer whatever comfort or
attention may still be in my power to bestow. Though absent from
you, I have heard of you and I have waited anxiously but in vain to
receive your permission to approach you. I have waited till the
reports of your medical attendance allow me to delay no longer. You
do not know your son, not even by sight, if you refuse me admittance
now I have too much reason to fear that in this world we shall not
meet again. I therefore once more come near you to implore you to
see me, to forget, to forgive and allow me to attend you, that I may
prove the duty and affection of a son.

It was a hard heart that when dying could refuse a plea like this from a
child. After the death of the third Earl, James repeated the story in one of
his letters to Lord Lonsdale[3], adding the following words:

To say I can regret such a father would be hypocrisy, but I have the
consolation of having done my duty towards him and I fervently pray
his God may forgive him, as I do.

The use of the possessive pronoun "his" before "God" strongly suggests
that James' idea of God was very different from that of his father.

In the Earl's will, James received £10,000. He now set out to rejoin his
regiment in Cambrai; he went via Paris, from where he wrote to Earl
Mansfield on 15 January 1817, and was back again in England in September[4].
From Meryon's *Additional Memoirs*, we can confirm that in September and

---

[3] Cumbria Archives in Carlisle, DLONS/L/1/2/60.
[4] In another letter to Lord Lonsdale (kept under the same catalogue number as the
one written after the death of the third Earl), written on 12 September 1817 from
Cambrai, James says "I expect to be in England about the 20th".

October (and possibly longer) James was in Wimbledon. Meryon wrote the following for 27 September 1817[5]:

> Colonel Stanhope, Lady Hester's brother, passed through London on his way from Cambrai, and, by a note he sent me, said he was gone down to Wimbledon. I could have wished to have seen him, as Rundell & Bridge, the silversmiths, had charged Lady Hester with a locket, never yet paid for, which had been sent to her when at Beilth. I called at their shop, and one of the partners, a lame person, when he found out what country I had recently come from, shewed me over the warehouses. This partner was a very keen man, and questioned me a great deal about the practicability of selling the Pigot Diamond to the Sultan, or to Mahomet Ali, Viceroy of Egypt, or to Ali Pasha of Yannina, with all of whose names and reputed treasures he seemed to be perfectly well acquainted.

This is also confirmed in a letter Meryon wrote[6] (presumably to Lady Hester). He was trying to find a good school for his daughter Lucy[7], and on Lady Hester's recommendation (and at her expense) was looking for one Miss Miller:

> Sunday October 5th
> I set off after breakfast to Merton in search of Miss Miller. On alighting in the village I ascertained after much enquiry that Miss Miller had removed from Merton ten years before to Petersham, where she kept a girl's school. As I was bent on finding her out for Lucy's sake, and as there was no conveyance short of a post chaise across the country, I resolved to walk the whole distance which is seven or eight miles, as they told me at the inn, perhaps to frighten

---

[5] Meryon, *Additional Memoirs*, p. 89.
[6] This text forms part of the section he entitled *Portions omitted of the Additional Memoirs*, and as such was physically cut out of the main body of the letter; his letters were often written over several days, which is why the date is included in the middle of the letter.
[7] In March or April 1809, a nineteen-year-old girl called Elizabeth became pregnant by Meryon. He makes no mention of her in any of his surviving writings. We do not know if they were a couple, or if she was just someone he met casually – we do not even know her surname. Early in 1810, she died while giving birth to Lucy Elizabeth, who was brought up by Meryon's sister and brother-in-law in Rye while he was away travelling with Lady Hester. He initially told Hester that Lucy was his niece, although he eventually took responsibility for her education and even planned on taking her with him to the Lebanon to meet Lady Hester.

me and keep me there. The road was beautiful. On my right for some distance I had Lord Spencer's grounds at Wimbledon[8], where Colonel Stanhope, as I told you, is now stopping.

James retired from the army in 1818 on half pay[9]. Much to Hester's dismay, he entered the world of politics and represented Buckingham in 1817 and 1818, Fowey in 1818 and 1819, lost his seat, and then represented Dartmouth from 1822 to his death in 1825. Politics was of course different two hundred years ago from what we are used to today, but the way in which politicians insulted each other has remained the same; Thomas Creevey, a Whig, wrote in his diary when visiting the army in Cambrai in July 1818[10]:

> That cursed fellow Colonel Stanhope was there amongst others, who I remember as an opposition man 3 years ago, but who now is in Parliament and a government lick-spittle. He made up to me cursedly, but I would not touch him.
> …
> I found Master Stanhope there again, and he wanted me to dine with him, but I would do no such thing. He has no talents; he is all pretension and impudence.

Creevey does not say why James was in Cambrai with the army, although the most logical conclusion is that he was there professionally and did not retire from the forces until later in the year.

James' entry into the world of politics caused a reaction in his sister Hester as violent and difficult to comprehend as his own at her relationship with Michael Bruce. She wrote to Doctor Meryon as follows:

---

[8] In the manuscript Meryon includes a footnote at precisely this point, but the text of the footnote is lost.

[9] Newman, *Stanhopes*, p. 197, incomprehensibly says that James was appointed ADC to the Duke of York *after* he retired, despite the fact that Hester had mentioned the appointment in 1814. Hamel (*Hester Lucy Stanhope*, p. 191) says, quoting "the Meryon MSS" (no specific reference given) that the appointment was made "as soon as peace was made", the peace in question referring to the peace with France after the Peninsular War but before Waterloo.

[10] Sir Herbert Maxwell (ed.), *The Creevey Papers, a Selection from the Correspondence and Diaries of the late Thomas Creevey M.P. born 1768 died 1838* Vol. I (London, 1904), p. 277.

Not a word to James about America[11]. I am so angry – so afflicted –
at his having become a creature of Lord Buckingham's! Why did he
not remain quite independent? What had he to do with parliament?
But alas! My advice has all been thrown away, not only upon one,
but how many! I cannot think of it. Oh my God![12]

On 3 March 1818 Dr Meryon visited James Stanhope, in relation to Dr
Newbury, who had now arrived back in England after his failed adventure
as Lady Hester's replacement physician for Meryon himself. This is what
he says in his diary:

Saw Colonel Stanhope, who told me that he had sent for Dr
Newbury, and the conversation which took place was to this effect.
Colonel Stanhope said that I have requested you to come here so that
I might reason with you, for if I had summoned you in my character
of her brother you and I must have blown each other's brains out.
You recollect that our agreement, before you went, was "If you
return dismissed by Lady Hester, she not being pleased with you, I
was not to pay you your passage home". Such is now the case. After
much discussion Newbury said he was a ruined man. He consented
at last to write an apology satisfactory to Colonel Stanhope which
Colonel Stanhope sealed up in his presence telling him that so long
as he heard nothing reported to have been said by him against Lady
Hester that paper should remain sealed[13].

James Stanhope was also made aware of Meryon's possible return to his
sister. He was enthusiastic, and even offered to pay him £100 towards his
travelling expenses. Meryon rejected the offer, although much later in life
regretted it:

This was another of those foolish actions which I have been silly
enough to commit through life from a desire to appear disinterested
in money matters or else from being really so. Thus a Captain Pasha
at Constantinople, whose wives I had attended, ordered his treasurer
to place down before me a canvas bag of dollars as big almost as a
gallon, which I declined to accept. Yet, as we advance in years, we
come to regret such sentimentality, and discover that fair earned

[11] Lady Hester at the time was entertaining the idea of emigrating to America, more
specifically to Virginia, another of her plans that was never followed through.
[12] Quoted in Guscin, *Good Sort of Man*, p. 65.
[13] This passage is repeated, with minor variations, in the *Additional Memoirs*.

remuneration should not be lightly rejected, since a competence for old age is a provision that should always be kept in view, to say nothing of the maintenance of a family. Many great characters have shown at some period of their lives to grasp at pecuniary emoluments, which were their right, considering that they thereby shewed no undue love of gain: but some, like Burke, who wished his pension to be antedated, suffer their avarice to injure their reputation.

Doctor Meryon did visit Lady Hester in 1818, via Switzerland (on a mission to find some servants for her), and 1819; in the short time he spent with her she was deeply critical of James and the fact that he had gone into politics (although as always with Hester, she tended to criticize those she most loved and needed when she was agitated by some other matter, as was clearly the case here)[14]:

> Thursday, April 19
> This day gave rise to a conversation more distressing than can be imagined. Lady H. had requested me to look over her banker's account, and I had arranged it for her perusal. On seeing the balance she burst into tears, and quitting the saloon said she was destined to the martyr of the stupidity of those around her. Such an observation as that was always the prelude to reflections on England & the English, in which she gave vent to her grief after many painful recollections of that country. When she came back I told her that whilst we were at Geneva I had written her brother James word that young Miranda[15] was going to accompany me to Syria. She broke out – "What business had you to acquaint him with my affairs? What are my concerns to him?" throwing at the same time a glass (from which she had just been drinking some water and which she still held in her hand), in a state almost amounting to madness, on the ground. "I never wish to see him again: it would drive me distracted. He never will become the soldier that Charles was. He may be correct in his duties and a man of business; but that won't do. Great minds are born so. We are created with a certain number of grains of talent, sense, feeling, courage; and nothing we can do will ever change this. For instance, one man will be so born that, when he stands before a

---

[14] Meryon, *Additional Memoirs*, p. 43.
[15] The son of Sebastián Francisco de Miranda y Rodríguez de Espinoza (28 March 1750 – 14 July 1816), commonly known as Francisco de Miranda, a military leader and Venezuelan revolutionary, who died in suspicious circumstances in a Spanish prison.

king, the king shall fear and will not know why: yet the thing farthest from that man's thoughts will be the intention or desire of inspiring that fear. He can't help it, nor can the king: but so it is". "But look at James" (she continued) "who writes to me about Mr Somebody (I'm sure I forget such people's names, indeed I never try to recollect them) and his post chaise and his liberality. Why, good God! What does it all mean? He rides with the Duke of York! Ah! If it had not been for me – the Duke of York indeed! I should like to know, if it had not been for me, if the duke would have taken such notice of him"[16].

The Additional Memoirs contain further passages related to Hester's displeasure about James' political adventures[17]:

Lady Hester's reflections on her brother James's conduct in politics were to the following effect; and it is to be presumed that Conservatives & Liberals, Tories & Whigs are upon most occasions guided very much by the same chart.

"Instead of lying by" she said, "as I advised him to do, he must needs attach himself to people who wanted to make a slave of him; and, not choosing to do this, he disobliges them, having already in the first instance disobliged ministers by going against them, and thus losing a fat place which they might have given him, if that had been his wish. If instead of this he had kept himself quiet, and pretended he did not like the present state of things, by & by there would have been those who would have said 'I don't know, affairs don't go on well'; they would have looked around for a man to head them, and they would perhaps have fixed on James as a fit person for their purpose, and he might then have made a figure in the world. Now he is nobody but the duke of York's aide de camp, and when he loses that, there is an end of him.

In all this not one thought is given to the welfare of the people, to the management of the finances, or to the sincerity of the motives which should guide a statesman. All that is looked to is to measure the chances for a rising man which lie open to his ambition".

Lady H. went on. "I have no longer any confidence in mankind. To think that Lord Buckingham, a man of 70,000 a year, should never once offer to contribute a farthing to my comfort! And yet half

[16] Meryon, *Additional Memoirs*, p. 43.
[17] Meryon, *Additional Memoirs*, pp. 187-188.

of his life he never moved a peg without consulting me. And now that he has me no longer to consult, see what he is – a poor foolish man, who goes half way in a thing, and then has not courage to pursue it.

You ask me sometimes why I make myself miserable. Why, isn't it enough to make one so, that one can't have one's own way with one's own things without using as many artifices as one would to cheat another out of his property? Ah! James, and Mr. Murray, and old Coutts and all of them little think how I have tricked them. I shall tell them of it. I shall just add four more lines to the letter I have written, and then have done with them forever. The French are not quite what I like; but, as for England, it is a blot in the Creation, a place God made on Saturday night when he was tired of work, where a person is to be asked why he goes to bed with his wife, and can't whip his own child when he likes.

And who are these that pretend to dictate to me? Why, James I treated like a foot-boy; and when I was twenty years younger than I am now, if he asked Mr. Pitt leave to do anything, even *he* would say 'I don't see any impropriety in it, but I must ask Hester' – and am I grown a fool now?

As for James, he is quite lost! What stuff his letters are filled with, about the magnanimity and I know not what of someone, who pays his post-horses. Why, what can his notion of magnanimity be?"

She then related to me a dream she had had concerning him, which she obviously intended I should interpret in its plainest sense. She dreamed she had returned to England, and was on some occasion parading the streets and haranguing the mob. Of these some applauded and some hooted her, but she smiled at them and felt unconcerned; but, turning round, she saw in the midst of them her brother James, who was in the act of pelting her. That he should unite with the scum of the people against her she felt was so cruel that she could not help crying, and she wept bitterly.

There was a final chapter in the *Additional Memoirs* that Meryon never got round to editing, and so as it is no more than a collection of anecdotes it was not included in the published edition. He entitled it *Anecdotes of Mr. Pitt's time to be severally placed*, i.e. it is a collection of various stories from various different times, which had he lived, Meryon would no doubt have included in their correct chronological order in the book. This chapter contains the following text:

Don't talk of James as a friend. I shall not suffer him to live under
the same roof with me. Not he, nor any soul living, knows my true
character. No one knows what you do, because I choose to tell you:
but as for those I have had to do with, the world is as ignorant as Old
Horn[18]. Many a time have people abused me before persons who,
they thought, hated me, when those were the very people who would
have overturned kingdoms for my sake. Had James married the
greatest strumpet that ever walked the streets, my conduct would
have been very different towards him. It would have been a dagger
to my heart that he had ruined himself in such a manner, but I should
not have gone writing stuff like a madman[19].

Unfortunately, there is no context given; in the passage included Hester
refers to James' marriage (the words "Had James married the greatest
strumpet that ever walked" can only be understood as meaning that he had
married *someone*; if he had not been married when Hester said this or
Meryon wrote it, the words would have been "Were James to marry the
greatest strumpet that ever walked"), so it can be assumed that she was
talking after July 1820. She also talks of James as a living person, which
means it must have been before 1825. The problem was that Hester and
Meryon were not together at all from 1820 to 1825; Meryon returned from
the Lebanon for the second time in 1819, and did not set out again until
1827, on an epic journey that took him and his family almost three years to
complete. This most probably means that Meryon remembered the words
but misplaced them chronologically in his works; they were most probably
uttered before Meryon first returned in 1817, although he mistakenly made
what Hester said sound like James was already married.

Meanwhile, we can only assume that James maintained his good
relationship with the Mansfield family and with Frederica in particular,
although as there was now no need for letters as they lived relatively close
to each other, there is no documentation. In 1819 the Mansfields set out on
a Grand Tour of Europe; Frederica kept a diary which was very detailed at
first, but her enthusiasm for it gradually faded out. She never once mentions
James in the diary, and yet at the same time they were writing assiduously
to each other.

---

[18] Meryon's own footnote: Old Horn meant the Drûz woman, a faithful servant, who
wore a horn on her head as all the Drûz married women do.
[19] The words from "Had James.." to "...like a madman" were encircled in red by
Meryon and marked "Omit".

James seems to have accompanied them at first, and in stages; the clues in their correspondence[20] suggest this, but provide only a few dates and even fewer explanations[21]. He was definitely in Paris with them just before the journal starts on 15 June, as in a letter dated 20 January 1820 Frederica says "I remember you telling me at a ball in Paris that you often, when you went home, read the Collects". There was no other occasion when they could have coincided in Paris.

There are three volumes of the diary[22]: all top quality hardbound notebooks and excellent paper, especially the third volume. The first volume is divided up by dates, like a traditional diary, while the second covers the part in Italy already narrated in the first, but is divided up by cities. The third volume is a very fair copy made by Frederica herself, and given by James to his mother-in-law after Frederica's death. The first volume bears a title inside: "Frederica Louisa Murray, Paris, June 15th 1819". All three copies end with the entry for 24 January 1820, although both the trip and the diary lasted some months longer (when later copying out Frederica's letters from Italy, James would often summarize and write "vide journal", for dates after this). The rest of the journal was probably lost; the first volume (which is the original copy) ends mid-page, and there are numerous empty pages at the end of the fair copy, and no other reason why the rest of the story should have been omitted.

Frederica opens by saying that they left Paris on 15 June 1819 (see Figure 6.7) and went to Compagne, travelling fifty-nine miles in seven hours. The next day they travelled no less than seventy-two miles, through Cambrai and Valenciennes, and then on 17 June eighty-six miles to Brussels. They went to the church of St Michael to hear the *Te Deum* in commemoration of Waterloo. The next day they visited Waterloo and saw all the monuments, giving thanks for those who survived; the diary does not mention James at all, but as it does not even mention him after Frederica

---

[20] Frederica's letters to James are filed under U1590 C266/4-7, consisting of four little books. James copied the letters out just a month after her death, in February 1823. Copying her letters must have been an attempt at exorcism for James, a way of dedicating his time to her even though she was no longer physically with him. The first book is entitled *Lady Frederica Stanhope, Extracts from Freddy's letters and journal, February 1823*.
[21] Frederica's diary starts on leaving Paris on 15 June 1819; Glover, *Eyewitness* p. 206, says that Frederica and her parents were "accompanied by James Stanhope", although that when they visited the battlefield at Waterloo just three days later he was no longer with them. This is confirmed by a later letter, in which Frederica mentions that James left them in Paris.
[22] U1590 C266/1, 2 and 3.

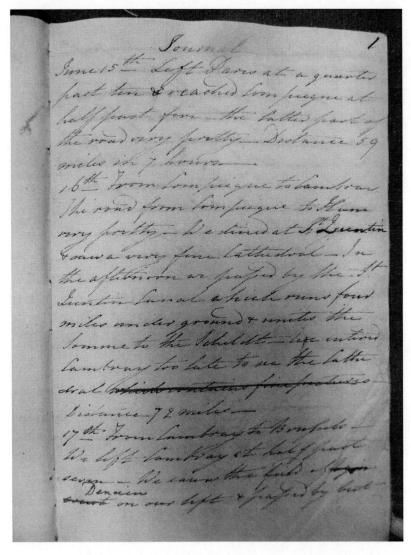

Figure 6.7 – The first page of Freddy's original journal

agreed to marry him, and when they were together, then it would hardly do so at the beginning, when the Mansfields were at Waterloo. James was not with them at Waterloo; in addition to the letter mentioned above stating how he left them in Paris, they would surely not have needed a local guide for

the battlefield had James been with them. The local guide showed them
where the officers fell, where they stayed the night before, etc[23]. Frederica
informs us that the Belgians commemorate the Battle of Waterloo on 21
June; they saw the place where Napoleon addressed the Imperial Guard.

They stayed in Brussels until 5 July, where James must have rejoined
them before they left. They then visited Genappe, where under a bridge
Wellington and Blucher met after the action on 16 June. On 6 July they
travelled 44 miles to Liege, then to Cologne, which they left on 13.
Frederica describes in general all the churches, houses and gardens they
visited, and at the end of each day is an assessment of the inn – "Inn very
good", "Inn not good", "Inn bad" (e.g. 28 August, the inn was very bad and
dirty) – and includes interesting historical details, such as the dates when
churches were built.

She rarely mentions the people she was with (James is not mentioned
even once), and includes very few personal or amusing funny details; 18
July is an exception to this. She writes:

> In the evening a most extraordinary mad or drunk Englishwoman
> who came to ask Papa to subscribe to a lottery of a picture – nothing
> could equal her impudence, she made us laugh excessively.

On 20 July she tells another story:

> We had been at home about a quarter of an hour when we heard a
> noise which we imagined was the Scholars but on looking out of the
> window perceived a light coming out of the window of my room; we
> went in immediately and found the curtain in flames, water however
> was quickly brought and the fire extinguished without other damage
> being done other than the loss of the curtain, but if it [had] been a
> few minutes longer undiscovered might have been dangerous.

Whenever she could, Lady Mansfield played the organ in the churches
they visited in Germany. In Offenburg (30 July) Frederica rather unkindly
tells us:

> Mama played on the organ and after she had done, the organist gave
> us a sample of his talents in a sonata which he fancied he played with
> great execution; but I never heard anything half so ridiculous.

---

[23] The battlefield tourism industry was in full swing just four years after the actual
battle.

Frederica also seemed to be much amused when her mother fell into a river in Laufenburg on 1 August:

> We then went up a hill from whence[24] fell a little cascade. Mama, attempting to cross a plank across this cascade, fell in, but catching at a post was saved with only a few bruises.

On 5 August they were in Zurich, and fifteen days later in Lausanne, which Frederica described as an "ugly town". She was "much disappointed" with Geneva, "it being uglier than I expected". In the entry for 26 August we learn that the Mansfields were accompanied by the Barnetts, a family related to Frederica's mother and one of whom would later play a significant role in James' life. They went to Voltaire's house in Ferney; Frederica was "very much disappointed in it – Voltaire's bedroom remains unchanged but there is nothing in it that reminds me much of him. At the end of the terrace in the garden are some silly pillars with the most ridiculous inscriptions, the view was not as pretty as I expected".

Even though it has never been perfectly clear at what stages and for how long James accompanied the Mansfields and their daughter Frederica on their Grand Tour in 1819 (the Tour continued into 1820 but James was definitely back in England in November 1819), a collection of dated watercolours produced in 1819, which at the time of writing this book were for sale at an art website, do indeed show us exactly when James was with the Mansfield family in July and August 1819.

According to the accompanying text on the aforementioned website, the sketches "have a rustic quality, the sense that they were done in the field rather than polished after the event – a sense enhanced by their pared back colouring and the coarse texture of the sketchbook wove"[25]. The first is

---

[24] "From whence" is one of Frederica's favourite expressions, and although common is technically incorrect. The word "whence" means "from where" by itself.

[25] The text also dates the paper used and some of the buildings depicted: "The paper supplier is 'Smith Warner & Co 211 Piccadilly', dating it to 1800–1820 (the company moved to 208 Piccadilly in 1821). Smith, Warner & Co was a leading artists' supplier of the day, and was one of three businesses singled out in 1811 by the drawing master and Royal Academy exhibitor John Cart Burges as having brought watercolours to the greatest perfection. Many notable artists used their paper, including John Varley, Eugene Delacroix and J.M.W. Turner, examples of whose work bear the Smith Warner stamp from 211 Piccadilly. These sketches can be more narrowly dated by their subjects to between 1818 and Stanhope's death in 1825: one drawing shows the fortress citadel at Huy in Belgium which was rebuilt by the Dutch in 1818, and one shows students of the University of Bonn (Kurkölnische Universität) which had closed in 1797 and re-opened in 1818".

entitled "Street in Brussels" and is dated 4 July (1819). The Mansfields left Brussels on 5 July; Freddie's diary entry for 22 June reads "From then till July 5th nothing to say, having been nowhere"[26], while 5 July starts with the words "Left Brussels". James had therefore rejoined the Mansfield family in Brussels and continued with them from there.

The next dated sketch is from 6 July, entitled *Meuse Marche les Dames*. Marche les Dames is very close to Namur, on the road to Liège, and which according to Frederica's diary is precisely the route they followed that day. Her diary entry reads "The road by the side of the Meuse under masses of high rock was beautiful". Two days later, James sketched the waterfall of Coo; Freddie makes no mention of this particular waterfall in her diary, although she does say that she was drawing all morning, and even though she went out in the evening she came back very quickly because it got cold and so she spent the evening at Lady Bristol's. James is never mentioned by name in the diary, but the fact that Frederica says she spent all morning drawing and one of James' drawings dates from precisely this day seems to suggest they were together.

Frederica's diary entry for 16 July reads "…and below it the village of St. Goar. Opposite is the town of St. Goarshausen and above it on the rock the Castle of Katz". James then drew Sankt Goar on 15 July, and the castle of Katz too, although this particular sketch is undated. On 22 July Freddie tells us that she "went to Castle Heidelberg, from whence I took a sketch of the newest part of the building". James too sketched the castle on the same day; no doubt they were drawing together.

The next and last dated watercolour in this collection is from the waterfalls of Giessbach in Switzerland (see Figure 6.8), although James' note on the back of the image is mistaken (it says Heidelburg, 22 July). The image is clearly of Giessbach, and must have been produced on 17 August 1819, when in her diary entry Frederica says "We stopped to see the magnificent falls of the Giesbach, of which there are seven", and from there they spent a few hours in a small cottage, where an old man and his four children entertained them with music. It is precisely on this date that James made some changes to the original text of Frederica's diary, crossing out some words and adding others[27].

---

[26] The fair copy of the diary, produced later, adds that the reason why Frederica did nothing these days is that she was ill.

[27] Frederica says "There was a simplicity and feeling in all these people which was quite affecting, and I shall ever regard the two hours we spent in this little cottage as some of the most [word crossed out by James, now illegible] happy I have ever spent". In addition to the word he crossed out, James also changes "we spent" to "we passed", and adds the following words at the end of the sentence; "their weeping at

Figure 6.8 – James' watercolour of Giessbach Falls

Scotch not Italian music". Frederica no doubt enjoyed the music and the setting, but the fact that they were among the happiest hours of her life strongly suggests that it was because James was there too, and they were in love with each other.

In the months of July and August James and Frederica fell in love with
each other, as can be gathered from their later correspondence. In a letter
sent to James from Rome on 26 March 1820, Freddy reminds James of what
seems to be their declaration of love at Secheron; according to her diary they
spent a week at this town, from 21 to 28 August 1819. She says:

> How little Mama knew me, dearest, or rather knew my attachment to
> you at Secheron. The day she was displeased with me for having given
> you my hair, she said "and if it suited and you could not marry him and
> that afterwards you were to marry another, for though I dare say you
> think it is impossible now, you would not find it so, should not you feel
> uncomfortable from the reflexion you had given your hair to another?"
> Do you think I would James? I did not and were it then as I feared I
> might have to do it afterwards, but no – if I never had seen you again
> after you left us at Paris, do not think I could have married another. I
> soon saw and I believe you did too that our parents were quite surprised
> at the degree of affection we had for each other – particularly with me,
> for how I could conceal it I do not myself understand.

Things came to a head on between 29 August, when they arrived in
Chamonix, very close to Mont Blanc, and 22 September, when they set off
for Italy. More precisely, it seems to have been on 10 September that James
proposed to Frederica; in the same letter from Rome she says:

> I am surprised how I authored[28] the joy of the 10th. Good God, the
> expression of your face! And when you pressed my hand to your lips
> and said "Will you say yes, Fred? We shall be poor but happy".

Even so, there seems to have been some doubt at first[29], as Frederica
goes on to say,

> I cannot yet bring myself to think with composure on the possibility
> of me having failed – the agony I felt those 5 days no-one is aware
> of, and I danced with what a heavy heart God knows! I can enter

---

[28] The word is unclear in the MS as the original reading was altered in darker ink. A
dot was inserted above the fourth from last letter, but must surely be ignored as the
only English word that ends in "thired" is "outhired", which does not fit in at all.
[29] Possibly that Lord and Lady Mansfield did not at first approve of the union, until
James had some money and property to look after their daughter; this would explain
the importance of the inheritance from Joseph Banks and their gratitude to him.

your feelings with respect to the library[30] and shall feel the same whenever I go into it. To have met you and not to have been allowed to love you, to have felt that I debarred you of all happiness not only by my means but in the society of my parents, oh James, I should have sunk under it. Though I knew not the extent of my gratitude to Sir Joseph I feel as if I was not half grateful enough for the happiness I possess through his means. How shall I ever be able to express my gratitude – he must see it reflected in our happiness in each other.

When James was back in England, he corresponded regularly with Frederica. In a letter dated 21 November 1819, he sent her some verses he had written, which contain the following verses:

For mental anguish well I know
Can blanch and furrow my cheek
And Fred in vain mid age's snow
The likeness of her love may seek;
But were my head with age as hoar
As that huge peak which saw our vow
My heart would cherish her the more
Not more!! As tenderly as now.

The line "As that huge peak which saw our vow" seems to mean that he proposed to her in view of Mont Blanc.

The diary then continues; there is a subtitle on 22 September - *Journey to Italy*. Six days later they went to La Scala in Milan; "the opera was not a good one but some of the singers pleased me much, the orchestra is very large but wants effect, the ballet was very bad". Frederica also saw the Last Supper by Leonardo da Vinci. She loved Genoa, and on 15 October arrived in Bologna.

On 19 October the Mansfields set off for Florence, and were in Pisa on 28 October. On 3 November the entry is limited to "Saw nothing worth relating", and two days later "Saw nothing worth mentioning".

In November the diary entries become much shorter, sometimes no more than two or three lines per day. This is most probably because Frederica was now much more interested in James than in Italy and much too busy writing to him to write in her diary. One of the entries even reads "From Nov 18th to Dec 5th saw nothing new".

On 10 December they left Florence for Rome, on 15 they visited St Peter's,

---

[30] Frederica refers to James' visit to Joseph Banks and the inheritance he received, which meant they would not be poor at all. Of course, in September 1819 this had not yet taken place, but it had when Freddy wrote the letter in March 1820.

and on Christmas Day they saw the Pope in his chapel[31]. From 28 December the diary jumps to 22 January 1820, and a few lines later the first volume of the diary comes to an abrupt end. Volume 2[32] is undated except for the beginning (October 1819), and is divided up rather into cities, repeating some of Frederica's previous comments and adding new ones. Volume 3[33] is a fair copy of the first volume of Frederica's diary, given to Lady Mansfield by James in 1824.

James entitled the fair copy *Journal 1819-20*, while the fifth Earl Stanhope (James' nephew), who organized the family papers, added the following words under the title

> Journal of Lady Frederica Murray, afterwards Lady F Stanhope, till p. 56 the writing appears to be hers, and from there onwards her husband's, Col. J. H. Stanhope.

The fifth Earl would appear to be right in his appraisal; the handwriting up to page 56 is indeed a careful and elegant version of that in the original diaries (compare Figure 6.7, the first page in the original diary, to Figure 6.9, which is the same in the fair copy), while James adds other texts to it at the end. On two pages that were left blank at the beginning, James wrote as follows:

> To the Countess of Mansfield
> To the best of mothers, who in a daughter worthy of her, and excellent in all things, formed the most pure and perfect mind, on the model of her own;
> To her who committed the happiness of that precious charge to the most grateful and blest of men;
> To her, who has been his most sympathising fellow mourner, and his steadiest comfort, under the heavy but all-wise dispensations of the Divine Will;
> To her, who has wept with him, but not repined, and who unites with him in humble and pious hope of being joined with her in a blessed immortality, this imperfect memorial of happy days (now past!) is presented as a mark of his love, his respect and his veneration.
> By her affectionate son,
> J H Stanhope
> Kenwood, February 15th 1824

---

[31] In a letter to James Frederica describes the Pope as "very pale and much bent". The Pontiff at the time was Pius VII, who was seventy-seven years old, and had suffered and aged much under Napoleon and the humiliations the emperor subjected him to.
[32] U1590 C266/2.
[33] U1590 C266/3.

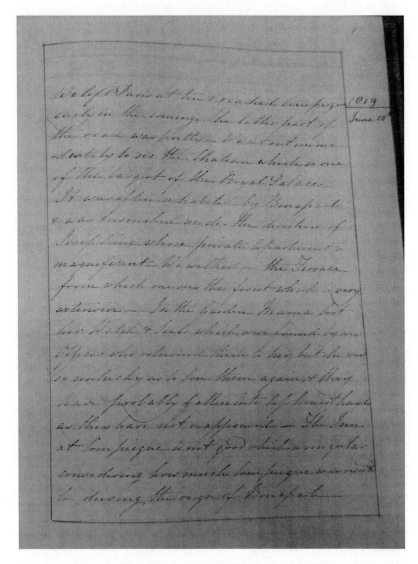

Figure 6.9 – The first page in the fair copy of the diary

Frederica considerably rewrote her own words in the fair copy, as can be seen by comparing passages from the first volume to the text in the fair copy. The text we have already seen concerning the drunk lady reads as follows in the original diary:

In the evening a most extraordinary mad or drunk Englishwoman who came to ask Papa to subscribe to a lottery of a picture – nothing could equal her impudence, she made us laugh excessively.

It is considerably expanded and changed in the clean version:

In the evening a most extraordinary Englishwoman who was apparently either mad or drunk paid us a long visit, for the purpose of asking Papa to subscribe to a lottery of a Titian which she said was in her possession. Nothing could equal her impudence and ignorance excepting her pretensions to learning; she amused us very much at first, but we soon became impatient to get rid of her.

Another text in the diary that was considerably rewritten in the fair copy concerns Frednerica's reactions to the University students in Bonn on 13 July. The original diary reads thus:

There is a university in Bonn and we have been much amused in seeing the students go past; they are most strange figures; one particularly who had long hair on his shoulders, a beard and no shirt, with a dirty green coat.

She rewrote it as follows:

There is a university in Bonn and the students wear the Teutonic dress; they caused us much amusement from their extraordinary appearances, they all looked exceedingly wild, very dirty, with long hair straggling over their shoulders, beards of many days' growth, in linen and most singular coloured coats.

One of the details that stands out on reading Frederica's diary is the family's relationship with the Roman Catholic religion. All of Freddie and James' letters, writings and other documents show a profound Christian faith, which given the moment in history and the fact that both Lord Mansfield (Frederica's father) and Lord Stanhope (James' brother) held seats in the House of Lords, lead us to the natural conclusion that all such religious feelings were contained well within the Anglican Church, not the Roman one.

Roman Catholics in England two hundred years ago were subject to all kinds of restrictions[34]; it would take an extremely devout Catholic to waive all the privileges enjoyed by a family like the Mansfields in order to declare one's faith. And yet as Frederica's diary advances, a different picture comes to light.

Just about everywhere they visited, there are legends to tell of Catholic saints and miracles; they visited numerous relics and made no objection to their supposed authenticity (for example, the skulls of the three Magi). In Germany, Frederica makes a specific point that one of the churches they visited was Protestant; this might have been worthy of mention in a purely Catholic country, such as Italy, but in Germany it seems to suggest much more that the rule was to visit Catholic churches, and this was an exception.

In Switzerland they visited a convent for no architectural or artistic reason, but rather for the sole purpose of conversing with the nuns, who were "very civil to us". In Milan, the family went to mass on 3 October, and on 17 October went to high mass in the cathedral (although Frederica does say that the Cardinal was "quite ridiculous"). On 31 October they went to mass in the morning, while on 24 December they went to midnight mass in Rome, and on Christmas Day they again heard mass, this time in the Pope's private chapel, where they saw the Pope. On 26 December they went to Vespers.

Visiting the churches in Italy in itself is something that huge numbers of tourists do; it says nothing about their beliefs or lack of belief. Noting down the Catholic legends in a personal diary without making any comment on the credibility of the stories strikes us as something more inclined to belief

---

[34] Cf. Norman S. Poser, *Lord Mansfield: Justice in the Age of Reason* (Montreal, 2013), p. 350: "The Toleration Act of 1689 did not free Roman Catholics from the restrictive and punitive laws. They were prohibited from gathering together to practice their religion; holding any form of government employment; inheriting, purchasing or owning land; sending a child out of the country to be educated; possessing a weapon, other than what was necessary for the defence of their house or person; coming within ten miles of certain localities, including London; and bringing a legal action or serving as an executor of an estate or legal guardian of a child"; J. Steven Watson, *The Reign of George III 1760-1815* (Oxford, 1960), p. 58: "Roman Catholic squires in the country were left in peace as eccentrics, even when they might make papists out of their social inferiors in the village. But they played no part in politics"; Llewellyn Woodward, *The Age of Reform 1815-1870* (Oxford, 1962), p. 328: "Although the worst of the penal laws had been repealed, and catholics had the right to vote, if otherwise qualified, they could not sit in parliament, or hold important civil, judicial or administrative offices under the Crown".

therein; but going to mass on repeated occasions could seem to suggest that
the family were in fact Catholics, even if in secret[35].

Outside of the diary, there is little to back this idea up. Lord Mansfield's
great uncle, the first Earl Mansfield, was (as he had to be in order to hold
the position of Lord Chief Justice) a member of the Church of England,
although "he kept his religious beliefs to himself" and was a "staunch
supporter of religious freedom for others"[36]. He defended Catholic freedom
to such an extent that in the anti-Catholic Gordon riots of 1780 his city house
was burnt to the ground. There was definitely a tradition of religious
freedom in the family, although there is absolutely no hint or accusation
anywhere that the first Lord Mansfield was a practicing or even secret
Catholic[37].

The tradition clearly continued in the family, despite the outward shows
of devoted Anglicanism. When Frederica married James, the ceremony was
Anglican, and when she was dying, she was attended by an Anglican
minister. This would have been unthinkable for a devout Catholic. There is
nothing in her numerous writings outside the diary to even suggest she or
the family might have been Catholics. Her father, who accompanied the
family on the Grand Tour and to all the churches and convents and masses,
made a remarkably anti-Catholic comment in the House of Lords in 1827.
The Catholic question (i.e. emancipation) was a sensitive political matter,
and it was even believed that George IV was about to grant it (which in the
end he did). He firstly denied any such thing (which might be taken by a
cynic as a guarantee that he was going to do it), but did not manage to
convince the Protestants:

---

[35] This attitude (i.e. going to mass) contrasted directly with that of other people on
the Grand Tour; cf. Brian Dolan, *Ladies of the Grand Tour* (London: Flamingo,
2001) p. 168: "A notable dissimilarity between France and Britain besides the
architectural majesty of the cathedrals was, of course, religion itself. Many in Britain
were seething with anti-Catholic sentiment, encouraging many travellers to ridicule
the rituals and beliefs abroad, and dismissing them as superstitious if not savage",
and Jeremy Black, *The British Abroad: The Grand Tour in the Eighteenth Century*
(Stroud: The History Press, 2009), p. 264: "The sensual and physical appeal of
Catholicism to tourists, who believed the religion to be irrational, evil and spiritually
corrupt, posed a difficult problem of balance for them".
[36] Poser, *Lord Mansfield*, p. 349.
[37] Poser even suggests that Mansfield tended rather towards atheism or deism; his
last will and testament makes mention of God, but Poser states, "But this may have
been less a declaration of a personal belief in God and the divinity of Christ than a
conventionally religious way of referring to the end of his life".

In the House of Lords, the Earl of Mansfield suggested that, had King George III still been King, he would never have consented to the formation of a government which was to contain a preponderance of 'Catholics' like Canning[38].

It is hard to see how a Catholic could have made such a comment, unless he was under suspicion of precisely that and wished to publicly show that it was not so; but there is no evidence to suggest this was the case.

The only evidence to make us think the family might have been secret Catholics is the diary that Frederica kept for the first half of the Grand Tour, and yet in one of her letters to James it seems very clear that they were not in fact Catholics. The letter is dated 26 March 1820, and was sent from Rome. Freddie tells James that they plan to go to the Miserere, which "although it is a Catholic ceremony it is very impressive"; this seems to clinch the matter. The Mansfields were not declared Roman Catholics, but just like the first Earl Mansfield they seem to have been very open-minded and clearly had no problems attending ceremonies perfomed by ministers from both branches of the Christian church.

It is no easy task to establish when James returned to England as the surviving documentation is contradictory. Frederica wrote him on 5 December (she was still in Florence), saying that it is eight weeks since they parted. If her memory was serving her correctly, this would mean that James left on 10 October. This is confirmed by a later letter, written on 10th April 1820 (again in Florence, but of course she had not been there all that time), in which she says "It is now six months since I parted from the dearest, most angelic, the most beloved of human beings, from my own James". Frederica's memory was excellent with dates; it can therefore be stated with confidence that James left the Mansfields on 10 October. On 10 October the Mansfields were in Genoa, and Frederica's diary entry shows a very busy day taken up with several different visits. She, of course, makes no mention of James or of his departure.

Frederica's first letter to James (now back in England) from Italy is dated 27 November 1819, sent from Florence, although she says therein that she has already received two from him. James' first surviving letter to Frederica begins on Sunday 7 November, at 2 o'clock (unfortunately, one very important letter from before this date is lost, in which, from what we can gather from later letters, he must have expressed some kind of doubt or misgiving about their future, and possibly even suggested that he and

---

[38] Christopher Hibbert, *George IV* (London, 1976), p. 722.

Frederica should not be married). The letter dated 7 November opens "My
best beloved, my dearest Fred" and continues:

> Such sacred and homefelt delight, such certainty of waking bliss I
> never felt till now!!!! How little do we know who are our friends,
> when I expected least I have obtained all. The transition from agony
> to joy is so overpowering that I am crying like a child, but gratitude
> to Providence and to my dear benefactor, and the reflection of the
> pious joy and gratitude which will fill the warmest and most
> affectionate of breasts on reading this.
>
> …
>
> When I came into my room just now I fell upon my knees and
> humbly thanked God for these blessings unlooked for.

The first impression on reading these lines is that he is referring to his
engagement to his "best beloved, dearest Fred", and has overcome his
doubts (whatever they were) expressed in the letter now lost, but he is
actually talking about a sizeable inheritance from Sir Joseph Banks[39]. Banks
has left him his estate (when he and his wife died), which is worth £10,000
a year. This is why he fell on his knees and gave thanks to God[40]. As
explained above, it is possible that Frederica's parents had withheld their
permission for the marriage until James had some income above that of half-
pay from the army. The letter continues:

---

[39] Sir Joseph Banks (1743 - 1820) was an English naturalist, botanist, and patron of
the natural sciences. Banks made his name on the 1766 natural-history expedition to
Newfoundland and Labrador. He took part in Captain James Cook's first great
voyage (1768–1771), visiting Brazil, Tahiti, and after 6 months in New Zealand,
Australia, returning to immediate fame. He held the position of president of the
Royal Society for over 41 years. He advised King George III on the Royal Botanic
Gardens, Kew, and by sending botanists around the world to collect plants, he made
Kew the world's leading botanical gardens.
[40] Cf. Newman, *Stanhopes*, p. 200: "The estates of Revesby Abbey in Lincolnshire
were the property of Sir Joseph Banks, the eminent botanist. Banks had no children
and his nearest heirs were his first cousin, Louisa Stanhope, whose mother had been
Joseph Banks's aunt, and his wife's family, the Knatchbull-Hugessens. It was for
long understood that on his death his landed estates would pass to the Stanhopes,
and it was in this expectation that Charles, Louisa's second son, had been given the
additional name of Banks. On his death James became the eventual heir, subject to
the life interest of Lady Banks. Sir Joseph died in 1820, and Lady Banks in 1828".
Hester expected to receive part of this money, but never did.

Oh beloved, may I not say that holy name of wife, I never expected riches, all I hoped for was just enough to give me the power of making you happy and I trust we shall never be spoiled by fortune's smiles as we have never been beat down by her frowns.

There is one reflection which gives me greater and more heart-felt transport than I can express, which is that you accepted me as a poor soldier, to have in his hardships and console him under difficulties, perhaps to partake in his poverty. The world, its wealth, its honour can never equal the value of this, which will abide by each of us to our latest moments that neither ambition or rank or wealth entered into our calculations. What you loved in me I know not except you saw into my heart, how affectionately and truly it was devoted to you; what did I not find to love in you, who as your parents said had never given them (or any human being) a moment's pain and who possess[es] all that care ...

...

I have been so dreadfully agitated and harassed that although my mind kept up, I am grown thin and have been very bilious, but with the peace of mind and joy and sober certainty of waking bliss, I shall be soon as I was when in such happiness with you. I fear my last letter must have made you most unhappy, for if you bore the trial as I wished, expected and trust you did, you will never in future regret it. My mind has been so harassed that I did not fulfil certain intentions to say, but be assured that I will the first opportunity and that I have made many good resolutions of behaving worthier [of] you which I hope to keep better than any I bother to have made. These last two days I have hardly dared to look at the locket, for I felt as if I was looking on a friend and upon my best consolation, which was to be taken from me. Oh, how shall I sleep tonight if joy does not keep me awake. I have hardly shut my eyes since my return from C or eaten. I found wine keeps me up. I look back on the past as a frightful dream; I shall write every fort[night] to you and once every week to my mother and father. That I should even use these words... My chief misery has been in the idea that I had been deluding you under false hopes and that I had widowed your affection and blighted forever the fairest prospect of a woman's happiness, domestic felicity.

A man has ambition, study and a thousand means of banishing reflection but a woman has but her heart as her treasure and her connubial home and duties as the end of her being, and to think that all this was blighted by your James was more than I could bear to dwell on. I keep your 12 o'clock accurately by the best station clocks, when 12 at Florence it is ¼ past 11 here, and at Rome 5 to 7 minutes past, and I will keep the time. And now may heaven bless you, my dearest, my beloved F, hope of my life, guardian of a virtuous carrier. How happy you are now!!!!!! Affectionately yours forever, your own.

Only think what use I may be of to my, to <u>your</u> sister.

...

Pray pray pray write every post and tell me all you do, but first all you think and feel; whenever I put 123 I mean God bless you, 123 123 to part in such sober certainty!!!! Keep this letter forever and if you find me ever spoiling and unlike what you expected, show it me and it will be my cure !!!!!!!!!!!!!!! 123

What seems to have happened is that James was overcome by some kind of doubt, probably not about his feelings but about his ability to look after and care for Frederica, and he expressed this in a letter which is now lost. Then he received the news of his inheritance from Sir Joseph Banks and everything changed; he would now be able to care for Freddy as she deserved. He would even be able to take care of Hester and her debts, and just as Freddy's family was now his own too, so Hester is also Freddy's sister too.

Luckily, Frederica received the above letter before the first one, as she says "I have this instant received your second letter, which is the first I have ever had from you"; although when she answered she had clearly read the first one too. It is even possible that she is trying to say that she didn't recognize him in the first letter and so doesn't count it as coming from him. Her answer reads as follows:

I have this instant received your second letter, which is the first I have ever had from you; I first heard the glad tidings of our happiness from your letter to Perfection, for as I am not to mention a dearer name what letter can I share – the sudden transition from grief to joy was almost too overpowering and it was some time before either of us was sufficiently composed to fall upon our knees and pour forth our heartfelt thanks to the Almighty – oh my dearest J. who were ever so happy as we are, not only happy in our mutual attachment but blest with parents and friends whose kindness we feel, but to whom we can never sufficiently prove our gratitude.

Even to you who can best suppose it, I can never express all their kindness to me when I was anxious and unhappy – indeed I am now almost afraid that I did not exert myself as I ought to have done and diminish their anxiety – much indeed was I cast down by your first letter and at 12 I no longer dared to say "such sacred and homefelt delight", but I said "God's will be done" instead, and most fervently did I pray for you.

Dear old Sir J. how little did I think when I read his voyages and he told me the story of his great apple stick, that he was one day the great promoter of our happiness, and the Duke too, what kindness – the manner in which he spoke of those most dear to me will ever deeply and gratefully be felt by me.

I cannot tell you the pleasure it gave me to hear you had had letters from Hester – the idea that I may be the cause of giving her pleasure is a great, great delight. All you say about her is indeed like yourself and the snowball rolls on faster than ever.

Sad indeed was the night we parted, that word farewell, "for in that word, that fatal word, howe'er we promise, hope, believe there breathes despair"[41]. My want of feeling when I came through the worm has been seriously reproved by Car__. Poor little thing, how happy she will be when she knows it, I play at nasty pig with Emmy for fear she should forget you.

What is it you mean by being so superstitious? I believe that I am improved in my singing but I shall never be able to give any but you pleasure.

What a difference to our last journey will this be to Rome, but what will it be coming back? I cannot tell you what I feel at going farther from you, but I am not sorry to leave Florence. I never heard of Mr. Stump before.

I hope you have taken care, both eyes are to be seen, my bust has been done but you would not like it, my little eyes were never meant for a bust. What a risk you ran in leaving town – the D. is not wrong as to my opinion on that subject. I cannot help being very anxious about the signature of the will, and when I see the B^{ts} I am more so.

I felt a perfect wretch when I was dancing away at balls and affecting the gay, when I knew you were passing the most anxious and trying moments. What I know will give you great pleasure is that Perf. is decidedly better than she has been for months, notwithstanding all her anxiety, which I assure you was almost as great as my own.

---

[41] Frederica is quoting Lord Byron, *The Corsair*, Canto I, Stanza 15 (1814).

I am so afraid none of your friends will think me worthy of you, and indeed no more I am, except from the greatness of my attachment to you and my desire of making you happy.

I must now conclude and in the full confidence that no stupid letter ever gave so much pleasure before, and indeed very few wise ones, there's a modest speech for you. Almighty God bless and preserve you, dearest and best. I will endeavour to be worthy of you. I take the sacrament tomorrow, and with what peace of mind, content and gratitude! I shall think of you next Sunday as doing the same thing – once more God bless you.

Again in reference to James' first letter, the one that seems in some way to have expressed doubts about his future with Frederica, she wrote about it again from Rome on 29 January 1820:

It did not affect me less for two months having gone by since I ought to have received it. If I had got that letter first I should have written a very different answer, for I felt all the time I was waiting that I was not expressing my feelings. Yes, my dearest, I will keep that as well as all your other letters for ever, and if ever, as you say, you should alter, or in other words si vous faites l'impossible, I will shew them to you.

James wrote again on Wednesday 10 November, explaining that:

Though I wrote a long letter my best beloved just two days ago, I feel that I have as yet said nothing ... Every instant in the day am I dwelling on what you must have gone through and what you will suffer when you receive my first letter, but then my imagination flies forward with the wings of joy and pictures to itself the smiling gratitude and pious bliss you will feel when you receive the first letter from my hand and see that you are to be mine ... When you get to Rome let me know all you do.

James tells Frederica that he has had his picture painted and sent it out to her; she should receive it by 5 December. His words were:

It will be done on 19th and if there is a carrier on that day it will go and you will receive it by 5th Dec. or at least by the day I leave, on 8th. Think of my being the possessor of that dear picture!!! 123 a million of times. I am going to dine with K. Adios.

James writes much more about what he is doing, rather than how much he loves Frederica, although at the end he adds "… for you are all to me, the glass which reflects the past, the power which supports the present, the light which brightens the future. Forever your own J. Write every post!!!!!! Hope was scarcely sufficient to repel the dread of uncertainty and the regret of quitting you … God bless you dearest Freddy!"

His next letter is dated Sunday 14 November, in which he expresses his feelings and thoughts about his fiancée:

> … my character and conduct: these Freddy are yours, these were the only possessions I had to tempt you to be mine, and to you I shall trust the improvement and perfecting of them during rest of my life.
> …
> To tell you how you are connected with every thought and even every common occurrence would be useless, for I know you can find the model in your own breast.
> …
> … and as I go by the shops I think when I have money I will buy that for my Freddy.
> …
> I am looking forward with great impatience to the 24th, when I may feel assured you are happy, and the 19 following days will be painful to me: but how happy shall I be about the 8 of next month when I receive your first letter and <u>continue twice a week to receive them.</u>

He tells her that he lives in a snug comfortable house with two rooms overlooking the Tower. He has parade at ten and at two goes to the painter's (presumably so the artist can finish the portrait he said he would send her). He then goes to the Travellers[42] and dines out there. Then at ten he trundles back home, reads for an hour or so and then goes to bed.

---

[42] The Travellers Club is a gentlemen's club founded in 1819. According to the club's website it was founded for "gentlemen who had travelled out of the British Isles to a distance of at least five hundred miles from London in a direct line. Membership was extended to foreign visitors and diplomats posted to London. The original concept of The Travellers Club by Lord Castlereagh and others dates from the return of peace in Europe following the Napoleonic Wars. They envisaged a club where gentlemen who travelled abroad might meet and offer hospitality to distinguished foreign visitors. Arrangements for the establishment of The Travellers Club were finalised at a meeting in the spring of 1819, attended by distinguished diplomats, travellers and two future Prime Ministers (the Earl of Aberdeen and

James continued this letter two days later, saying "No letters which is a great disappointment but I trust in God you are all well. ... 123 123 my dearest Freddy, ever affectionately, your own James".

The next letter is dated 17 November:

> I only sent off my last letter yesterday but as I have no pleasure equal to chatting to my beloved F I take up my pen when I have a little time for fear I might not be able to write at length if I have to postpone it to the last.
>
> I must now go on with a little account of what I have been doing and seeing, for if I were to keep to what I feel towards you and the joy which possesses me at my good fortune I could fill folios and might bore you at the end.
>
> I have just received a letter from Dr Meryon who is in quarantine at Marseille on his return from Syria, who is bearer of letters but will not be at home for 2 months[43]. He gives a very good account of my sister's health and of the calmness of her mind and comfort of her situation, which you may imagine gives me the greatest pleasure.
>
> I dined yesterday at the Travellers. I can hardly yet persuade myself that all this is reality and that so soon, so comparatively soon we are to be happy, and that we shall have no dread for the future.

Viscount Palmerston). The head of Ulysses was adopted as the Club device. It was first housed at 12 Waterloo Place but soon outgrew the space, moving to 49 Pall Mall. In 1826 money was raised to lease part of the grounds of Carlton House and Charles Barry, who later designed the Reform Club next door and the Houses of Parliament, was appointed as architect". John Martin Robinson, *The Travellers Club: A Bicentennial History 1819-2019* (Marlborough, 2019), p. 12, says that the club dates from May 1819. The first chairman was Lord Auckland, while on the first committee was the Hon. Lt. James Hamilton Stanhope; this is why he went to have dinner there; "These soldiers, scholars, landowners, travellers and statesmen were all men of taste and ideas". In the same book, p. 247, we learn that in the 1930s the Earl Stanhope, the historian, was on the General Committee. In 1960 (p. 297), it says that the Earl Stanhope, who had been a member for fifty years, died. This date is mistaken; the sixth Earl died in 1905, and the seventh in 1967. No direct member of the family died in 1960.

[43] This was Meryon's visit to Lady Hester in 1818-1819, when he went to Switzerland to find some employees for her, took them to Lebanon and then had to bring them back as neither party could adapt to the other. The adventure is recounted in Meryon, *Additional Memoirs*.

He wrote again on Sunday 21, and presumably included the following
verses for Frederica (she refers to the poem in a later letter)[44]:

To the quiz[45] in a blue cloak on his travels
Full many a month must pass away
E'er I like thee may cross the [..]ain[46]
And hail the soul-transporting day
When I may clasp my love again.
But thou ere yet that waning star
Shall rise anew o'er Albion's isle
Will reach her sunny home afar
And feel her touch and meet her smile.
Then if with pressure kind she hold
Thine image to her heaving breast
Though charms unknown you'll there behold
You'll meet I mean no stranger guest.
The tenderest love with truth combined
Sense, feeling, worth her bosom fill
But mid these treasures first you'll find
By fancy drawn, thy copy still.
If e'er o'er thee she breathes her vow
And wonders there for once and mute
And chides thy "cold and changeless brow"
Bid her not this to me impute;
For if our thoughts must make us speak
And tell the language of the soul,
She must for mine around her seek,
For long they've scaped from my control.
And if the heart the lips must move
And bid the eye with rapture roll
She may herself thy faults remove
And add my heart – she has the whole.
I envy thee creative art!!
Thy power immortal and sublime

---

[44] The poem is kept separately from the letters, under U1590 C263/3, but dated 22
November 1819 and clearly meant for Frederica. The verses also refer to the portrait
that James sent her.

[45] "Quiz" here means an eccentric person.

[46] The word is unclear in the MS. The first two letters have been overwritten with
what looks like an "r"; the last three letters are "ain". Judging from the poem alone the
word could very well be "main", but this is difficult to maintain from the manuscript.

Which fixes life's most happy part
And baffles sickness, care and time.
For mental anguish well I know
Can blanch and furrow my cheek
And Fred in vain mid age's snow
The likeness of her love may seek;
But were my head with age as hoar
As that huge peak which saw our vow[47]
My heart would cherish her the more
Not more!! As tenderly as now.
When placed beneath her speaking eye
Thy gaze will motionless appear
Then tell her with like constancy
On her my soul is fixed from here.
Be there my sylph, to dry such tear
Record each smile, improve each grace
And calm her gentle bosom's fear
Till I in transport fill thy place.
Then when holy bands entwine
My life with hers (no more to err),
To make her blest, the task be mine!!!
My fondest hopes to equal her!!!!

On 24 November, James wrote:

I fear you will find me a bore in my happiness.
      …
      I went to the H of L last night and heard the debate. Lord Gray
was so ill and exhausted that I could hardly conceive he was capable
of so much exertion as to make the eloquent speech he did; it was a
Spanish olla, fish, flash and fowl, past, present and future all jumbled
together with a very piquant sauce.

He signs off in Spanish this time, "hasta el fin". Freddy's first letter in
the copies James made is dated 27 November (and numbered the first of her
letters), although by 24 we have six letters from James to her in Italy, in
addition to the first one which is now lost. It is highly improbable that from
17 October, when James left to return to England after they had agreed to

---

[47] I.e. Mont Blanc. According to Frederica's diary, she reached Chamonix on 29
August 1819, and then she writes nothing until the journey into Italy on 22
September.

be married, until 27 November, that Frederica would not have written anything at all to him. These first letters must have existed and are now lost.

This is shown to be true in the letter James wrote on 28 November, in which he says he had received a letter from her the day before, i.e. the same day on which she wrote her first surviving letter. After this letter they came thick and fast, and the terms of endearment became more and more pronounced as time went by.

On 29 Frederica writes "Oh, what I felt when the sound of your wheels died away for I heard you go". The religious aspect of their relationship is so intense that it almost seems exaggerated; "I never felt so contented or so much attached to you as when we knelt down together, I never before felt so certain that our prayers and good intentions, although mingled with weakness, were accepted by the Almighty".

In the same letter she writes in reference to Hester, "you, I may say we, can never do too much for her", and "I am sure she will love me if I make you as happy as I hope to do". She expresses their belief in the afterlife; "If as you say the 'Spirits of the Blest' can look down upon the world, with what joy will my dear Grandfather and godmother see (as I trust) their granddaughter not unworthy of them".

Even though I have interspersed their letters in a more or less chronological order, we should of course not forget that letters from England to Italy and vice versa could at the time take several weeks to reach their destination (sometimes just a week, it depended on whether the sender could find suitable transport, and very often two or three letters would arrive together – letters to and from Hester in the Lebanon were sometimes received over a year after being written), and so even though Frederica might write on 27 November and James on 28, he was clearly not writing in response to hers.

Freddy's letter of 3 December contains the following passages:

Only four weeks more and I shall have finished if not the happiest year I have ever passed, the one which has prepared the greatest happiness for me in futurity.

...

At this time five years ago you were suffering agonies, and now you are well; at this time three years ago you sent me your drawings and verses, and for the last two years we were in the néant produced by crushed and blunted feelings, and now! Oh dearest James, I feel that I am not half grateful enough for my happiness and I pray most ardently that I may never forget all the blessings the Almighty has bestowed on us and never be unworthy of them.

This letter is most interesting as it tells us something about James and Frederica's courtship, when they met and how James went about conquering her. We should not be shocked at Frederica's tender age; if this letter was written in 1819, James sent her his poems and drawings three years before that, in 1816, when she was precisely sixteen years old. We do not know which poems he sent her (if his intention was to win her heart, we can safely assume he did not send her any of his military poems); but they had been aware of their feelings for each other for the two previous years, since 1817, when Frederica was seventeen years old, and had to cover them up until now.

In her letter dated 5 December, from Florence, Frederica refers to an alabaster lamp that Hester has sent to James, and says she can imagine how he feels receiving presents from her. She says that she used to feel anxiety about dancing with this or that person, or who she sat next to at dinner, but now all this is indifferent to her and she cares only for the post coming. He asks her in his letters what she is doing; "I do nothing all day but think of you, write to you and dream of you". She refers to what she perceives as her physical defects: "My nose and mouth are still as large as two of their species[48], but I never was in better health, la santé du bonheur".

She had been to the theatre in Florence: "They then proposed a comparison between the four seasons and the 4 ages of woman. This she did quite beautifully. In her description of the 2nd age, which she begins at 20, but which I began, I think, at 15, ..."; again, this is a clue as to when James and Freddy first fell in love, or started their relationship, in whatever quality. In her previous letter, Frederica said they had been covering up their feelings since 1817, but now she goes back two years further, and says that she fell in love with James in 1815, when she was just fifteen years old and he was twenty-seven. He had seen Pitt and Sir John Moore die, he had fought at Corunna and Waterloo, he had been seriously wounded in the service of his country; all this must have seemed quite wonderful to a fifteen-year-old girl.

She continues her description of the theatre:

> She never described a woman surrounded by her children, receiving from them in her old age that kindness and care with which she had formerly nursed them, and having spent a virtuous and happy life in this world, looking forward without dread to that death which is to reunite her to a beloved husband and open the gates of everlasting happiness!!!! This, dearest James, is what I trust we shall feel, and

---

[48] The woman in the portrait at Kenwood House, reportedly Frederica's mother, also has a large nose.

although deprived of imagination and poetry, is I believe more congenial to your feelings than her beautiful but worldly description.
...
It is now 8 weeks since we parted, I have knelt down every Sunday and said the same prayer we did together, I shut my eyes and fancy I still see those eyes filled with tears, not only of sorrow but of pious hope.
...
People sometimes ask me if I shall be glad to return to England, I say yes! They shake their heads and say you will not be so when the time comes – what do you think, my dearest James?

The portrait James sent out to Italy had arrived by 8 December, as Frederica writes excitedly:

I have got it! I have got the image of the greatest, the best, the most perfect of mankind, of one by whom I have the happiness to be loved and whose happiness is the first wish of my heart, of me of whom it will be my pride to call by the dearest name a female heart can know, and that name created and sanctified by religion. Oh my dearest, my best beloved James, what pleasure can ever equal what I felt in receiving your picture, except me again seeing the original. It is like, very very like, but still I am not satisfied – the mouth has not that angelic expression which if only momentary I can remember for four months and is one of the greatest pleasures my memory can know, even if hope were excluded. But I gaze on those eyes, which I have seen beaming with delight whilst blindly adoring one whose only merit is in knowing the value of the almost faultless being she adores, and gaze on those eyes which when I last saw them were dismal with grief at parting from one so loved and then lifted up to heaven imploring the protection of the Almighty and expressing gratitude for the past, hope for the future, or whatever might happen resignation to an all-seeing Providence.
I am not contented with the mouth – it was done when you were smiling and yet it does not smile. And I have said nothing of the verses, of those verses so full of feeling affection, memory, hope, those verses which although they flatter me, do not increase my vanity but my gratitude. How well my dearest love have you described that inward resemblance which neither time nor circumstances can diminish or alter. I got your picture just as we sat down to dinner and I am afraid C & G saw I had a parcel. I ran into Mama's room to

open it and had hardly strength – it was as if I was afraid of seeing you. All three think it excellent and are very much pleased with the verses, but what can I say of myself? Wait till you get my picture and in your own breast you will find my feelings. How shall I carry it, when may I dare look at it is now my only distress – we go the day after tomorrow.

Thursday – I have just been saying how do you do to you my dearest. Every time I look at it I am more and more pleased with it, I cannot describe the pleasure I have in it – that old cloak! The black hand was not put on as I had intended but never mind. I sometimes think all that has passed is a dream, to think that I possess your picture. Oh my dearest, what a beautiful letter is your last. Why do I, who feel as you do, find it utterly impossible to express my feelings, what would I give to write as you do. You will be ten days without letters. It seems as if I was flying from you. Adieu, your own little Freddy.

Meanwhile, James wrote on 5 December and again mentioned the letter that caused such dismay to Frederica and her parents (he calls it his "dismal epistle").

I received yesterday the letters of both our parents in answer to my dismal epistle and from what they felt I can guess what must have been your feelings when it was communicated to you; I had feared that my letter of the 8th could have by raising your hopes made your disappointment much worse, but my dearest love, could I be otherwise with such a sentence before me as the H's. Hope is they say always sanguine but such an answer could have even cheered despondency – what I would not have given or give if the letters of yesterday had not contained the account of how you knew it: from the 19th to the 24th.

On 12 December, James says:

I was not disappointed my dearest love, in my expectations, as your first letter arrived yesterday evening, the expressions you make use of towards me are like yourself and you can better imagine that I can express my gratitude.

You think I wrote unconnectedly: could I retain my senses under such a change.

I believe your affection is even greater than mine, but you never could feel what I did and I deeply regret my letter is lost as I expressed myself at length, and begged you to keep it forever.

I recollect telling you in that letter that the greatest cause of my happiness was you having accepted me as a poor soldier to have in my difficulties, and I could not help indulging in some feelings of pride, in which you will participate, but that it is was [sic] not to solicitation, to pity, but to character that I owed it, for in becoming my wife you have nothing else to be proud of except you can be in knowing none was ever more tenderly and more truly loved.

Surprisingly enough, writing on 12 December, James tells Frederica that her first letter had arrived the day before, whereas he had said exactly the same in a letter dated 28 November, i.e. that he had received a letter from Frederica the day before. This is further proof that James' numbering of the letters is not perfect and there must have been several more letters that are now lost.

On 15 December 1819 Frederica and her family were in Rome:

What a million of things that little word Rome expresses! What a million of things worth notice it contains, from the monuments of ancient grandeur which have been respected by their usual enemy time, and the stupendous fabrics of more modern days, down the small and imperfect frame that contains the greatest and truest affection for you that ever mortal bore to another, whose every feeling, every thought and every action is influenced by the desire of pleasing and being worthy of you, down to one who hearing of any sacrifice made by affection in ancient times, feels that were it ten times as much, it would be no sacrifice but a pleasure so that it were for her beloved James – oh my dearest James, will you believe that in my first view of this city of cities, my feelings were not of admiration and delight at our arrival in this labyrinth of wonders, but were looking forward to the happiness with which I should leave it to go and meet my James, to gaze again on that being so tenderly loved, so long and so hopelessly cherished.

She loved the trip from Florence to Rome, despite the fact that two maids were ill and couldn't attend them. They stopped in Perugia; she says she would have loved to spend more time there. In Rome they visited St Peter's (she was very impressed), the Forum, the Coliseum and the Piazza de Spagna.

> Oh my dearest, how your expressions of affection delight me, I have often told you you love me better than I thought was in the nature of man – I knew you were very much attached to me but never expected or even dared to hope you would be in love with me.

She still keeps going out, even though she feels a bit guilty about it on his account, but she does it for her mother (it sounds a bit like an excuse, although in her case it was probably true), so as not to give her a "foretaste of their separation" i.e. when she marries James.

Frederica openly admits her emotional state in her letter dated 18 December:

> As for me, I am quite in the sillies[49], for whenever I see anything that astonishes or pleases me, I feel the tears come in my eyes, though I have now luckily a little cold, which carries it off.

She only looks at the picture when she is alone:

> I am very unlucky in my room, which is the passage room of the whole family; I can only look at you after everyone is gone to bed, or get up before I am called in the morning to get a trembling peep. Perhaps it is as well though, for if it were in my power, I believe I should do nothing else all day but gaze upon it.

Two days later she wrote again:

> Oh my dearest James, how I look forward to our meeting. I have already tried to calculate when we may reach our own dear country, and I think it cannot be before the last day of June or the beginning of July. You say 'our 10th anniversary of 12 July'. If this means what I fancy it does, it is next to impossible, if not quite so – everything will be so tedious and we shall think then 10 times more so.

In previous letters James said he had started sending her sketches and poems in 1817, and Frederica said that she had entered the second age of woman (i.e. with James) in 1815, when she was just fifteen years old, and

---

[49] Frederica wrote "silly's", which I have corrected.

now James refers to another anniversary, on 12 July 1820, and says it is a tenth anniversary. This would take the date back to July 1810, when James was with his regiment in Spain and Frederica was no more than a ten-year-old girl. There is no evidence from that he even knew the Mansfield family in 1810, although as always, the *argumentum ex silentio* is never definitive; even if they did, a twenty-two-year-old soldier could not have noticed a ten-year-old girl in any kind of romantic way. It is also impossible that any such anniversary could have been on 12 July, as on this date James was in Spain.

Another possibility is that they were already talking about the date of the wedding, which makes sense, as Frederica talks about returning to England at the end of June or the beginning of July; in the end they got married on 10 July, but 12 could have been a first plan, and if we look at what James actually wrote we see that he was humorously referring to their tenth anniversary in the future. The letter Frederica quotes from is dated 1 December;

> I wish I could have a talk with you if it were no longer than by the side of the island of Corsica under those beautiful[50] for then I might tell you what I feel and all I could say!!! As it is, you must take the will for the deed, and as I dare not pursue the now old story of how truly I am devoted to you, I will go on with a good day, detail (i.e. if the bottle don't [sic] upset again[51]) as if we were in our tenth anniversary of 12ᵗʰ July 1820.

On 24 December Freddy wrote "I always say that 3 years and a half is a long while to be absent from one's country". She had been absent for six months and had no plans to remain abroad for another three years; she must therefore be referring to James and his time in the Peninsula. She says she doesn't like the mild weather as it reminds her it is winter in Italy and as it is only winter it is still a long time till they will meet again – "I know this is silly but I do not see why I should not be silly as well as you".

They saw the Pope (Pius VII, aged seventy-seven at the time), which led Frederica to talk about her own beliefs:

> How different are my religious ideas become in the last 5 months. It is true that when I was unhappy I always had recourse to prayer, but I was then very far from the peaceful bliss I now feel.
>
> …

---

[50] A word would seem to be missing here.
[51] Earlier in the letter James describes how he spilled a bottle of ink over the letter he was writing to her.

How I pity you my dearest James for reading my stupid letters –
after you see I am well you can find nothing more worth your notice.
I must however claim a little indulgence for this as I have been
interrupted 13 times – I hope to write more rationally on Thursday,
but all my sense is deep in the Tower. Adieu my dearest.

The letter Frederica wrote on Monday 27 December is an essential part
of the collection as it provides further details of how and when their
relationship started:

My interest in you was so early, for I remember the first time you
were at Kenwood, in July 1814. I was sorry not to see you go to
church, and hoped you would follow in the last carriage and when
you did not arrive I felt quite disappointed. Is not this very singular
for I hardly knew you! And it would never have come into my head
with anyone else. I think I may date the commencement of my
attachment to you as early as this, though I was but 14½. When you
were at Scone the 2nd time you once said "Hereafter" – what an effect
those words had upon me, I think I must be a very odd person for I
had the depth of feeling and confidence of Corinne, and yet in some
things all the simplicity of my age – how we shall enjoy going over
all this together at Scone. What a good novel our history would make
altogether, yours from your infancy and mine from my childhood,
only it could be a little too improbable. I am such a different person,
I wonder anyone does not observe it, in the first place I am a fool,
for I think of nothing but you, and it is an effort to give my attention.
All I do is so painfully indifferent to me, but I envy you the
possibility of shutting yourself up and almost wish myself in the
Castle of St Angelo, for I have never either time or quiet, for I go out
scrupulously with Mama, though I believe I am often of no use to
her. Still the possibility of her wanting me would make me
uncomfortable at home.

    ...

I date the beginning of my happiness almost from Baden, for that
date we went to Eberstein, I thought I fancied I could discover in
your countenance that you wished me not to read the Strasspaper and
such was my respect for what I believed to be your wishes that I
would not have looked at it for the world, but I was very much
touched with the mute interest thus confessed – oh my dearest James,
how well I can enter into all the feelings of misery you describe on
the failure of our dearest hopes – mine were still more poignant for I

thought 'He has no friend to talk to, no gentle sympathiser and consoler of your sorrow, in short no father and no mother' – oh my dearest James, no praise you ever gave me was so flattering to my feelings now that I am composed enough to recollect it as the manner in which you announced your failure, repeating to me my own words and saying that they alone enabled you to bear our trial with fortitude. What affected me most in your letter was 'Give her my saudades, in which there is more of memory than of hope – henceforth I shall send no other message'. These simple words, which as you intended had so much meaning to me gave absolute despair and when they asked me what I thought of it myself I said I felt your despair to be greater than you expressed. From that time I had incessant pain in my side, so much so that at times I could hardly move and yet was obliged to dance. I had never had a good night since you had left us, and now I scarcely closed my eyes and prayed and bathed my locket in my tears in dread lest it should be taken from me, and then when I did sleep, dreamt such horrible dreams that I wished I had never slept – at last, blessed be the day! Mama and Mademoiselle were making a trimming for me for the ball in the evening which I was obliged to appear to care about when the letters were brought in. Mama flies into her room. I waited a minute and was just following when she called me and told me happiness – I could not stand and she could hardly support me and we both fell in each other's arms against the bed, and it was some time before we had either of us had sufficient composure to fall on our knees and offer up our thanks to the Almighty. Perhaps I have told you all this before but I am totally unconscious of all I wrote to you.

Wed 29th. The post did not come in yesterday. It is in vain I repeat to myself that your account was bitter, still knowing that the complaint is to continue some days makes me uneasy but I am obliged to conceal my anxiety before Mama, who is lower than even I had expected. We did not dine at the Cs yesterday as we none of us felt equal to it. Although I trust all this anxiety is groundless I cannot help partaking of Mama's feeling that we always have such happiness that we must expect to be chastened. God's will be done – my spirits are so low that I can hardly see to write through my tears. It is only in your bosom that I can give vent to my feelings and if when you read this the worst should have happened (Oh God how can I write these words) you will at least see I am prepared for any dispensation of His power with which it may please the Almighty to afflict us that I trust to hear it with fortitude and complete resignation to His will.

Frederica finally (for us) provides specific information about their relationship. The first time James visited Kenwood was in July 1814, after his return from Holland. Frederica says that even though she was not yet fifteen years old she noticed him, and was disappointed when he did not go to church (this could have been because of his wound, or maybe his Christian beliefs were not so fervent before his relationship with Freddy). He also visited Scone with the Mansfields and so must have become quite a good friend of the family.

Frederica in this letter also gives us a rare insight into the letter that James described as his "dismal epistle"; the words "Give her my saudades, in which there is more of memory than of hope – henceforth I shall send no other message" (the letter was addressed to Lord and Lady Mansfield) suggest that James himself doubted either his own capacity to keep Freddy happy, or maybe even a blacker outlook on life arising from the incessant pain of his wound and his own nature. As Hester said in a letter, James had had dark moments of depression from his earliest childhood.

The comments written on Wednesday 29 refer to Frederica's brother, William David (1806–1898), who eventually succeeded as 4th Earl of Mansfield on the demise of his father. Just as the eldest son of the Stanhope family was known as Mahon until he inherited the earldom, in the Mansfield family the equivalent name was Stormont (often abbreviated in the correspondence to just St.); this brother became very ill when Frederica and her parents were on their Grand Tour, although he pulled through.

In some of his letters James kept the Mansfields informed about developments with Stormont; on 20 December he refers to him as "our brother" and says that he seems to be getting better. On 22 December the first thing in the letter is "St quite out of all danger", which obviously came as a great relief to the family in Italy. We have already seen several examples of James' great, almost compulsive generosity with people he hardly knew; he now tells Frederica of another episode of his giving:

It is true that the right hand should now know what the left hand does, but the same heart should not be ignorant of it. I had the opportunity of helping a poor woman whom I had seen at my ...[52] a few days before I left the Tower. A great [illegible] rode over her child, which

---

[52] There is a hole in the page at this point; the lost word began with "b" and must have had four or at most five letters.

lingered a few days and died. The man would do nothing and the wife banged the door in the wretched woman's face, she had not even a sixpence to lay her child out, so I gave her 5 pounds and got the particulars, meaning to go to the Lord Mayor but in the mean time the man came and apologised for his wife's conduct and gave her a pound and I believe it was the child's fault.

The letter written on Christmas Day is headed with the words "St going on very well!!!!!!"
Both wrote on 30 and 31 December with similar feelings. James wrote "This is the last day of a year which has laid the foundation of my future happiness, and which has been more full of pain and pleasure than any I ever yet passed", while Frederica wrote from Rome:

I have thought over all our prospects of happiness and I think the perfect confidence that exists between us is one of our greatest securities – no perfect love can exist without confidence – I never could have believed it possible that I could have loved a person to that degree, that their being ignorant of my smallest defect could give me pain, all this I feel to you.

I have always been accused by my sisters of not liking to acknowledge my faults, but with you I am quite the contrary, I consider your soul the reflection of my own but beautified and improved, and as such that what soils my mirror must have the same effect on yours. I think I cannot spend the small part of this year that yet remains better than in reflecting with you on the manner in which I have spent it.

The first thing I remember particularly in the last year is that I got no message from you on my birthday, not that you forgot it, dearest, do not reproach yourself with that, but Mama forgot it and it was near a month when she mentioned it by accident, although I was doing my best to forget you and never mention your name. This gave me such pleasure and at the same time such pain that I cried all night.

At Easter I took the Sacrament for the first time and I prepared myself for this with all the fervency in my power; on returning to my seat after taking it I prayed with the utmost earnestness that if the unhappy attachment I had so long cherished in my breast did not find favour in the sight of the Almighty that he would grant me strength to subdue it, but if it be possible, oh Lord let it be! But nevertheless Thy will be done!

I prayed that neither of us, even if we were never to meet again, might do anything the other would disapprove of, and most earnestly did I pray the Lord to dispose you to partake of his supper. After this I felt the purest happiness - I no longer repined at the fate that separated us but earnestly hoped that I might, if not in this world, be yours in Heaven!

...

I was dreadfully agitated when I heard you were coming with us, and was on the point of speaking of it to Mama, when I heard your voice at Brussels I cannot express the effect it had upon me – I clasped my hands, I found strength to rise and in my wild ecstasy I said "He is come, my spe[53] is come" and then quite exhausted with intending emotions fell back in my chair, for I felt too strongly it was not my spe that was come – you cured me then for from the moment you came I got better.

The next trial I had was hearing you and Mathilde sitting there, for when I gazed upon you I felt you had no separate religious interests from my parents, that no reason of virtue was the cause of our separation, and it was agony – as you know I begged her to leave off – when I was ill during your absence, when my patience nearly forsook me ...

In James' letter on 4 January, he says that he had been to the Sevenoaks ball for the first time in eighteen years. He talks about his own family: "I have ever wished to unite the disjointed members of my family and to be to them what others should have been. I have often to be the maker of happiness for that part of my family, and the supporter from distress of my other sisters" (i.e. Lucy and Griselda). He then continues the story of the woman whose child had been run over and killed, to whom he had given some money. She came again in great distress and said they were destrained on for rent and were about to be turned out into the street. He began to think that both Philip, his brother, and himself were being used, as Philip had given her nearly £20 the previous year under an idea that she was the daughter of a clergyman. James told her he would do no more and then found out she had also written to Philip, who with his usual kindness of heart had sent more money. James' lawyers did not live far from the strange place she lived in, so he went in search of the woman, to the "most blackguard holes" and found out that she was the most infamous impostor, not possessing the name or residing where she said but living in a house

---

[53] Possibly a corruption of the Latin word "spes", meaning "hope".

which sends so many of its inmates to the Old Bailey. Her whole story was false, and the man (supposedly the man who had killed the child) was tried for wilful murder and was sent to Newgate for six months.

According to their correspondence, the original plan was for James to go to Paris to meet the returning party, but a curious letter he wrote in Bologna, which contains no date, no addressee and no salutation, suggests that in the end he went to meet them there as a surprise. The letter mentions Frederica in the third person, and so was clearly not addressed to her, but it does seem to have been meant for someone in her entourage. The text starts:

> For fear of startling you or giving a shock to poor Miss Barnett or dearest Fred from an unexpected appearance, I write this to say that on this our seventh day we are here in good health and not fagged, and if my companion did not express a wish to stay here tonight I should not have given up the intention I had of your finding me keeping your place for you tomorrow at breakfast.
> ...
> I do not mean to start till 7 so that we may not break in upon your dinner, but I hope between 8 and 9 to be au sein de ma famille.
> ...
> I will send this on from the second stage from Florence, so within less than an hour after you receive it you will see yours affectionately JHS.

There are various reasons why this letter cannot have been written while in Bologna in 1819. James and his unnamed companion have been travelling for seven days; this letter is not dated, but we know from Frederica's diary that in 1819 she arrived in Bologna on 15 October, and left again on 18, and we also know that James left the Mansfields in Genoa on 10 October. His idea seems to have been to give a surprise to Frederica by turning up at breakfast, but his companion wished to stay in another hotel or inn so they changed their plan, and were now planning on showing up just after dinner. This, of course, is not compatible with his having left the family. If he had been travelling for seven days it would be now 17 October, and he would presumably be nowhere near Bologna.

It would also appear that James and Frederica had already agreed to marry, and that her family had accepted him, as he refers to the group as "ma famille". The expression cannot mean his family in England, as he had none to speak of in such a way, and seven days is not long enough for him to have travelled from Bologna to England. Frederica makes absolutely no mention of James' presence at Bologna, but this is only to be expected as she makes no mention of him anywhere in the journal. James says he plans to set out at 7 o'clock to reach his new family just an hour later, either by horse or on foot. He must therefore have been in or very near Bologna when he wrote this.

It is impossible to make this letter fit in with the dates in 1819, but there remains a further possibility. It could refer to the Mansfields' homeward journey in 1820. In favour of this, in one of James' booklets into which he copied Freddy's letters, there is another dateless entry entitled "Extract from her private journal at Bologna", whose text is not in any of the copies of the diary for her stay in Bologna in 1819[54]. It is clear that her journal continued to the end of the trip, although we now have nothing beyond January 1820. James was planning on meeting Freddy and her family in Paris on their homeward journey; it would seem that he travelled seven days from there to surprise them in Bologna, which is feasible. There is no reference to such an event in any of the couple's surviving letters, but it the only possible explanation for James' otherwise incomprehensible letter.

In Frederica's letter written from Rome on 26 March 1820, she describes how they are packing to leave; they are in a "hurry-scurry", although as it is Easter week, she would have preferred to be more "religiously employed". She says that they would be in Paris by Whitsunday; in 1820 Easter Sunday fell on 2 April, so Whitsunday would have been 21 May. On April 14 she wrote from Florence to say they would be in Paris later than expected. While in Florence, Frederica's aunt, Mrs. Barnett, died, leaving their daughter Lizzy with the Mansfields. Freddy suggests that James travel out to Paris with Mr. Barnett (the widower), which reveals who James' otherwise anonymous travelling companion was on this surprise journey to Bologna. There can be no doubt that he did travel out to Italy to meet Freddy, as there is in the manuscript collection (in the same folder as his letters written to Freddy in 1819) a poem written on 18 May 1820 in Venice. Once he had joined up with his future family Bologna, they clearly went to visit Venice before continuing on their journey back home. The poem in question reads as follows:

Nor poet's wish could frame a lovelier eve
Nor painter's skill could fairer tints bestow
Nor less unbroken could the waves receive
The mimicity on their gulfs below
Yet looked I not on dome, no marble pile

---

[54] It is highly unlikely that Frederica kept two different journals, one personal and the other less so.

It Mark's proud tower bright tipp'd with rays of gold
Not pomp nor grandeur of Palladio's isle
....
Yet still I fondly gazed on hues of heaven
But not for them on cloud or sea did seek
Perhaps I sinned, if so, be it forgiven,
I found them fairest on my Freddy's cheek.

Among the souvenirs that Frederica brought back from Italy with her were three miniature watercolours, two of which show the Strada di Santa Lucia in Naples (see Figures 6.10 and 6.11), while the third shows an eruption of Vesuvius dated 5 March 1820 (see Figure 6.12). There were major eruptions in December 1820 and again in 1822, but there can be no doubt that there was also a lesser volcanic action in March 1820. Frederica and her family rather unwisely went up quite close to the volcano while visiting Pompeii and describes the scene as follows in the letter to James written on 9 March[55]:

We were above an hour going up but we were amply compensated for all our trouble and fatigue, which was saying a good deal. When we came to the head of the lava, for we could not go up to the crater, nobody having been there for a month, but we sat down close to the small crater from whence issues the stream of lava running I should think about two miles in the hour – as we sat by the side of the lava, red hot pieces of lava fell among us; the lava on which we were sitting had been liquid three days before. We went down to look at a little crater which had only opened that morning – and every now and then we heard a great noise above us which was from the shower of stones sent up by the large crater. The lava was quite hot, so comfortable for we had been almost frozen, the cold was so intense … we were all the better for some bread, oranges and wine.

...

At length we began to descend by torchlight, and difficult as we thought the coming up, it was nothing to the going down. Part of the way was not disagreeable as we had only to stick our heels into the cinders and we slid down several yards together, but it was not quite so pleasant when large pieces of lava rolled down on our heels: my guide fell down and as I had his arm pulled me down with him and I

---

[55] The original letter has not survived, only James' copy in the fair copy of the journal; he might very well have embellished the style and vocabulary, but the actual facts remain unchanged.

slid down laying on my side about 30 yards but luckily for me, it was dark[56] and I was not much bruised.

...

I cannot describe the state of our chaussure, one side of my thick shoes was cut open quite through the stocking, my ankles were bleeding and I had several bruises on my legs.

It is not known exactly when the Murrays came back from their tour – Glover says it was early in 1820[57], but in the fair copy of Frederica's diary from her Grand Tour of 1819 and 1820, which James gave as a gift to Lady Mansfield, the long letter from Freddy to James telling him how they had visited Pompeii and Vesuvius and were currently based in Naples, dated 9 March, automatically precludes a return to England at the beginning of the year.

The main impression we get from the correspondence between James and Frederica while she was in Italy is that they made a perfect couple; they were hopelessly in love with each other and cared for little else in life, their love had a deeply religious aspect to it, and they were both open about their feelings and not at all restrained. More importantly from a historical point of view, the letters provide a great deal of information about when and how their relationship started, and about the Grand Tour undertaken by the Mansfields.

The Stanhope manuscript collection holds a power of attorney[58] for the transfer of £8,690 from the "Trustees of the Hon. James Stanhope's marriage to himself". The power of attorney is dated 23 April 1820, which shows that the wedding was already arranged (possibly the date too, although no mention is made of it).

The same file also holds a document called "Epitome on the settlement of the marriage of the Honourable Colonel Stanhope and Lady Frederica Louisa Murray", dated 6 and 7 July 1820. It is quite a long document and concerns mainly what will happen to the estates in Lincolnshire inherited from Sir Joseph Banks, depending on who dies first from among James, Frederica, any possible children they might have, Joseph Banks and his wife Dorothea.

Colonel the Honourable James Hamilton Stanhope and Lady Frederica Louisa Murray were married at the bride's house, Kenwood, on 10 July

---

[56] The dark was presumably lucky as nobody would have clearly seen her discomfort and disarray.

[57] *Eyewitness*, p. 206.

[58] U1590 C 262/2. The papers are held inside a folder sheet entitled "Papers relating to the marriage settlement of the Hon. J. H. Stanhope 1820".

1820. The evidence for the date is contradictory. Many years after the event, Charles Lewis Meryon tells us it was on 9 July[59], a Sunday (and is followed in this by many of the later books that give a date for the wedding[60]), while in a contemporary letter he actually says the wedding took place on 10 July. The letter in question was written to Lady Hester on 11 July; Meryon informs her that James had married Lord Mansfield's daughter just the day before, and that (as he had been told) they had gone to spend their honeymoon at Chevening.

This is further backed up by a note from James to his mother, sent from Kenwood on Friday (no month or year given). He refers to a letter he has received from his mother and which he has shown to Freddy, i.e. Freddy is now back from her travels. He goes on to say that:

> The marriage takes place here at 1 o'clock on Monday, and we shall reach Chevening by dinner[61]. I hope on the Monday following we shall have the pleasure of receiving you or you will open your house to us, for Freddy is impatient to be acquainted with you.
>
> Lord and Lady Mansfield join in everything that can be said kind, and Freddy sends her love.

In July 1820, 9 July was a Sunday and 10 was of course a Monday. James writes as if the event is imminent, and even though his mother was apparently not going to the wedding, James would hardly have got the day wrong so soon before the marriage. On the weight of the evidence, given that James wrote three days before the wedding and Meryon the day after, it seems safe to state that James and Freddy were married on Monday 10 July 1820.

---

[59] In a footnote of his own to his copy of the letter informing Hester that James had died, quoted in Guscin, *Very Good Sort of* Man, p. 93.

[60] E.g. Glover, *Staff Officer*, p. 3.

[61] Confirming what Meryon said about their spending their honeymoon at Chevening. The dowager Countess seems to have been very much excluded from the ceremonies and festivities.

Figure 6.10 – Naples

Figure 6.11 – Naples

Figure 6.12 – The eruption of Vesuvius on 5 March 1820

CHAPTER SEVEN

MY GREAT CALAMITY

Frederica became pregnant almost immediately after her wedding; given their profound religious beliefs and the fact that they had been apart since agreeing to marry, we can assume that at least Frederica was a virgin on marriage (she was just twenty years old and had never lived apart from her parents), whereas James had travelled extensively and lived a soldier's life (although it is true that there is no record of any serious liaisons with other women before Freddy).

They seem to have lived a quiet domestic life for the rest of 1820 and most of 1821. Their son was born on 13 May 1821, and named James Banks (Banks was doubly in honour of James' brother Charles Banks, and his benefactor Sir Joseph Banks). The weeks before the birth show us a curious side to Frederica's personality; the following letter is kept in the Stanhope collection[1], with a title written by Lady Mansfield: "This note was written by my beloved child to her husband nearly seven weeks before the birth of her first child which took place 13 May 1821".

> London, 26 March 1821
> What is my spirit in writing this? To attempt to cheer the heart of one whose warmest affections will have received their death blow ere he can open this. Oh almighty and most merciful God, grant this last proof of my affection for him (who by thy grace made me enjoy a state of happiness no mortal had ever known) grant that this last proof of my affection may be pure from all the deceits and vanities of this world and which may be calculated to make him repeat being separated from me, what we never craved repeating while together, thy will be done O God!
>
> Almighty, Merciful Father, grant the prayer thy unworthy servant pours up to Thee – support I pray Thee and comfort my afflicted James. Grant him I beseech thee patience in his sufferings, and humility of spirit to acknowledge thy chastening with gratitude.

---

[1] U1590 C 269/1.

Grant that he may so spend his life on earth that he may be worthy
of the joys of heaven, to which I (though in humbling) aspire.

My dearest, my own, my best beloved James! Father of my child!
When I think that the hand that writes this will be cold and stiff and
thou canst read it, that the eyes that now glisten with affection will
be shut forever, that the lips that have so often assured thee of my
affection will be cold and motionless I confess I should die –

My James, I wish to comfort you for my loss, first let me thank
you for the perfect happiness I enjoyed with you and let me beg of
you that as our souls are still in union although our bodies are
separate, that you will with me thank our maker for all the blessings
we have enjoyed. Remember, my dearest, our separation will be
short, and we shall meet again, never, never to part – I trust I leave
you a pledge of my love! Cherish me in it! Be not only a father to it,
supply the place of a mother, for you alone can supply that greatest
of losses.

Recollect, my James, that next to the loss of a wife, comes the
loss of a child. Think of this not only as to our poor little babe, but
as to our parents – go to them and comfort them, in trying to assuage
their grief your own will become more regulated and composed.
Take care of your health I conjure you, for my sake, yes, James, for
do I not live still in our child?

As Frederica did not die during or immediately after the birth of James
Banks, this letter can only have been written in preparation for what she
thought might happen. Childbirth was certainly risky at the time and a lot
of women did die, but the maturity and faith of a twenty-one year old woman
are profoundly evident in this letter. It would not be the last warning of her
own death that she wrote. There is no sign that James read or even knew of
the letter; it was clearly entrusted to Lady Mansfield, who would give it to
James if anything happened to Frederica. She seems to have donated the
letter to the family after both Freddy and James had left this world.

We have seen on various occasions how the love between James and
Frederica enjoyed a profound Christian aspect; this is even more evident in
the fact that they composed prayers together. A small red notebook[2] kept
inside a black velvet bag (see Figures 7.1 and 7.2) contains several of their
prayers. The leather cover has the following words written on it in black:

"Private memoranda 1819, Private 1823".

---

[2] U1590 264/4.

Figure 7.1 – The black velvet bag containing the prayer book

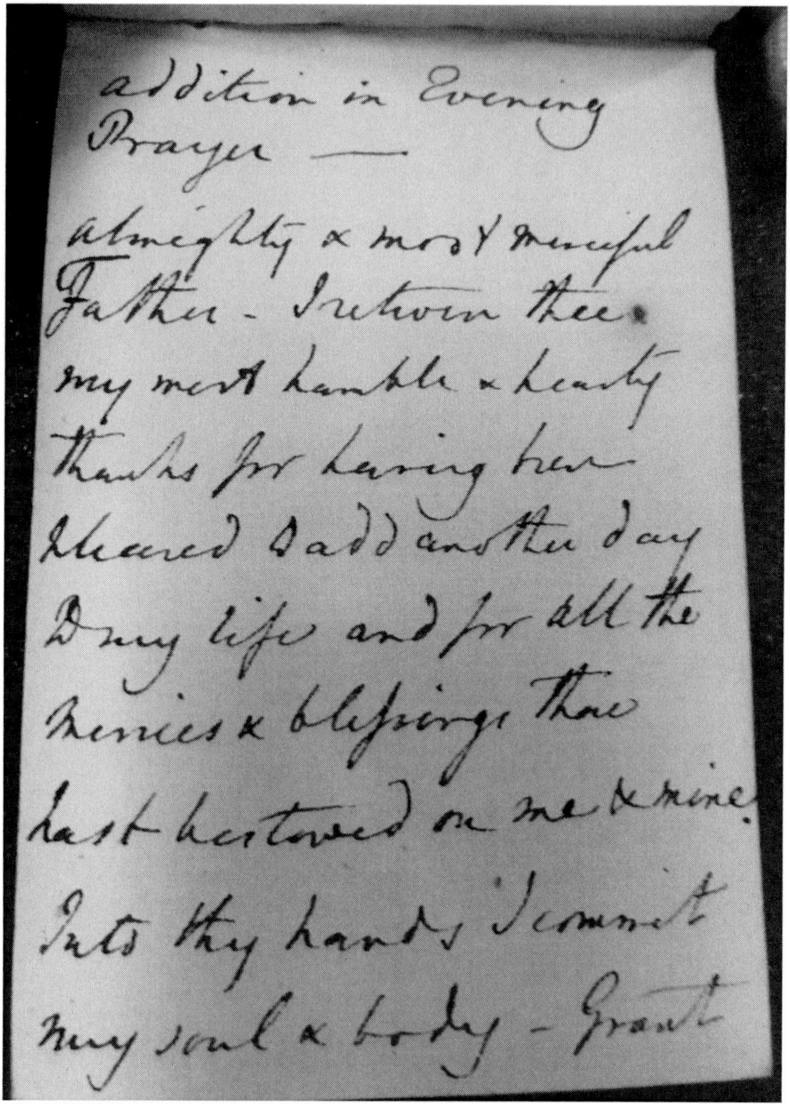

addition in Evening
Prayer —

Almighty & most merciful
Father — I return thee
my most humble & hearty
thanks for having here
sheared & add another day
D my life and for all the
mercies & blessings thou
hast bestowed on me & mine.
Into thy hands I commit
my soul & body — Grant

Figure 7.2 – A page from the prayer book

James was a devout Christian, as is evident from his surviving writings. His Christian beliefs were very much wound up with his patriotism as an Englishman; no doubt today he would be described as a bigot and racist, but such feelings were much more widely accepted two hundred years ago, even if they cannot be justified by today's prevailing thoughts. It would be, however, a mistake, here as in so many other cases, to judge people's feelings in the past by using today's standards as if they were any more correct than those of the past. We might find today's ideas more correct, but in two hundred years' time they might equally well have been replaced.

The inside cover contains the words J. H. Stanhope, 72 South Audley Street, James' and Frederica's London address (see Figure 7.3)[3]. The first page contains a heavily foxed and damp-stained profile pencil sketch of a woman, most probably Frederica (see Figure 7.4).

One of the most touching prayers is entitled "For our child" (James Banks), dated 1821:

Almighty God, we humbly beseech thee to bless our dear child with health of body and spirit. Defend him from all danger, protect him from all sin, support him under all the afflictions of this life, grant me thy grace that I may bring him up in thy faith, fear and love, that he may fulfil his duties to his country, his sovereign and Thee[4]: and that he may so hap through this state of trial that he may at length be received into everlasting life through the merciful mediation of Jesus Christ our Lord.

I beseech thee o Lord to make me truly grateful for the great blessings and perfect happiness I have enjoyed and under all the future dispensations of thy will, even in that of withdrawing, which o God in thy mercy avert!, from me this dear pledge to bestow on me thy grace that I may bear my afflictions with perfect resignation to thy will, with fervent gratitude for the past and with increased hope and confidence in thy future mercy.

---

[3] The house is now a Grade-II listed building, designed in 1736 by Edward Shepherd, and probably stuccoed c.1830 with an extra storey added. The house has four 4 storeys, a basement and a dormered mansard. The house has associations with the French Royal Family in exile during the Napoleonic Wars, as it was the London residence of the Comte d'Artois (later Charles X) from 1805 to 1814.

[4] The order possibly shows James' priorities; first England, then God.

Figure 7.3 – 72 South Audley Street, James' residence in London

Figure 7.4 – A profile of Frederica

The prayer was originally written in the first person plural "we" and "us", and were no doubt changed to the first person singular "I" and "me" after Frederica's death. This could be a sign of James' bitterness even towards his God.

After James Banks was born, his father did travel, as part of his political responsibilities. One of the prayers was written during his time away from home:

> Prayer during our separation Dec. 1821
> Almighty God we humbly beseech thee during this our separation to grant us, thy unworthy servants, thy merciful support that we may increase in virtue and mutual affection, and preserve ourselves in purity both of body and soul. Strengthen us in all our good resolutions, protect us under all temptation and from all danger.
> Bestow on us the peace and calm and contented minds and grant that after having fulfilled to the best of our powers our several duties we may meet again with blameless consciences to live according to thy word in the blissful hope of everlasting life through the mediation of Jesus Christ our Lord.

The letters James sent give us an idea of his travels. The above prayer shows that he was away in December 1821, and did not go home for Christmas as he wrote to Freddy on New Year's Day 1822 (the letter does not say where it was written); on 15 January he wrote to his mother from Dublin, and on April 6 Frederica wrote to him from Kenwood (so he was away, but we do not know where). James wrote to Frederica from Boston (in Lincolnshire, where he was visiting the estates inherited from Sir Joseph Banks) on Wednesday 12 – the only month in which there was a Wednesday 12 in 1822 was June – and she wrote to him again on 4 July from Kenwood (the envelope shows that James was still in Lincolnshire). He wrote to Frederica from Exeter on Thursday 8 (which in 1822 could only have been in August), and there are no further letters between them, which could mean that he was back in London with his family for the rest of the year. Frederica gave birth again in January 1823, so James must have been at home some time in April or May, and no doubt spent time at home between his different journeys, while at least for Christmas and New Year in 1821 Frederica went to Scotland with her family (and presumably with James Banks too).

It is clear that she had recently had a miscarriage, as her letter to James on New Year's Eve 1821 says:

I believe that all is for the best, the Almighty in his mercy ordained that my child should not be born. Perhaps it might have died and caused us greater grief than now, perhaps it might have been sickly and have lingered in misery.

James' letter on New Year's Day also refers to the miscarriage:

Another year has passed my best and sweetest Freddy. I have offered up my very grateful thanks to the Providence which has enabled me to live thus far as to be able to look back with satisfaction at the past year.

I am grateful that you have had no pain, we must be very careful next time and James must be doubly aimable till we have a companion for him, I am rejoiced to see how well you bear the disappointment – like my own Freddy!!

At the end of the letter he adds what would seem to be a new lovers' code word for them: "zu zu zu zu!!!".

In April 1822 James Banks fell ill while his father was away, as Freddy tells him:

The dearest of babies is not quite right again, my own very best darling – he has not slept well for the last three nights, and last night was very very restless, but his bowels are better.

...

Baby has had a good sleep but is rather feverish and I do not feel quite easy about him as I can see no cause for this restlessness and fever unless it is from weakness.

...

Adieu my very own best dearest, your own silly little Freddy. Do not fidget yourself about Baby for it is nothing.

James answered her from Dartmouth (he was in Dartmouth as it was his constituency from 1822 to 1825):

Your letter today my very dearest makes me as you can imagine still more anxious to get home. It is very trying upon me, little darling, but I am almost glad there is a reason for his feverishness and restlessness.

Poor little babies, what they have to go through, and what anxious hearts parents must have till they get over the few first years. I will not fidget myself but hope humbly for the best.

Kiss our poor little dear, bless u bless u, my best, my sweetest Freddy, your own faithful and ever affectionate own own own James.

Included in the Stanhope manuscript collection with this letter is a version of the prayer described above for James Banks; it is written in the first person singular, which could either mean that James composed it while he was away from home and sent it with the letter (which would explain why only he is praying and not Frederica with him), or it is a copy he made of the prayer after Frederica's death.

Some of the letters are undated, with just the day of the week in the header. One of them, written in Dartmouth, narrates how James had been canvassing his constituency: "I have been calling on the voters". Frederica would probably not have been overly pleased to hear that "I have seen in my rambles this morning two very pretty young ladies". He signs off "How I shall count the days till I am again in your arms, zu zu".

In the next letter he explains how he stays up late talking to his host, telling him about Hester. For some reason his electorates love the fact that he has been to Newfoundland; he eats and drinks very well (lots of John Dorys). He calls his wife "Frity", and says "As you tell me not to fidget myself about baby I will not, but I do not like this return of restlessness, and on that account am additionally anxious to be back but cannot get away before Thursday".

Frederica's letter to James dated 4 July (she was at Kenwood with her parents while James was in Lincolnshire), contains an abbreviation that we tend to associate more with mobile phone text messages: "It came into my head that I had not told u" (just as James had written to her in his letter). She expresses her love: "James, James, I cannot live without you", and signs off with their new term of endearment: "Your own zuzu, Freddy".

A colour drawing of a woman is included in the collection at this point (see Figure 7.5), although we do not know if this was sent with the letter, given that James says in a later letter that he has her picture, it could be a depiction of Freddy. The woman has downcast eyes and a distinctly sad expression.

In August, when James wrote to his wife from Exeter, she was at their London residence on South Audley Street (suggesting that his absence was not prolonged, as when it was she tended to go and stay with her parents at Kenwood). He describes the journey and the other passengers, showing that he used public transport:

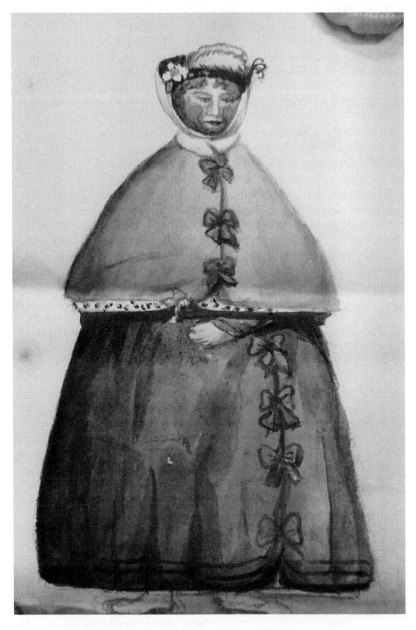

Figure 7.5 – A sketch of a woman (possibly Frederica)

You see, zu zu, I am only thinking of coming back.

...

In the morning two rosy schoolboys got in, one sick, no handkerchief between them. We will manage this better when Master James goes to school. Then we got a Quaker and then a fine old farmer of 40. I read the New Quarterly, the stupidest ever published.

...

What a comfort it is having your picture to look at[5],

Good night sweetest, kiss our darling as I am now kissing you, James zu zu zu

Towards the end of the year, as Frederica's pregnancy advanced, James no doubt stayed with her in London and/or Kenwood. On 15 October he wrote to his mother to inform her that Lady Mansfield's brother, the Dean of York, i.e. George Markham, had died on 30 September 1822. He tells her that Freddy expects to be confined in January:

She continues as well as possible and as for our dear boy, he is every day more intelligent and more dear: he is crying papa with all his might at this moment to make me hum his top and ride him my foot. I shall be so glad to show him you again for you will hardly know him to be the same child.

On 5 November 1822 he received a letter from Dr Meryon (who was again planning on returning to Hester, although it would in the end be five years before he actually left[6]); he answered the same day:

I have received your letter this morning, and must express, if I can, how deeply sensible I am of the value of that devotion to my sister, which has prompted the kind offer of returning once more to Syria. I need not tell you how much pleasure it will give me to know that

---

[5] This could mean that the sketch of a sad woman with downcast eyes mentioned above is Frederica.

[6] The delays in Hester's correspondence with Meryon and his consequent uncertainty about leaving England again resulted in his taking employment, this time with Sir Gilbert Heathcote (the first man Lady Hester ever danced with, as she later confessed to Meryon) for five years in London. His profound sense of duty to his new contract, his marriage to Eliza in 1823 and the situation with Narcisse (the French opera dancer he had a child with in 1821) no doubt made him unwilling to return to Hester, and he must have told her so (although without explaining any of the reasons other than his new professional situation).

she is again accompanied with so faithful, tried and attached an attendant. At the same time how far it is for your own interests is to me a great question, and how far anything I can ever do can assist I will now inform you. You must consider this *entirely secret* and I must *request your promise you will never mention even to my sister this communication.*

Lady Hester has of late been spending even more money than formerly, has expended the sum received from Lord Chatham, and has drawn the full amount of all I can advance 'till Lady Banks's death: and has at this moment drawn on her account till midsummer next. How far her finances in these circumstances can stand the additional expense of your going out, and your salary, you must be as good a judge as me. I shall give you a hundred pounds for your journey, which is all I can afford.

I have told Lady H. candidly, repeatedly, forcibly that I can do nothing more till Lady Banks's death, who may live one month or ten years. My expenditure now is hardly covered by my income, and I owe to others not to embarrass myself, when I may be so long before I come to my property. If therefore you leave Lady H. before that event, or if she, by pursuing her present line of expenditure, gets bills protested, and into distress, I cannot assist. Deeply as I shall deplore it I shall have the consolation of knowing I have done all to avert it, and that it is not arrived without frequent warning and ample time to economize.

When Lady Banks dies, Lady H. will be, by the arrangements I have made, so well provided for that there will be no difficulty in her, during her life, making you an ample provision. Should you continue with her during her life I should be happy, after Lady Banks's death, and on anything happening to my sister, to give you whatever annuity I can afford, up to £300 a year, not being less, however, than £100 a year.

[text cut out][7]

I have been, do you see, most explicit. I wish you to think the matter over most maturely before you go. I shall be in town in a little more than a month[8], when we will talk it over.

---

[7] When Meryon was preparing the final manuscript of the *Additional Memoirs* (an activity no doubt cut short by his death), he quite liberally cut parts of the text out and pasted them elsewhere in the manuscript, or just threw them away.

[8] They were possibly planning on spending Christmas at Scone.

On a flyer attached to the manuscript of the *Additional Memoirs* are the
following words; when working on the text many years later Meryon added
the words "put aside, forgotten why".

Lord Stanhope in all probability considered himself exonerated
altogether from a claim originating in a half-sister's troubles.
Besides, there never had been any cordiality between them; and Lady
H. considered her brother, Lord Stanhope's, conduct, both in his
politics and towards herself, far from praiseworthy. Colonel James
Hamilton Stanhope came to an untimely end by suicide, and his
intentions towards the author were therefore never fulfilled[9].

After Christmas and the New Year, Frederica was seriously ill. By 9
January 1823, she knew she was dying. She had already considered this
same possibility when she was just a few weeks away from giving birth to
James Banks in 1821, and had written a letter to James, presumably to be
delivered to him only if she did not survive the ordeal. She did survive this
first birth, but this time she knew that there was no hope; the doctors had
been honest with her and her letter to James expresses this openly.
Surprisingly enough, the textual history of the letter is quite complicated;
this is due mainly to James' habit of amending texts he copied, adding to
them, deleting parts and "improving" the original text.

Fortunately, we have the original copy of the letter as written by
Frederica[10], kept inside a beautiful silver box with the initials JHS engraved
on it (see Figure 7.6). Once the box is opened, the letter is wrapped in a
piece of paper containing the following words: "James – to be opened within
a month after my decease". On 9 January Frederica had not yet given birth;
the baby was born in the early morning of the 11th. The text of the original
letter is as follows (see Figure 7.7):

London, 9 January 1823.
My dearest and best husband, my own beloved James, I write this
to express my gratitude for the happiness you gave me, happiness,
dearest James, such as no mortal ever felt. It is a feeling of great
happiness to me and I am sure will be a consolation to you to reflect
that by no thought or action did we ever disturb that felicity which it
has pleased the Almighty to permit us to enjoy. I do not repine at my
death, dearest James, and notwithstanding all my happiness I feel

---

[9] Neither was Meryon's part of the bargain, namely to stay with Lady Hester.
[10] U1590 C274/5.

more for the grief I know you will suffer than sorrow at quitting all I love. I certainly would have wished to have been your prop through life and the guide and instructor of my dear children, for I trust I shall leave more than one pledge of our happiness. I do not ask you to control your grief for their sake, nor for mine, dearest beloved, but as a token of submission to the divine will. It is my fervent wish that you should embrace the first opportunity of taking the sacrament. When we last took it on Christmas Day, how earnestly did I pray for resignation for you – I know the blow will be a heavy one – I have only to think what I should feel were I to have lost you – dearest, God's will be done!

No human creature ever passed three and twenty years so happily; whether I have passed them so as to please the Almighty I know not, but I die in hopes that my intentions will be mercifully received and that for the sake of our blessed Saviour I may be admitted to everlasting happiness and that I may there be joined by my James, my children, my parents, by all I love.

Oh, if it is permitted to souls to look down to influence mortals, how will I watch over my James. If spirits are allowed to hold communion ere the last day, how will I glad the spirits of your brother, Mr. Pitt, of all you have loved by telling them that every day spent by you is a step to joining them in the regions of bliss.

For my dear children I feel solicitude but no fear. I leave them under the care of such a father, my mother will be a mother to them. I leave them to your care, to Mama's and to Elisabeth, in whom I have implicit confidence. If she marry and have children she will let my children be as brothers and sisters to hers.

No-one can be more fitted to the education of children than you are, dearest James. If I have a girl and that it should not hurt your feelings, call her after me, and let Mama be her godmother – pray, dearest James, be particular in the choice of a governess, and unless it be perfectly necessary from you or Mama not being able to take care of her, I would rather she has no governess after she has attained the age of fifteen. As for my dear little James, who has been the joy of my life, keep him with you till old enough to send him to Westminster; dear child, tell him how his mother loved him. Tell him how happy his affectionate caresses used to make her, and how grievously disappointed she would be if he did not fulfil the promises of his infant days. If I have a son my prayer is that they may be such brothers as you and Charles were.

Figure 7.6 – The silver box in which Frederica's last letter is kept

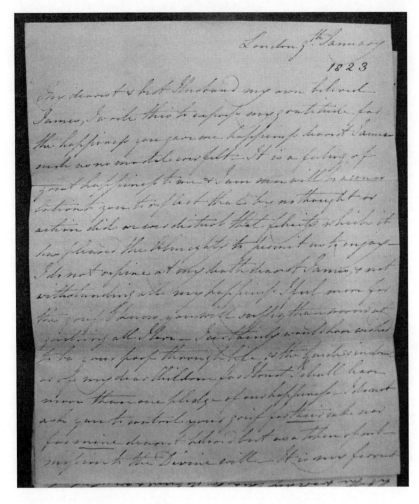

Figure 7.7 – The first page of Frederica's last letter

In the event of a war, dearest James, do not seek it as a relief from grief, but as a duty that I, had I lived, would have begged you to perform. Exert all the energies of your mind for the sake of your Freddy, and now, my dearest James, I must touch upon a tender point, but one I have much at heart. I have often spoken of it to you. Can you better prove your attachment to me and to your children your gratitude to God for all the blessings heaped upon us than by preserving your virtue? I believe this can only be accomplished by your marrying again and therefore I earnestly wish it. It may perhaps not add to your apparent happiness, but if it causes you to lead a good life, it will add to your real happiness. Do not let the worldly idea of its being a want of affection to my memory deter you – I do not expect anyone will make you as happy as I trust I have done, but I earnestly wish such a woman should be found. Whenever you have found a person likely to suit you, disclose the state of your heart truly; if you do not feel in <u>love</u> do not pretend it but own that esteem and attachment are all you feel. Should you ever disagree or should anything be disputed never say what I should have done or felt. Think of me as a sister, speak of me to her as you have done of Charles and Hester to me. Do not be surprised or hurt if you should discover any jealousy of me or my memory, her very love for you would cause it. Do not continue to wear the locket if it should seem to hurt her if you wear it, let her hair be worn on the same chain as mine, it is my wish.

I trust you will consult my parents as you would your own in the choice, they shall know it was my wish you should remarry. I am sure the wife you will have will be fond of my children, and I feel no fear or anxiety in their having a stepmother, if she should have children make no difference between them and take care no-one else does through the mistaken notion they are not cherished as they ought to be. This is not written with forced feelings but on mature, serious and I trust religious considerations. Trust to no-one but yourself the religious education of our children. I will now subjoin a few wishes which are not be considered as necessarily binding but subject to your better judgment.

I wish you to give Mme. Bourillion 20 guineas yearly instead of ten. I wish while you continue unmarried to give half of what you would give besides in charity for my sake. I leave you the picture of Mama to be left after your death as you think it will be most valued. I wish you to have it copied in miniature for Miss Murray and given her from me. My Bible I leave to you. My prayer book, if I have a girl, I wish to be given to her the day she is six years old; it was given me by my mother at the same age. If I have a boy you may do as you please with it.

As to my jewels – if I have a son they are to be distributed among my sisters with the exception of one set of coral for Hester Taylor another to Lizzy Barnett, the ring with Mr. Pitt's hairs to James, the one with yours to any other son. If I have a daughter the jewels will go to her with the exception of the set given by Lord Glenlyon[11] which I desire may be given either to Elizabeth Carrhine or Georgina, and some trinket that I have worn to each of my sisters. The cornelian vinaigrette to Mama, it was given me by her mother, and I beg she will leave it to my daughter if I have one. I wish that my hair should be given to my father, my three brothers, and in suitable amounts to Lucy Stanhope[12], Hester Taylor[13], Fanny Cathcart and Laura Mackenzie and that the rest may be properly taken care of for my children. If my sisters wish for more they may have it. Miss Murray has some and I also wish Mrs. Goodenough to have some in a trinket and that some memorial of me should be given to Gisela Robert.

Carrhine's bust I leave to you, your picture to my children. I leave everything unmentioned to you to be disposed of as you think proper, given away where it will be valued for my sake. I wish tokens of my regard to be given to the servants and also to Winbridge and Mary. If there is any wish contained in this you do not approve of I beg and entreat you will not comply with it.

Pray be a watchful guardian and observer of dear Stormont, tell him it was my wish and desire and that I trust he will be the same to my sons. Give the hair of my last born babe to Mama in a heart like the one containing James's, the stone bearing a reference to the name. And now my husband, my friend, my own James, father of my children, adieu until we meet forever.

---

[11] Most probably Lieutenant-General James Murray, 1st Baron Glenlyon KCH FRS (29 May 1782 – 12 October 1837), styled as Lord James Murray until 1821, a British Army officer, Member of Parliament and peer.
[12] This obviously cannot be Lucy Stanhope James' half-sister, as she died in 1814. It must be Catherine Lucy Wilhelmina Stanhope, born in 1819, who by marriage became the Duchess of Cleveland, visited the places related to her aunt Lady Hester and wrote a book about her.
[13] Newman, *Stanhopes*, p. 189, tells us that Lucy left three sons and four daughters, but no names are given. Hester Taylor must have been one of these seven children; she must have been a favourite of Freddy's as nothing is left to any of the other children.

I trust this letter will not have given you pain, but comfort as it has done me in writing.

Almighty and heavenly Father, look down with merciful eyes[14] on me thy unworthy servant who here says and from her inmost heart the divine words of thy blessed son, "Lord, if it be thy will, let this cup pass by me, I pray thee, nevertheless not as I will but as thou wilt – thy will be done. Almighty God, I praise thee, I laud thee, I magnify thy holy name and thy word. I thank thee for all the blessings I have received from thee. I deliver up my soul willingly into thy hands, trusting that thou wilt forgive my sins and accept of my contrition – I say, I trust with unfeigned repentance – Lord be merciful to me, a sinner – Lord, receive me in thy mansions of bliss, not for my sake but for that of our blessed Saviour Jesus Christ.

Strengthen, I beseech thee Almighty God, the weakness of my husband, my parents, of all who mourn my loss. Grant them thy grace to support this infliction of thy power with proper resignation. Almighty God listen to my prayers for the earthly, but still more for the eternal happiness of my husband, my parents, my children and all my friends and of my enemies if I have any, but I trust not. I believe I die in charity with all men. I trust that I earnestly repent of my sins.

Almighty God, I beseech thee, protect all I love for the sake of thy beloved son Jesus Christ our Lord. Amen.

Frederica Louisa Stanhope.

There are two copies of this letter, both made by James. The first is on sheets of paper[15], while the second is to be found in the last of the four miniature books James copied of his wife's letters to him[16]; these booklets consist mainly of her letters sent from Italy before they were married, although this, her last letter to him, is also included. There are some minor variations in the wording, although both copies omit the details of what Frederica left as legacies for other people[17], and what is much more significant is that the copy made on paper omits the whole section about Freddy's making James promise to marry again[18]. This would appear to be

---

[14] The later copy omits the words "with merciful eyes".
[15] U1590 C265/1.
[16] U1590 C266/5.
[17] The sentence "I will now … instead of ten", the whole section from "I leave you the picture" to "not comply with it", and the sentence "Give the hair … to the name".
[18] From "I believe this can only be accomplished" to "I trust religious considerations".

some kind of attempt at denial by James that the promise had ever been made, at the very least a wish to avoid reading and copying it; given the terrible consequences the promise had later on, this is hardly surprising.

On the same day, after this letter to James, Frederica wrote a farewell letter to her parents (see Figure 7.8). On the outside of the folded paper it says "To my dear parents, to be opened whenever they think proper". The letter itself reads as follows:

> My dearest parents,
> I cannot express my gratitude for the affection and happiness you have blessed me with during my happy life. Forgive me, dearest dearest parents, all the faults I have been guilty of towards you; believe me, they proceeded from harmless imperfections and not from my want of affection. I fear I shall pain you by touching on a subject which gives <u>me</u> no pain except in fearing it may give you some. It is my earnest wish that James should remarry. I have expressed this wish to him and begged him to consult you on his choice. For <u>my</u> sake I intreat[19] you that you will regard her not as the wife of your <u>son-in-law</u>, but as the wife of your <u>son</u>, and treat her accordingly. Pray, pray encourage James to marry. I believe it to be the only chance of his happiness. I leave my children to your care, and his, and also to dear Elizabeth.
>
> Dearest, dearest parents, do not give way to sorrow. Recollect how happy I have been, and that I leave 8 brothers and sisters to console you, I am content to die, I die happy, and have lived happy – God bless you and preserve you and all I love. When James marries let it be known <u>I wished it</u>.
>
> With confident hopes of meeting again, adieu dearest parents.
> Your most affectionate daughter
> F. L. Stanhope.

The baby was born and died a few days later (named Frederick); Frederica never saw or held him, and indeed his death was concealed from her. She asked to see the baby but was always given an excuse. At this time James wrote to his brother Philip:

---

[19] An old spelling of "entreat".

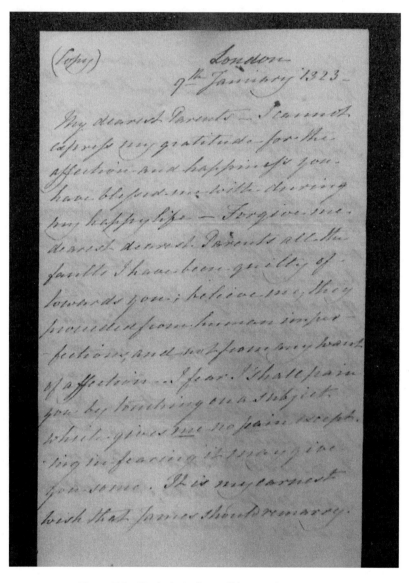

Figure 7.8 – Frederica's farewell letter to her parents

The baby is very ill also with inflammation. I have sent to have it baptised. It is rather better since then. Freddy is no better, I fear it will not do. A great change has taken place for the worse, I am afraid of being left alone so come and stay with me altogether till the end come. Dear brother I know not what will happen.

In the month following Frederica's death, James wrote an account of his wife's last illness and death[20]; he tells the story much better than anyone else ever could, and so his account is now given in full.

The Narrative of my Wife's Last Illness finished on her Birthday, 15 February 1823

On Thursday 9 January I attended the Duke of York at the consecration of a new church and was out nearly the whole day. When I returned I asked Freddy what she had been doing; "writing letters?"

"No, something for you which I have long meant to do. Here they are" (giving me some papers), "you may open them now if you like to see if you approve of their contents, or not, as you think best".

Seeing they were instructions in case of her decease, I said "I will read them now; you are very right to do so. I was making my will at the same time that our settlements were preparing and I did not think I should die the sooner on that account. Only tell me one thing, have you any fears or presentiment?"

She said "Of course there is always some risk, but I have no fears or presentiment".

I read them before her. The perusal of them affected me deeply; for no-one could read such angelic sentiments without tears. I kissed her affectionately and thanked her for writing it as I found I had never known her before and that I loved her ten times better than ever I did.

I then sealed them up and put them by. I must here mention that on the 7th and 8th she had suffered great agony from the toothache. Granville said he could not allow the pain to go on as it would be detrimental both to herself and the infant and on seeing Parkinson it was decided to take it out. She bore the 2 pulls, which were very severe (the tooth breaking the first time), with her usual fortitude.

On the 9th she was particularly well, there was a peculiar calm and serenity of countenance, manner and voice which struck me so

---

[20] U1590 C269/2. There is also a fair copy of this document, kept together with the original.

much that I told her of it. We passed a most happy evening, but went
to bed early. At about half past one in the morning of the 10th she
woke me saying she felt unwell and that certain symptoms had
appeared. Mrs. Smith was to come on the 10th, I sent off immediately
for both her and Dr Granville. When they came, they said it might
come on or it might be postponed for day or two. The 10th passed,
she being up, but keeping her room. She was in very good spirits, I
stayed with her all day but went early to bed for her sake. At about 1
on the morning of the 11th Mrs. Smith woke me to tell me that Freddy
had been ill since half past 11 and that it was time to send for
Granville, I did so and went up to see her. She rejoiced as her pains
grew stronger, asked for her chain and locket and put it several times
around her neck. When Granville came I retired and at 10 past 2 he
gave me the glad tidings of an excellent delivery and a fine boy. Her
pulse fell to 60 immediately after; as soon as I could I saw the baby,
a beautiful fat child, like his brother in face but stouter. He cried
lustily and seemed quite healthy. I then saw Freddy, kissed her and
wished her joy; she said she felt quite well. I would not let her talk
and left her to write my letters and notes to announce the happy
event. Granville was obliged to go some miles out of town and came
at a little before 2 and said her face was flushed, and that she had a
little fever, that it was too soon for fever to come on and that he
should change her medicines and send some cooling ones. She asked
me if I had finished my letters and hoped I had not mentioned her
not being quite so well and repeatedly said she was so glad there was
no post on Sunday (next day) for on Monday we should send good
accounts. Granville returned at half past 5 and finding the fever
increased, determined on bleeding her, to which she willingly
agreed. She complained of a heaviness in her head and laid in a sort
of stupor. Mr. Tupper came immediately and took 24 oz of blood.
They said they never saw blood in a higher state of inflammation, it
was yellow and fuzzy. She felt immediately relief and said her head
was better. At about 9 Granville and Tupper returned and thought it
advisable to take 12 more ounces of blood. Her pulse, which had
been at 140, now sank to 120. Some remedies were now
administered which brought away some faeces of a very bad
description which was singular as her bowels had always been open
and her stomach in good order. During the night (Dr Granville and
myself) determined to call in Dr Baillie and Clerk. In the meantime
30 leeches were put on her stomach as there was a degree of tension
and they were afraid it would turn from general to local

inflammation. Drs Baillie and Clerk came as the leeches had nearly done sucking and ordered them to be taken off. They said we had mastered the inflammation but that it was a case of exceeding hazard, that she had youth, a good constitution and a good delivery in her favour, but they would not encourage much hope. I sent for my brother who came and stayed with me without quitting me a moment; I never can do justice to his kindness. His affection, the judgment in his conversation supported me throughout this dreadful trial.

In the meantime on the Saturday evening the poor baby was affected in the same manner by inflammation in the bowels. He had had all the natural passages the day before and there seemed no reason why he was ill. Mr. Tupper since said "It seemed as if God had but first breathed life into him and then withdrew it again".

Every remedy was resorted to, he was frequently put into hot water, he was relieved by a plentiful motion and seemed better on Sunday morning. A wet nurse was obtained for him, the baby took the breast and slept nearly two hours. My hopes revived, but spasms came on and he became worse. I thought it right to send for a clergyman who baptised the child by the name of Frederick (the Duke of York having kindly consented to be the godfather of my next child). The baby lingered on and on Sunday evening the poor infant was removed from this world, I trust to that kingdom which we are told is composed of such innocence and purity.

During the time of the violent inflammation Freddy occasionally wandered, had strange and horrible dreams, but always became collected on anyone speaking to her. After the leeches her pulse, though still very quick, became so low as hardly to be felt, her body was very cold, but she was perfectly collected.

Every means was used to keep her extremities warm, I frequently rubbed her feet. The only relief she seemed to feel was from my laying beside her on the bed. She made me put my arm round her neck and she frequently slept in the position. As her weakness increased she complained of the pains of her bones and particularly of weakness in the back. She asked frequently about the children and expressed a great anxiety to see them. I said that Baillie had positively prohibited it, that she was to be kept quiet and that I could do nothing without the doctor's consent. At 3 o'clock on the Sunday I had sent an express to Lord and Lady Mansfield at Becca and I calculated on their arriving by 10 o'clock or 12 at the latest on Tuesday morning (they would have arrived sooner but the express was somehow several hours too long upon the road). On Monday morning I told her I had received a letter from Lady Mansfield, stating that they only meant to remain one night at Becca and would be in town a day sooner, I did this to break their arrival. During all this time I was in a state of alternate hope and fear as the doctors gave their opinions. I tried not to hope and endeavoured to prepare myself but hope still held her place. One of the most painful duties I had to perform was to appear with a calm countenance before my beloved wife, when I had just left the cradle of my dying child.

When the child was first taken ill, she remarked a change in my countenance (which was more on her account) and asked me what was the matter. After this I was wonderfully supported, was always cheerful near her and she never suspected the illness of her child. She several times repeated her written wishes and continued to ask for the children. When Dr Baillie came I proposed that she should see James, but that we should say the baby was asleep. In the meantime she thought of everything and to prove her filial affection predominated desired Tupper to make her mother consult him about a complaint with which she was troubled. In the evening (Monday 18th) she was put into a hot bath, she was very faint in it but at 10 I laid down beside her and she slept on my breast quite tranquilly till 12. Dr Baillie at 9 on Monday evening told me that as sixteen hours had passed without her being worse, if she could go on so for 12 hours more he should entertain great hopes. Mine revived!!! When she woke at 12 she became restless, everything passed through undigested and I saw a change had taken place. I called up Granville who saw it was hopeless. I went downstairs for a short time to recover myself. During all this time, she fancied she should like different things and we were desired to try everything. She asked for every sort of wine, porter, arrowroot, grapes, figs, but disliked everything when she tasted it. At 6 she asked for me and when I came said "Why did you not tell me I was in danger?" I said "I meant to have done so whenever I was permitted".

She desired a clergyman to be sent for and saw James, kissed him repeatedly and implored a blessing on him. She took leave of him with a smile that partook of heaven. She asked to see my brother, shook hands with him and took leave of him. She desired to see Stormont, who had gone home with Lady Cathcart; I sent for him, when he came (about 8) she joined our hands and begged I should take care of him and given him advice and begged him to follow my example through life. She again pressed to see the baby, I solemnly promised she should see him when he woke. She often asked afterwards whether he was awake but never expressed impatience again. The clergyman arrived and we took the sacrament, Stormont with us. She followed some of the prayers faintly and said Amen to all. I attended the clergyman into the other room and when I returned I found she had written her name (it was all she could do) in the guide to the altar of Bishop Wilson and dated it on Xmas Day when we had taken the sacrament together. I told her her parents were expected that morning. She said "I shall not see them for all is dim, but I may feel them still". She told me to take care of myself and to have the baby baptized by the name of Frederick William and if I liked to add Pitt. She desired ten guineas which had been left her as a legacy to be laid out in a bracelet like that she had ordered as a present to her mother for her birthday and to be given to Miss Murray. The former only came home on Monday morning. She asked for it, I unpacked it, she called for a candle and examined it minutely but evidently with difficulty and then told me to put it on. I fastened it on the left arm, I said "I will give it to your mother", she answered in a strong voice "not till I am dead". I told her and I remember I said with a smiling countenance that we were parting but for a time, that we should meet in heaven, that my study should be to live so that I might be worthy of meeting her. If resignation, piety, hope and confidence was ever expressed on any countenance it was stamped on her by a smile which is my comfort when I recall it and which I can never forget. She then said "Marry", I answered "I swear that rather than relapse into a state of sin, I will fulfil your wishes", she smiled upon me and appeared quite satisfied. She said "Do not give up your liking for music and keep your fondness for Handel".

She desired to be remembered to Clanwilliam and to Mr. Stanard with "tell him not to be so violent". She then said how much I had improved her, that she did not wonder she was unpopular when a girl, that Lord _____ was right, that she forgave him and desired me to tell him so with her remembrances. She said soon after "Do not be too fond of a joke". I have omitted stating that at intervals I knelt down by her bedside and we prayed together[21].

She urged me to support myself and be a comfort to her parents. She complained of a terrible gnawing in her stomach and said it was like the pangs of starvation. As the morning advanced she became more and more anxious for the arrival of her parents and frequently

[21] This sentence is written in a different colour ink (i.e. was probably added later) and also ends the page half-way down.

asked what o'clock it was. She desired to be lifted up and there was such a change I thought she was going, but she rallied, it seemed as if filial affection detained her vital spent till her wishes could be fulfilled. She saw James again and remained with her hand in mine and occasionally took Stormont's in the other, looking at Granville, her maid Stewart and Mrs. Smith alternately and smiling upon all. She offered to take off her ring; I said "I will take it by and by", pointing to her wedding ring, she said "No, not that, you must marry". I answered "If I ever do, it will be with that ring".

I then got a Bible and I solemnly swore rather than to return into a state of sin, I would marry and I repeated this oath by her side after her spirit had departed. At about 12 o'clock she asked "Are they arrived?" I said "No, but they must be now on this side of the tunnel". She said "I wish they would come in time for their sakes for it would be a comfort to them". And I do not think she spoke afterwards. She asked for a pair of scissors and attempted to cut a lock for me from her forehead, which with my assistance she fulfilled. This I placed in her locket since and I shall wear it till my death. She continued to breathe softly and occasionally opened her eyes and a faint smile played on her countenance, but she became weaker, the colour changed and at 20 minutes past one her pure spirit departed and I felt myself alone[22].

If there is a belief in goodness, piety and virtue, in the confidence of a life well spent and of every duty fulfilled, if there is truth in the promises of the Gospel and in the resurrection of our blessed Saviour, I must not permit myself to indulge in selfish regrets, for she must now be enjoying through the merciful intercession of our redeemer the rewards of her excellent life, in happiness which shall not end. May the Almighty grant me in his great mercy that blessed as I have been by the love of that perfect being, blessed as I am by being the father of our sweet boy, blessed as I shall ever be by the record of her excellence and by the recollection of her virtues, I may bear this severe visitation with proper resignation and that I may so steer through the storms of life as to reach in safety that haven of rest where she is already anchored and to be joined in everlasting happiness with those I have loved and lost.

I wish this paper as well as the last letter of Freddy in case of my decease to be given to my son. I adjure him to study them and on the

---

[22] The date of Frederica's death was 14 January 1823; only Glover (ed.), *Staff Officer* p. 2 records it incorrectly, giving the date of her death as 14 September 1823.

anniversaries of his mother's birth, marriage and death, as well as on mine, to seclude himself for a while to peruse them. If he ever finds himself strongly tempted by sin, if ever his conscience is ill at ease, if ever he feels he is not in a state of grace with God, <u>I entreat him, I command him to read the blessed words of his sainted mother and they will reclaim him. Let him strive to imitate that he may meet in heaven!!!</u> If he marries and has offspring I bequeath these papers with the same wishes and prayers to his children and his children's children.

Frederica comes across in this narrative (and also in her farewell letters) as something of a saint, heroically facing up to her own death at the age of twenty-three; if we had nothing else to judge her by we could be excused for thinking that James had embellished her image in his own grief and love. However, in light of Frederica's own letters and statements, we can confirm that she did indeed die a most noble death, fully convinced she was going to a better life in heaven, and that James would one day join her there. In many ways, James and Freddy were the perfect couple; hopelessly in love with each other, irremediably happy in each other's company, unashamed to proclaim their love to the world, and both fully persuaded of their eternal happiness and joy in the afterlife.

One aspect that catches our attention in the narrative written by James is the belief in bleeding as a possible remedy for certain sicknesses. Bleeding (or bloodletting) was a common practice at the time, although medical experts were just beginning to realize that it was actually more harmful than beneficial. It was based on the ancient medical ideas of humours in the body, and was abandoned in most of Europe in the late eighteenth century and in the rest of the world towards the end of the nineteenth century. James' half-sister Hester insisted it did her good, while Charles Lewis Meryon, her physician, with exact medical precision, always argued the opposite. Placing leeches on Frederica's stomach to do the job sounds like anything except serious medical practice.

In another document contained in the same folder as the copy of Freddy's last letter, James added the following words as a first epitaph:

Sacred to the memory of _____ 1823
Her life was all purity and happiness
Its pious close like the slumber of a child
Her own prayer will tell what she wished to be
The mourners she has left feel it is what she was

To be a pious Christian, a faithful, affectionate and tender wife, a dutiful and grateful daughter, a kind sister, the mother to my children which my mother was to me, the friend of the poor and needy, to have true charity, to live a godly life on earth, and to die in the blessed hope that my sins though many may be forgiven, and that I shall enter the gates of everlasting happiness there to meet or wait for those I love. This is the life and end for which I pray.

To His all wise and all righteous will
who thus early withdrew her to himself
a resigned, afflicted but grateful husband bows!!!
Cheered by her memory
incited by her example
He waits in humble hope for a united immortality.

Inside another folded piece of paper, with no writing or any kind of indication on it, but kept together with all the papers related to Frederica's death, is a long lock of dark brown hair, which we may safely assume is hers (see Figure 7.9). Also included are two silhouette profiles of a man and a woman (see Figure 7.10); the man looks very much like the known engraving of James, and so we may also assume that the woman is Frederica.

Frederica died without knowing that her second child, Frederick, had died before her[23], leaving James to bring up their son James Banks and face the greatest challenge of his life – living without the person he most loved. He received numerous letters of condolence in the weeks following Freddy's death, kept in a folder entitled "Letters on my great calamity 1823"[24].

Some of the letters are almost akin to what might be expected today; two of his friends write to him and advise him to travel and meet them;

Pray pardon me if I intrude too soon upon your grief – I do not pretend to offer consolation yet you may like to hear that an old friend sympathises most sincerely in your dreadful misfortune. The last time I saw you you were so happy, with such bright prospects, and all is over, but you have a little boy left, he will be a great comfort to you, the feelings of a father will be kept alive, and they are the most agreeable that enter the human breast – if you can part with him

---

[23] Once again, Haslip, *Lady Hester Stanhope*, p. 229, is mistaken in the details; Haslip claims that James' wife died and left him two small children, whereas Frederick had already died before his mother.

[24] U1590 C284/1.

for a while leave him with Lady Mansfield and make a rapid excursion on the continent .... I shall be at Paris towards the end of March, either let me see you there or write to tell me how you are.

Figure 7.9 – A lock of Frederica's hair

Figure 7.10 – Profiles of James and Frederica

One friend recommended travel to take James' mind off his suffering, while another, who had clearly suffered the same kind of tragedy, told him that travel was in fact quite useless:

> My religion taught and commanded me not to murmur against the will of God – I have never once done so – but it did not command me nor teach me not to suffer or not to feel the heavy finger of God laid upon me.
>
> The first counsel I have to give you, my dear Stanhope, is to take care of your health and not destroy it by incipient and long-continued indulgence in sorrow as I have done mine. I have lived to repent of this and I now wish for that health I used to have, for the sake of the dear child whom I am to bring up. The first thing that did me any good was occupation, and although I shrank from it at the time, I now know that the government of the case saved my life – you <u>must</u> get some occupation – but it must not be a mere everyday sort of one – it must be <u>new</u> in its kind to you as mine was to me – one which will bring no associations of the past, nor of the object you deplore – Fr – although she was present herself daily and hourly to your mind, the

grand thing is to prevent that image and idea from mixing itself up habitually by association with everything you do, and all day long – you must look for something which will move you, which involves a responsibility, which makes others depend in some degree on your exertions, and although you cannot perhaps fall into a great government as I did, you may find out something else, foreign to your former habits.

A mere journey, such as I am now taking, is of no use – it has done me more harm than good. It has left me too much time to return to my sorrow.

The letter is addressed to James at Kenwood and as was customary, bears a black wax seal. James had presumably moved in with his parents-in-law, and apparently divided his time between Kenwood and South Audley Street.

Another letter came from Harriet Charlotte Beaujolais Campbell, the daughter of Colonel John Campbell of Shawfield and Islay and Lady Charlotte Bury, who married Lord Charleville in Florence in 1821. She might have met Frederica when she was in Italy in 1819 and 1820. Lady Charleville was a minor author; she died in Naples in February 1848, aged 46. The letter is addressed to James at his London house, 72 Audley Street, and is dated 16 February 1823:

I listened to every account of your perfect happiness and of the excellence which preceded it yearly and of the dear baby which confirmed it, with the joy of a mother. I dreamed on my return to England of finding in your wife another friend.

Shall the great eternal light alone reveal to us how and why such things are permitted?

My dear friend, may this be the only calamity as it most surely be the heaviest that you shall ever know; may time soften its weight and may your children prove a blessing to you.

I will tell you I was during two years in danger of losing Lord Charleville and his son …. but they survived.

Therefore my dear Colonel Stanhope, may that God who watches over excellence and that blessed spirit who loved you and now rejoices in eternity sooth and comfort you.

The psychology of death and condolences was not as developed as it is today; it can hardly have been of any comfort to James to hear how Lady Charleville had almost lost her husband and son, but only almost.

Griselda wrote to James from Paris on 27 February, where Mahon (who continued using this name even though he was now the Earl Stanhope) had been and had just left. As always, she writes in a vastly superior style to any of her siblings, acknowledging the uselessness of trying to comfort him:

> It is perhaps better to avoid entering on this mournful subject, on which my sympathy can do little towards alleviating your affliction, and may only awaken some feeling of wretchedness lulled for the moment to tranquil resignation; but allow me, my dearest James, to entreat you that however deep the wound you have experienced, and none can conceive it better than myself, not to indulge in a melancholy pleasure in nourishing grief and dwelling upon those objects which minister to it. Human nature cannot long resist the effect of those desponding passions which debilitate all its energies.

There was also a condolence letter from Richard Heber[25], dated 3 April, and another from Emily Napier, the sister of the three soldiers Charles, George and William, saying "momentary as our acquaintance was, I saw enough to appreciate the extent of your loss".

James was a generous and giving character all his life, and as on other occasions there was always someone ready or willing to take advantage of this. Even in his present state of grief, or possibly even because of it, on 12 March an otherwise unknown Elizabeth Joyce wrote to James, on black-edged paper, firstly expressing her great sorrow at his loss. Her address is given as 4, Cottage Place, Kentish Town. The style is a poor attempt at a kind of literary language, and is plagued by anacolutha and incompleteness:

> My dear Sir,
>   With emotions which I will not attempt to describe, I have only within these three days received the intelligence of your heavy and irreparable loss, scarcely excusable, as perhaps it may be, to intrude upon the grief which has now taken possession of every thought, I know nevertheless that your goodness will admit of this expression of my sincerest sympathy in an affliction which all acquainted with your truly generous feelings must conclude to be overwhelming. Every surrounding object recalls the image of what is gone, every tender recollection enhances the magnitude of the loss, and the

---

[25] Thereby proving Glover (ed.), *Staff Officer* p. 2 wrong: "but by all appearances he [i.e. Heber] never wrote back".

moment of feeling will and must flow on, uncontrolled by reasonings or by precepts, the lenient hand of time only can mitigate and subdue.

After trying to win his confidence in this way, pretending to feel sorrow at his great loss, the woman continues as follows:

I sincerely hope you will not think me impertinent in requesting your friendly aid and assistance in my humble appeal to your brother's benevolence for some assistance in educating the youngest child of your old and faithful tutor, believe me my dear Sir that this appeal is made only from the strong necessity of putting him to school and not having the means of so doing, he is now nine years of age and hithertoo [sic] I have done all in my power to bring him forward, he is a boy of excellent abilities and possesses a fund of useful information far beyond his years – as I often walk as far as Caen Wood I will take the liberty of leaving this letter and the one enclosed to your brother at the lodge, hoping at the same time you will lend me your kind assistance and that you will have the goodness to read my address to your brother before you convey it to him, by so doing you will for ever [sic] oblige me and if the warm and tender spirits of the departed hover o'er us, that of your old and faithful tutor will smile a grateful tear upon your exertions to serve his child. Believe me my dear Sir that I still cherish the most lively recollections of old times, and that I am with sentiments of sincere esteem. Your gratefully obliged friend, Elizabeth Joyce[26].

Finally, there is a letter from General Graham, Lord Lynedoch, who James had served as ADC.

Many thanks my dear Stanhope for your letter, which I found here on my arrival yesterday evening. The account you give is as satisfactory as it was possible to expect, under such circumstances of distress. There is undoubtedly grounds of comfort in the considerations which you notice – as there was opportunity of trying all that could be attempted, which might not have been the case where the sad

---

[26] As pointed out to me by Col. Alastair Mathewson, Elizabeth Joyce has the same name as the widow of the Reverend Jeremiah Joyce, tutor to the 3rd Earl's children, who was arrested at Chevening in 1794 and taken to the Tower on a charge of high treason. Her youngest child was a girl called Hannah, but as Hannah was adopted by her late father's schoolfriend shortly after he died it is possible that the new youngest in the family, as it were, was the son in question.

event was so sudden – there is however in peaceable times and many
women particularly, something in that very circumstance that is
awful, and creates more horror than when death is apprehended. I
trust Lady Mansfield's exertions for the sake of others will not cause
any reaction injurious to her health, but instead of a gay and happy
house, home must long bear the stamp of melancholy and fear.

The rest of the letter is taken up with a description of Lynedoch's
upcoming stations, and news related to other people they both knew.

There is also a letter from John Stonard, who had been one of James'
tutors (and of the other children at Chevening), dated 26 February 1823.

I am heartily glad to hear that your dear little boy is to be brought up
by Lady Mansfield, at least during his first tender years. It will be a
consolation, though sometimes doubtless a melancholy one to her
and a real satisfaction to yourself, who know so well what is to be
expected from her maternal affection and her sound judgement.
Besides it is much to be desired by you and by your friends for you
that the ties which unit[e] you to so worthy a family should not be
weakened by separation.

The rest of the letter is filled with Stonard's personal news and recent
political events that affected him.

The daughter of the Stanhopes' family lawyer, Mr. Murray[27], also wrote
to James offering her somewhat distant condolences: "Oh let us remember

---

[27] Some years earlier Lady Hester had tried to set up a match between Mr. Murray's
daughter and her physician, Charles Lewis Meryon, who had recently returned to
England. Meryon, however, was more interested in a French opera dancer, by whom
he eventually had a son, Charles Meryon, the tormented but brilliant engraver who
lived in Paris and died there in a lunatic asylum. Meryon has the following to say
about Miss Murray; Guscin, *A Very Good Sort of Man*, p. 67, quoting Meryon's
diary: "In May I find myself escorting Miss Murray about; but, with every wish to
follow Lady Hester's good advice in proposing to her, her plainness of figure and
face deterred me. I expressed to the father some such intention, and he told me to
wait a little while until we had seen more of each other. I followed this advice the
more readily", and again on p. 167: "I followed this advice more readily because I
had made an acquaintance with an opera dancer who lodged above me with her
mother at No. 8 Warwick Street. Her name was, as inscribed on the bills of the
theatre, Madame Narcisse Gentil, but in reality Pierre Narcisse Chassepoux ... I
spoke French, had been accustomed much to foreign manners, and in the usual
jostling which takes place in a small lodging house had from a bow got into amicable
speaking terms with her. Her mother, who was her cook, her dresser, and the caterer

what we are born for and look sanguinely forward to what I trust is in store for us".

Finally, on 16 January, just three days after Freddy's death, and if James was in a fit state to remember, the anniversary of the deaths of his brother Charles and his commander in chief Sir John Moore at Corunna back in 1809, another letter was written by J. Harrington, clearly known by James but not a close friend as the letter opens with the words "Dear James Stanhope". Rather than offering any kind of consolation, Harrington simply asks James to keep him informed; "Pray let me know how you do under such severe affliction. It made me quite ill and we are all sincerely sorry for the loss of poor dear Lady Frederica".

James' sister Hester never wrote to him, although she later rued this lack of contact. On 30 July 1823, she wrote as follows to Meryon:

> James's loss – the General's death – all has afflicted me beyond description. I heard of James' affliction six months after … He considers me as a sort of poor mad woman, who has once loved him, therefore he is kind to me.

In a state of bereavement, especially when both wife and child had died, it must have been comforting to James to have received all these letters, although in the end they were all ignored and had no real effect on him. The loss was simply too great to bear.

In the little book of prayers written by James and Frederica, one of the orations dates from just two days after Frederica died:

> Prayer for my great calamity, 16 January 1823.
> Almighty God, dispenser of all good, but hastener of hope[28] in mercy look down upon me with pity and grant my prayer. Receive

---

for their small events, always accompanied her to the opera house, and, waiting there until the representation was concluded, brought her home. I was in the habit of going there too, and the more I went, the more I was let into the secret doings there by conversing with Narcisse at home, so that by degrees I took the office in part of escorting her home, but I never was asked to remain in their room, and almost always dismissed at the room door. A salad with some porter and bread and cheese was the homely supper to which they would sit down. The worldly apothegms of the mother with the strong sense of the daughter contrasted strangely but advantageously with the general character of the English. I was attracted to them, and perhaps Miss Murray was in consequence neglected".

[28] This text was written in great anguish after Frederica's death, as is evident from the handwriting and the disjointed nature of the feelings expressed. This clause in

into eternal happiness the souls of my departed wife and child. She passed through this world unspotted, pure and holy. Forgive the sins of our frail nature and receive her who lived according to thy word, and died in faith, hope and charity into life eternal through Jesus Christ our Lord.

Grant, o God, that the innocent being who became a Christian[29] before he left this world may share with those whom we are told from the kingdom of God, in the mansions of the blessed.

On 3 February James wrote to his mother:

My mind and spirits are indeed as they have been from the beginning, just what I should have wished them to be; I am calm and resigned. I felt and feel that the happiness I had is gone for ever, but I have the consolation of thinking that every regret must be selfish. The blessed being who is gone before me passed twenty years of perfect happiness, the joy and pride of her parents.

I am satisfied she in in heaven – I have many duties yet to perform, her place to fill if I can in the education of my dear boy, and I have so to live and die that we may meet in happiness for ever.

She desired some of her hair to be given you in a locket, which I have got for you and will keep till you come over. The dear boy is quite well. Lord and Lady Mansfield as well as can be expected.

We know very little about how James spent his time over the next two years. He divided his time between his London residence and his parents-in-law's house, Kenwood. He copied out Frederica's letters, wrote the above account of her last illness and death, made additions to the fair copy of her diary and gave it to Lady Mansfield as a gift, and anything else he could do in relation to her. He also wrote to his brother on various occasions; he has the following to say (on black-edged paper) in 1823, on a Tuesday, but no month or date is given:

Thank you my dear brother for your kind letter, which found me better in every way. My natural sleep, appetite and functions of the stomach are returned and I am perfectly calm. How shall I ever thank you sufficiently for having consoled and supported me under the most agonizing moments. I try to employ myself about little bequests

---

the MS reads "but hastener much as are hope in mercy", with the words "much as" crossed out. I have corrected it as I see fit.

[29] In other words, was christened.

of the departed saint and in the fulfilment of her wishes find consolation, but the first of all my comforts is the recollection [of] how we lived and she died. I am glad to hear you are coming to Kenwood. The longer you can stay there the more pleasure I shall have.

...

The baby is not well, but all from teeth, he is so cross that he lets nobody come near him.

A letter dated July 1824, also from James to his brother, shows that he was planning on travelling to his estates in Lincolnshire, and is thinking of the future; "at any rate I shall acquire a knowledge of the estate which will be of great importance hereafter".

On 3 September 1824 he wrote to his brother from Stapleton:

I cannot delay my dear brother wishing you joy of your safe return and thanking you for the kindness you have had about my books – I fear it will be long before I am capable of reading them, for I found German very difficult, did not like my master, liked other avocations better, pursued it slackly and gave it up. I mean however to take to it again when I come to town for the winter and will then have a master two or three times a week.

He tells Philip that he has been to Wales, Warwick and Birmingham, and finds his health and spirits improved.

I think I shall keep little James entirely at Kenwood for Granville does not wish to inoculate him till the winter and I shall be very shy of exposing him at all before that is done, for from many things which have lately occurred I doubt the efficacy of vaccination as to a total prevention – I long to see my boy again for nothing can compensate for his absence but I thought it was a matter of duty to change the scene a little. He is wonderfully well and thriving more than I express.

The Duke of York had insisted he see a surgeon about his wound, which was now troubling him again, and he did:

He gave me exactly the opinion I predicted, that nothing could be done except an abscess came on, that the ball was lying between the spine and ribs and that the bones were probably exfoliations, that I should think of it as little as possible and live as usual but take care of keeping my stomach in good order.

Lady Mansfield is surprisingly improved both in health and spirits and we begin to look like old times.

…

I have I find taken your German grammar among my Don Quixotes, which it much resembles.

He spent Christmas 1824 and New Year with the Mansfields at Scone in Scotland. In another letter to Philip he says that he had planned on spending some time at Chevening, but was prevented "by an attack of my wound, which so perfectly unhinged me that I was obliged to give up the idea and get a brother ADC to take my duty with HRH". He consulted surgeons in Edinburgh but they all say there is nothing they can do. His niece Catherine was healthy:

I am glad to hear so good an account of Catherine and that she is all Lady S can wish. My little boy is very thriving and stout and much improved here in every way.

The time in Scotland was positive, as on 3 January 1825 he said that his pain had been getting much better and he hadn't had any for the last ten days. After his time in Scotland the whole family came back to London.

In a letter dated 12 Janaury 1822, sent from Scone to James while he was in Ireland, Freddie wrote (referring to herself):

The pious Christian, the faithful, affectionate and tender wife, the dutiful and grateful daughter, the kind and affectionate sister, the mother to her children that her mother was to her, the friend of the poor and needy. To be meek, mild and religious, to have true charity, to live a godly life on earth and to die with the hope that though her sins were many they may be forgiven and that she shall enter the gates of everlasting life and happiness, there to meet or wait for her James. This is the life and end for which she prays!!!

After she died, James added the following words:

And this the Almighty in his mercy has granted, to remain the brightest example, the best hope and the sweetest consolation of a widowed husband.

CHAPTER EIGHT

THE IMPOSSIBLE PROMISE

After Frederica's death, rather than recovering from his loss and taking refuge in their child, James spent the rest of 1823, all of 1824 and the first few months of 1825 in profound mourning. One of the first things he did was to commission a monument for his late wife. The result (see Figures 8.1 and 8.2) is a beautiful marble life-sized effigy of Frederica, breast-feeding a child (which is James Banks, as she never saw Frederick after he was born), which in fact is the only likeness we have of her (apart from a silhouette, which is not meant to be descriptive). The monument is at the church of St Botolph's (see Figure 8.3), very close to the main entrance into the Chevening estate. The church is open to the public, and even though the marble effigy can be readily seen, the Stanhope Chantry is usually locked. The inscription reads as follows:

SACRED TO THE MEMORY OF THE RIGHT HONOURABLE LADY FREDERICA LOUISA STANHOPE, DAUGHTER OF THE EARL OF MANSFIELD, AND WIFE OF THE HONOURABLE JAMES HAMILTON STANHOPE, WHO DIED IN CHILDBED JANUARY 14TH, 1823, IN THE 23RD YEAR OF HER AGE.

HER LIFE WAS ALL PURITY AND HAPPINESS, ITS PIOUS CLOSE LIKE THE SLUMBER OF A CHILD.

HER OWN PRAYER WILL TELL WHAT SHE WISHED TO BE. THE MOURNERS SHE HAS LEFT FEEL IT IS WHAT SHE WAS.

"TO BE A PIOUS CHRISTIAN; A FAITHFUL AFFECTIONATE AND TENDER WIFE, A DUTIFUL AND GRATEFUL DAUGHTER, A KIND SISTER; THE MOTHER TO MY CHILDREN WHICH MY MOTHER WAS TO ME; THE FRIEND OF THE POOR AND NEEDY, TO HAVE TRUE CHARITY, TO LIVE A GODLY LIFE ON EARTH AND TO DIE IN THE BLESSED HOPE THAT MY SINS, THOUGH MANY, MAY BE FORGIVEN AND THAT I SHALL ENTER THE GATES OF EVERLASTING HAPPINESS, THERE TO MEET OR WAIT FOR

THOSE I LOVE; THIS IS THE LIFE AND END FOR WHICH I
PRAY".
TO HIS ALLWISE AND ALLRIGHTEOUS WILL, WHO
THUS EARLY WITHDREW HER TO HIMSELF, A RESIGNED,
AFFLICTED, BUT GRATEFUL HUSBAND BOWS. CHEERED
BY HER MEMORY, INCITED BY HER EXAMPLE, HE WAITS
IN HUMBLE HOPE FOR AN UNITED IMMORTALITY.

The monument was the work of Sir Francis Chantrey (1781 – 1841),
England's leading sculptor in the Regency period. One of his best-known
pieces of work is the statue of George IV on horseback in Trafalgar Square.
The sculpture of Frederica was commissioned on 17 January, just four days
after her death, but was not finished until 1827, after James' own death[1].

---

[1] Cf. N. B. Penny, "English Church Monuments to Women who died in childbed
between 1780 and 1835", in *Journal of the Warburg & Courtauld Institutes*
XXXVIII (1975), pp. 318 – 319: "The beholder, and above all the original bereaved
patron, although in this case he did not live to see the sculpture completed, is
encouraged to entertain the idea that Lady Stanhope is not dead but simply asleep
with her child. But, of course, he is not deceived and such solace could only be
partial and bitter. Further reflection, assisted by his faith, might then encourage him
to accept the image as a metaphor for the rest he hopes she has attained in Heaven.
Thus the monument is susceptible of a pious interpretation, but for its initial impact
it depends on a denial of death which need have nothing in common with Faith. The
only contemporary criticism of the work seems to have been that the tomb-chest was
too high and the child was virtually bald. Chantrey was particularly pleased with the
work, but according to Maria Edgeworth, who wrote a rhapsodic account of the
monument, it was never publicly exhibited because of family sensitivity over
Stanhope's suicide". Maria Edgeworth (1768 – 1849) was the prolific Irish writer;
the account referred to can be found in Augustus J. C. Hare (ed.), *The Life and
Letters of Maria Edgeworth* Volume 2 (London, 1894), p. 223: "The white marble
monument of Lady Frederica Stanhope is in the church; plain though she was in life,
she is beautiful in death, something of exquisite tenderness in the expression of her
countenance, maternal tenderness, and repose, matronly repose, and yet the
freshness of youth in the rounded arm and delicate hand that lightly, affectionately
presses the infant – she dies, if dying it can be called, so placid, so happy; the head
half-turned sinks into the pillow, which, without touching, one can hardly believe to
be marble".

Figure 8.1 – The monument to Frederica

Figure 8.2 – The monument to Frederica (detail)

Figure 8.3 - The church of St Botolph

Meanwhile, in one of the many letters sent by Dr Meryon to Lady Hester, dated on this occasion 22 February 1824, the physician has the following to say about Hester's younger brother:

> Of your brother James, of late, I know nothing. Yet I have no right to complain of him. He may think that I report his doings to your Ladyship, which may annoy him. Perhaps he considers me to be a stupid man, and therefore bars the door to all intimacy: but, notwithstanding, I believe he would at any time render me a service if it were in his power.

Hester had not contacted her brother when she heard of Frederica's death, although she seems finally to have acknowledged her feelings for him, despite everything. The following words are taken from a letter sent by Captain Yorke to Lord Chatham on 25 February 1825, just a few days before James took his life (and so given the time it took for letters to reach England from the Middle East, sometimes up to a year, we can safely assume that the message never reached him) "… and you can make it known to her brother James, of whom she never ceases to talk, and for whom she retains the warmest affection"[2]. Hester always found time to write lengthy and detailed instructions for absolutely trivial matters to her physician Charles Meryon, and yet despite her supposed affection for James, she never wrote to him when he most needed it.

On 17 September 1824 James wrote to his mother from Scone:

> I had been intending for a long time to write to you but could have told you nothing worth your knowing. My perigrinations have not been great. I spent a fortnight in Lincolnshire on business and joined the Mansfields on their way down since which except a week at Blair shooting or rather trying to shoot the red deer and a visit to Taymouth I have remained quite quietly here.
>
> As for myself I have had at different times a great deal of pain from the old cause. I have not seen any surgeon for nothing can do me good. As for my spirits I cannot say much. I over exerted myself last year and am paying for it now. I take no interest in anything but I hope this will mend and I can look to l'avenir for I trust in any consolations. My health is pretty good but both my mind and body have been sadly unstrung.

On Saturday 5 March 1825, James Stanhope was at Kenwood, the residence of his parents-in-law. Shortly before dinner, his valet could not find him to dress him, and raised the alarm. As James was not to be found, no doubt given his oscillating moods, which they were all very much aware of, they thought it better to leave him alone and had dinner without him. Among those at table was one Elizabeth Barnett, Lady Mansfield's niece, a friend of Frederica's (she had left her some jewels in her will) who had accompanied them on their grand tour a few years earlier. Presumably in agreement with the Mansfields, Elizabeth was also the woman who James was to marry, in accordance with the promise they had all made to Frederica on her deathbed. Of the numerous books on the Stanhopes and especially on Lady Hester, the one by Kirsten Ellis is the only one to mention the possible remarriage, and even then, only in passing as something reported in the newspaper[3]. The History of Parliament website also mentions the fact

---

[2] Quoted in Cleveland, *Life and Letters*, p. 237.

[3] Ellis, *Star of the Morning*, p. 351: "The London newspaper reported that he had been due to marry a young woman, who was at Kenwood that same day, but did not name her. He was thirty-nine". This last statement is something of a mystery; James was thirty-six when he died, and would have been thirty-seven in September the same year. The dates of his birth and death are undisputed. Glover, *Staff Officer*, p. 2, mistakenly says James died on 7 January 1825, and then even more mysteriously,

that he was to be married again, even giving the name of the future bride, Elizabeth Barnett[4].

That James had agreed to marry Miss Barnett can be definitively confirmed in a letter from James' half-sister Griselda, written to Philip, the fourth Earl, when she heard of James' suicide[5]:

> I wish to know whether Miss Barnett is the lady he was engaged to some years ago. He announced his intention of a second marriage to me in rather a gloomy manner as the consequence of a solemn promise he had made to poor Lady Frederica.

There is no record of James having been previously engaged to Elizabeth Barnett in any of the extant papers, and if this were so it would have been somewhat strange for her to have agreed to marry the man who had previously broken off their engagement to marry a relative and friend of hers; it seems much more likely that Griselda (who was not even living in England at the time) had become confused and made up her own story.

When James' absence after dinner became worrying, search parties were sent out. What happened then is best related in a short note sent by Earl Mansfield late that night to James' brother at Chevening (see Figure 8.4). The heading says it was written at "half past 2 AM" on 6 March; as the body was found the same night, Mansfield has followed the calendar rigorously and as it was after midnight when he wrote it was indeed 6 March; it was the night of 5-6 March.

> My dear Lord Stanhope,
> It is with the deepest affliction that I have to announce to you that your dear brother has destroyed himself. He was found last night suspended in his handkerchief and braces. Your apprehensions may have prepared you for this dreadful misfortune but although I shared them and have been in constant anxiety the blow has shaken me, as much by surprise as if I had no previous warning. The coroner's inquest will be called on Monday.

---

in a footnote states that "Hamilton" (an otherwise unidentified person) gives 5 March as the date of James' death.

[4] Cf. https://www.historyofparliamentonline.org/volume/1820-1832/member/stanhope-hon-james-1788-1825.

[5] U1590 C/279.

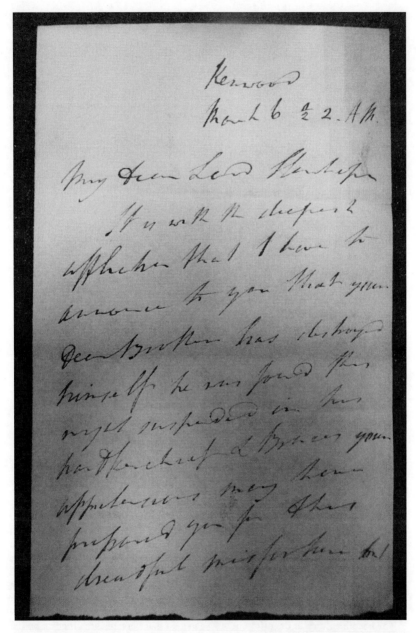

Figure 8.4 – Note from Earl Mansfield to Earl Stanhope

The fatal act had been long a contemplation, for the manner of it showed much forethought and determination. He was found suspended in a shed. He had not returned to dinner and we immediately began a search for him in every direction.

James' death and the finding of the body were recorded in various different newspapers; the accounts were cut out and now form part of the Stanhope manuscript collection[6]. There is no indication as to which newspapers published the accounts, nor of the date, although as the account includes statements by witnesses and the coroner's report, it must have been at least a few days after his death. The accounts are basically the same in all the different accounts, and read as follows:

INQUEST ON THE BODY OF THE HON. J. H. STANHOPE[7]
On Saturday night some of the most respectable families in the neighbourhood of Hampstead and Highgate were thrown into great agitation by the intelligence that Colonel Stanhope had been found hanging from a beam in one of the outhouses at Caen Wood, the seat of the Earl of Mansfield. Numerous inquiries were made into the circumstances of the death of the Colonel, but no information could be obtained. A coroner's jury was summoned with remarkable haste to meet at ten o'clock yesterday morning, at the Fox-under-the-Hill public house, Highgate.

The jury, upon being sworn, proceeded to view the premises where the body of the Colonel was found suspended. It is an outhouse in Caen Wood, at a considerable distance from the family mansion, where cattle are sheltered. The beam from which the body was cut down was about seven feet from the ground, and there lay across it a pair of braces by which he had suspended himself. The jury, after inspecting this spot, were conducted to the nearest lodge,

---

[6] U1590 C262/8. The title is "Account of the death of Col. The Hon. James Hamilton Stanhope". Other newspaper accounts are kept in a folder entitled "Extracts from newspapers on my poor Uncle James' death 1825"; James had no nephews or nieces via his brother Charles or his sister Hester, it is highly unlikely that the children of either of his other sisters would have enjoyed access to these papers, which means that it was one of his brother Philip's children who classified these papers; and given the historical mind and pursuits of the fifth Earl, we can safely assume he wrote this comment.
[7] The headlines vary in the different newspapers; other versions are "Inquest on the body of the Honourable J. H. Stanhope, who destroyed himself at the house of the Earl of Mansfield", and "Suicide by the Honourable J. H. Stanhope".

where they viewed the body, which was laid out on a bed. The deceased was dressed in a common walking dress with boots; his top coat was pulled down over the shoulders, his cravat was off, and there was a livid mark in the throat: a silk handkerchief which he had tied to the braces and fastened round his throat was exhibited. There were no other marks of violence on the body other than that just described.

The first witness called was William Wright, groom of the Earl of Mansfield. He stated that towards ten o'clock on Saturday night, in consequence of the very great alarm which prevailed in the mansion, he went, with several others of the servants, to search about the wood. He, as well as the rest, were apprehensive that something might have happened to the Colonel. After having searched several places, they went into the shed which the jury had inspected. Witness was the first that entered the shed, and he started back on finding the Colonel suspended from a beam. Witness's fellow servants cut down the corpse immediately. The extremities were quite cold. They immediately conveyed it to the nearest lodge, but life was quite extinct.

The next witness was J. Wheeler, who seemed to be in extreme grief while giving his testimony. He stated that he had been valet to the deceased upwards of 17 years, and had attended upon his master as usual on Saturday morning. The family usually dined at seven o'clock, and a little before that time the bell rang to dress for dinner. Witness went to attend his master, but was greatly surprised at not finding him, according to custom, about to dress. The deceased was then sought after in various directions, but no intelligence was gained respecting his unaccountable absence. The dinner passed over without his attendance, when fresh inquiries were made respecting him. There was an arrangement about the purchase of a house, in the disposal of which the Colonel was concerned, to be concluded on the Saturday, and Lord Mansfield, who was at home, conjectured that the Colonel might have gone to town for the purpose of settling the business. For the purpose of ascertaining whether this was the case, and from a feeling of uneasiness on the subject, his lordship ordered out the carriage, and drove to town; made inquiries at every place in which he thought his relative might have been retained, but returned without having obtained any tidings about him. The apprehensions of the family increased. Inquiries were made as to the last time he was seen upon the grounds. It was reported that about ten minutes after four he was seen going in a particular direction in the wood.

The wood was scoured around, as it was feared that the Colonel might have been seized with some paroxysm. The deceased had received a wound at the storming of St. Sebastian, in the Peninsular War. A shot had passed through the thin part of the shoulder blade – that wound had never been cured and occasionally gave him great pain. About two years ago his wife, the eldest daughter of Lord Mansfield, died, and his grief at the loss of her was very great. Of late, witness had observed that the deceased was very abstracted, was in the habit of sitting a long time as if in a state of stupor, and then he would suddenly start up as if from sleep or upon an alarm. Within a few days he had complained very much that he could get no sleep in consequence of the pain he endured. The deceased was in general very sedate in his manner.

James Alexander, an under-gardener in the service of Lord Mansfield, deposed that he was at work in the grounds, when, at about 20 minutes past 4 o'clock, he observed the deceased going towards the wood, in which the outhouse where he was afterwards found suspended was situated. Witness thought that the step of the deceased in going towards this place was remarkably hurried.

Dr Gilman of Highgate stated that he was called in on Saturday night to the house of Lord Mansfield. He found the body of the deceased not quite cold, but life entirely gone. He took the usual course adopted in cases of that nature, but with no effect. He judged that the body had been suspended several hours, and death was no doubt caused by suffocation. Witness had attended the family. The deceased had received a shot in the scapula of the left shoulder. Frequent exfoliations of the bone had taken place, and there was a rather copious issue. He believed that the spine was affected. In such cases, paroxysms of pain might produce temporary derangement. He mentioned one instance known to some of the jury, of Mr. Mitchell, an attorney, who, by a fall from a gig, injured a particular nerve, and was frequently taken with a fit of running several yards. The pain and nervous irritation created by the wound, acted upon by mental causes, might have produced temporary insanity. There was little doubt that the Colonel had laboured under considerable nervous irritation.

The Coroner summed up the evidence, and the jury returned a verdict to the effect that the deceased had destroyed himself whilst labouring under a fit of temporary insanity.

The Colonel was held in the highest esteem in the neighbourhood by all who knew him, and the unaffected sorrow of the domestics who gave evidence before the jury bore testimony to his worth as a master. He was remarkably pious, although from his early youth in the army, and he paid the highest attention to religious duties. He was in his 39th year and a Member of Parliament for Dartmouth. We understand that he was about to be married to a young lady who was on a visit at Caen Wood at the time the dreadful event took place. The Colonel gave up his establishment after the death of his wife, by whom he had one son, who is now living.

The other newspaper versions add further details on to the end of the account. One of them reads as follows, directly after the words "… now living":

There has been a succession of calamities recently in the mansion of the noble family. Only a fortnight since an old and highly valued domestic fell down dead. An event happened there a few weeks since, which created considerable talk in the neighbourhood. Towards midnight a noise was heard, or fancied, resembling a coach and four driving into the yard. Everyone in the house heard it, and conceived that Lord Mansfield had returned suddenly from Scone, where he had been spending some days. All the domestics, and every other person in the house got up, for the purpose of welcoming his Lordship on his return, but no carriage was found. The circumstance excited considerable astonishment and much wonder.

Another of the newspapers adds the following postscript:

FURTHER PARTICULARS
[From a correspondent]
At the siege of St. Sebastian this gallant officer (the Hon. Colonel James Hamilton Stanhope) received a grape-shot wound in the spine. Severe as the consequent sufferings were, it was, however, the decided opinion of the eminent surgeons by whom he had been attended that the ball could not, without imminent risk of fatal consequences, be extracted. Whether by the pressure of an extraneous substance, or by direct lesion of the nerves themselves during the passage of the ball, the result was that not only the spine was morbidly affected, but the whole nervous system partook of the injury. Occasional determination of blood to the head, and of late a temporary access of delirium, were among the results. These were, however, regarded, and probably with justice, as the effects or

accompaniments of the processes carried on by nature in the formation of abscesses about the spine. Exfoliation had taken place at different periods; and latterly an extreme sensibility to temperature, and an increasing impatience of cold in the extremities had become a marked symptom. About a fortnight back, after a sharp access of nervous disease connected with the wound, he was deemed convalescent; and was so much restored as to be able to pay a visit to his noble father-in-law at Caen-wood. On Saturday afternoon, restless in all probability from pain, and the indescribable sensations that come by fits and starts, where the nervous system has sustained a serious injury, he had walked out, and the most probable explanation of the melancholy sequel is that the exposure to the cold had brought on a sudden access of nervous bewilderment, and with this that overwhelming and instantaneous desire and resolve of self-destruction, of which so many mournful instances are fresh in the recollection of the public. The more mournful indeed, as in many cases the fit is so sudden, and so unprepared for by any precursive signs, as to baffle or preclude precautionary measures. The belief that the act in this instance, the resolve, or rather blind impulse of the moment, is strongly supported and confirmed by the circumstance, that in his walk to the shed, in which his body was found suspended, he must have passed three large ponds of water, that might have suggested a more easy and certain mode of destruction; and he had likewise at the time a penknife in his pocket. We have only to add that the event must have taken place some hours before it was discovered, the body having been found nearly cold.

The Hon. Col. Stanhope was brother of the present Earl Stanhope, Aide-de-Camp to Gen. Sir John Moore and Gen. Graham, and latterly to the Duke of York, and M.P. for Dartmouth.

The Coroner's certificate[8] (see Figure 8.5), giving permission for the body to be buried, is dated 7 March 1825. In May of the same year, the *Gentleman's Magazine* published the following obituary[9]:

March 5. At Caen Wood, the seat of his father-in-law, the Earl of Mansfield, aged 38[10], the Hon. Colonel James Hamilton Stanhope,

---

[8] U1590 C262/6.
[9] *The Gentleman's Magazine and Historical Chronicle* Vol. 137 from January to June 1825 (London, 1825) pp. 455-456.
[10] James was 36 when he died, but the newspapers seem to have thought he was 38.

MP for Dartmouth. He was the third and youngest son of Charles third Earl Stanhope, and brother of the present peer.

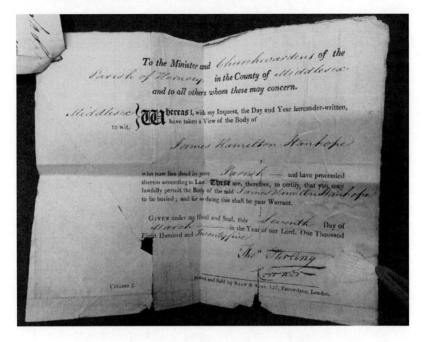

Figure 8.5 – The Coroner's certificate on James' death

His death took place with the following melancholy circumstances; at the siege of St. Sebastian this gallant officer had received a grape-shot wound in the spine[11]. Severe as the consequent sufferings were, it was, however, the decided opinion of the eminent surgeons by whom he had been attended that the ball could not, without imminent risk of fatal consequences, be extracted. Whether by the pressure of an extraneous substance, or by direct lesion of the nerves themselves during the passage of the ball, the result was, that not only the spine was morbidly affected, but the whole nervous system partook of the injury and frequent exfoliations of the bone had taken place. About two years since he had lost his wife and his grief for her loss was extreme. Of late he had appeared very abstracted, was in the habit of sitting a long time, as if in a state of stupor, and then he would

---

[11] It was actually a musket ball in the shoulder blade.

suddenly start up, as if from asleep or upon an alarm. Within a few days he had complained very much that he could get no sleep in consequence of the pain he endured. Afflicted in this melancholy manner, whilst walking in the park at some distance from the house, he entered a shed, formed to shelter the cattle, and suspended himself with his braces to a beam. His body was not discovered till some hours after, when, the household being alarmed, a general search was in progress. A Coroner's jury gave a verdict of "temporary insanity".

Colonel Stanhope was placed in the army at the early age of 15, contrary to his father's wishes, but by the advice and influence of Mr. Pitt, who was Earl Stanhope's second cousin by the marriage of his grandfather, the first Earl, to Lucy, sister of Robert Pitt, Esq. of Boconnock (the Minister's grandfather). The young soldier entered as Ensign in the 1st Foot Guards, Dec. 26 1803, was promoted Lieutenant and Captain, Jan. 14 1808, brevet Major June 21 1813, and Captain and Lieutenant Colonel in the 1st Foot Guards, July 24 1815. He served in Spain, Portugal, Flanders and France. In 1810 he acted as extra Aid-de-Camp [sic] to Lord Lynedoch, in 1812 was appointed a Dep. Assist. Quarter Master General; in 1813 an Assistant Quarter Master General in the Peninsula, and at the storming of St. Sebastian, as before mentioned, received what may be termed his mortal wound, however slow its effects were. He was, however, involved in the Battle of Waterloo. Beside the above-recited he served as Aid-de-Camp [sic] to Sir John Moore, to General Graham[12], and latterly to the Duke of York.

Colonel Stanhope was first elected to Parliament about 1817; he was returned for Fowey in the general election in 1818, but was not re-chosen in 1820. In that year he was, by the will of Sir Joseph Banks, appointed one of his four executors; and in the same year, July 9, he married Frederica-Louisa, eldest daughter of William, third and present Earl of Mansfield. She gave birth to one son, now living; but died, after a short union, Jan. 14 1823. Greatly afflicted at his loss, the Colonel thereupon gave up his establishment in South Audley Street. It was rumoured that he was about to enter into a second alliance with a young lady who was on a visit at Caen Wood, when the dreadful catastrophe occurred. The Colonel again entered the House of Commons in 1822, as M. P. for Dartmouth, and continued so till his death.

---

[12] The writer of the obituary seems not to have been aware that General Graham and Lord Lynedoch were one and the same person.

He was held in the highest esteem by all his acquaintance, and the unaffected sorrow of the domestics who gave evidence before the jury bore testimony to his worth as a master. He paid the greatest attention to religious duties, and was much addicted to Literature.

The evidence from Earl Mansfield's note and the reports in various different newspapers leave no room for doubt as to the place where James Stanhope hanged himself; in a shed or outhouse in the grounds of Kenwood. There seems to be no logical explanation of why some versions believe that he hanged himself from a tree[13]. It is remotely possible that Lady Hester Stanhope's doctor, Charles Lewis Meryon, was the origin of the tree legend. When talking of James' death[14] he quotes the Roman poet Ovid, Amores 1.12:17, in a footnote: "Praebuit illi arbor misero suspendia collo", which may be translated as "The tree provided him a means to hang himself, the poor fellow". Against this, however, it could be argued that the *Additional Memoirs* were not published until 2017, and it is highly unlikely that any of the above authors had access to the original manuscript; and if by some remote chance they did, it is even stranger that they did not mention the manuscript or use it for any purpose other than a detail such as this (especially as all of them are ignorant as to the circumstances of Meryon's second and extremely short visit to Lady Hester in 1819/1820, which it is the main purpose of the *Additional Memoirs* to explain in great detail). Furthermore, Meryon does not actually state that James hanged himself from a tree; he had spoken to James' valet, Mr. Wheeler, a day or two after the suicide, and so must have been well aware of all the details. It is much more probable that as on other occasions in his books, he simply included a

---

[13] Day, *Decline to Glory*, p. 301, states that James killed himself on an oak tree at Chevening in the middle of a storm; we have seen above, however, this book can hardly be taken as a history book. It is a mixture of half-truths and the writer's own fantasy. Haslip's *Lady Hester Stanhope* is in general a serious study, although the facts are also somewhat muddled for this episode (p. 229); "One spring day, his father-in-law found him hanging from a tree in the grounds of Ken Wood". It was not yet spring, the body was found at night and not by Earl Mansfield, and the name of the house is either Caen Wood or Kenwood (Lord Mansfield himself uses "Kenwood"). It would be difficult to make more mistakes in one short sentence. Brett-James, *General Graham*, p. 322, is undecided about the place but his words suggest he used Joan Haslip as a direct source: "On the morning of March 6th his father-in-law, Lord Mansfield, found James hanging – some say from a tree, others in a cowshed – in the grounds of Ken Wood, Hampstead".

[14] *Additional Memoirs*, pp. 293-294.

quotation from a classical author that bore relationship to the matter at hand. He never meant to say that James actually used a tree to hang himself from[15].

Mansfield, in his note to Earl Stanhope, claims that James had been long contemplating suicide, as "the manner of it showed much forethought and determination", and is followed in this by Kirsten Ellis[16]. This at first does not seem particularly logical - why would Mansfield conclude that James had planned everything? From his point of view, it must have seemed much more like a spontaneous act; James did not come to dinner, but rather went out for a solitary walk, and killed himself with what he had at hand, i.e. his braces. There seems initially to have been absolutely no forethought or preparation involved.

There is, however, evidence to suggest that James had indeed been planning his own death. In addition to the fact that everyone said that they had seen signs of it coming (although such comments are easy to make in hindsight), on the same day that he committed suicide, James wrote out a cheque for forty pounds (a considerable sum at the time) to Mr. Wheeler, his valet for at least the previous seventeen years (see Figure 8.6). This could be seen as a kind of farewell gift expressing gratitude for his valet's service. Secondly, in his will, James left Elizabeth Barnett the grand sum of £10,000, if he were to die before they were married. This seems to show beyond doubt that he had no real intention of marrying her, and at the same time was trying to compensate her financially for his guilt at leaving her in such a terrible way. Neither of these events show that he had "methodically prepared" his death, understanding "methodically" to mean the manner in which he carried out the act, but they do seem to prove that he had planned the moment. The fact that he did so just before sitting down to dinner with the Mansfields and his possible future bride could also suggest that this dinner was to see the formalization of his marriage to Miss Barnett and when he saw the moment at hand, he decided that death was the only honourable way out of keeping his promise. The plan was already there in his mind as a possibility, but the proximity of his engagement to Elizabeth also brought the actual moment of carrying the idea out right into the present.

---

[15] Cf. the apostle Paul in his epistle to the Galatians, 3:13, "Christ redeemed us from the curse of the law by becoming a curse for us, for it is written: Cursed is everyone who is hung on a tree", in turn a quotation from the book of Deuteronomy 21:23. Paul does not mean his readers to understand that Jesus was crucified on a tree or on anything other than a cross.

[16] Ellis, *Star of the Morning*, p. 351, James "methodically prepared his suicide".

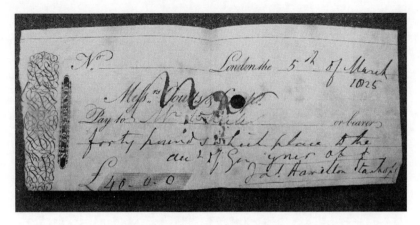

Figure 8.6 – A cheque made out by James Stanhope on the day of his death

In relation to Miss Barnett, there is a tantalizing scrap of paper inside a kind of silk purse[17], which when opened has the following words embroidered on it: "Souvenir d'une amie sincére" (a mistake for "sincère") (see Figure 8.7). The inside of the purse contains a pencilled sketch by James of a couple by a tree at the edge of a lake (see Figure 8.8), a piece of paper with the words "Memorials of Lady F. Stanhope", another with the words "The present of H.R.H. the Princess of Wales, her own painting, Dawlash[18] 1806" and what is presumably the painting (see Figure 8.9). The Princess of Wales in 1806 was Caroline of Brunswick, the estranged wife of the Prince of Wales who would later become George IV. If this little painting is by her (it is not certain that the information on the scrap of paper refers to this painting), it would indeed be memorable, although Frederica herself was only six years old at the time. The other scrap of paper shows the following words: "Miss Barnett by Harlowe". Unfortunately, there is no painting of Miss Barnett inside the silk purse; could the artist have been George Henry Harlow (1878-1819), famed for his portraits? The spelling of the surname is different, and Harlow would have been expensive; at any rate the portrait would have been earlier that this date as Harlow died in February 1819, and had spent most of 1818 in Italy[19].

---

[17] U1590 C 268.

[18] Dawlash is otherwise unknown as a surname or place name (apart from a town in Iraq, which is obviously unrelated). If "Dawlish" is meant it could be either a surname or the town in Devon.

[19] "G. Harlowe" is mentioned at various websites as the engraver of a portrait of Margarita Cogni, from an original taken at the request of Lord Byron, in 1829.

Figure 8.7 – The silk folder

The contemporary accounts of James' death seem to find it difficult to view suicide without some kind of "temporary insanity", as if no-one in their right mind could take their own life[20]. This was possibly for legal reasons; in England laws against suicide were still in force and could result

---

[20] James' suicide is even silenced in Canon Scott Robertson, "Chevening Church", in *Archaeologia Cantiana* Vol. 16 (1886), p. 121: "The celebrated marble monument, with a reclining figure, by Chantrey, represents the beautiful wife of the third son of the third Earl. She was Lady Frederica Louisa Murray, daughter of the third Earl of Mansfield, and she married Colonel the Hon. James Hamilton Stanhope, M.P.; she died young in 1823. Her husband could not live without her; he died in 1825".

Figure 8.8

Figure 8.9

in the confiscation of the successful suicide's property[21]. Earl Mansfield, in a letter to General Graham, now Lord Lynedoch[22], who James had served as ADC, seems to be of this opinion, also linking James' temporary madness to his incurable wound:

> He had felt much pain in the back, but had not slept for many nights … The pain in the back, the want of sleep and the pressure of the ball on the spine caused a deterioration of blood to the head and a paroxysm of delirium.

---

[21] Cf. Róisín Healy, "Suicide in Early Modern and Modern Europe", in *The Historical Journal* 49.3 (2006), p. 913: "The decriminalization process was even more protracted in England, with bodily desecration coming to an end in 1823, confiscation of property in 1870, and the remaining penalties not until 1961". Cf. also Jack C. Smith, James A. Mercy and Judith M. Conn, "Marital Status and the Risk of Suicide", in *The American Journal of Public Health* (1988), p. 79: "On the basis of our findings, we recommend that suicide prevention and intervention strategies should take into account the higher relative suicide risk faced by: 1) the surviving spouse (especially the surviving male spouse), when one partner of a young married couple dies".

[22] Letter dated 7 March 1825, National Library of Scotland, MS 3617, ff. 248-249, quoted in Newman, *Stanhopes*, p. 199. Graham first heard of James' death in a letter he received from Arabella Bouverie (née Talbot): "This day we have heard of Col. Stanhope's death – by hints and so on I feat he must have made away with himself, for the letter says he was insane. Oh! How dreadful! How poor Lady Mansfield will feel that God in his mercy took her child, before she could witness such a scene. Of course we shall have all in the paper tomorrow. You will be much hurt I am sure": Arabella clearly did not understand that Lady Mansfield's child, had she lived, would never have had to witness the scene because had she lived, James would not have killed himself. Cf. Brett-James, *General Graham*, pp. 322-323: "Lynedoch could not recall but how he and James, riding in Portugal, had crossed a river by a natural bridge formed by a large stone and had then lost their way, nearly broken their necks and nearly drowned in a ford; how the cannon-shot had whizzed over their heads when riding together outside Ciudad Rodrigo; how James had deplored the episcopal statues glaring down every alley of the Bishop's Garden at Castelo Branco; how at Oporto, while waiting for a ship to take him home to have treatment for the spectrum in his eye, he and James had stayed in the house of three Jewish brothers who were lace-makers and who not only fed the General and his aide magnificently, but also provided places at table for eight or ten friends and would never sit down without being requested to do so by himself. He had many recollections of James Stanhope, some happy ones, others melancholy, and now one more of the young men had died before his time".

Some authors attribute the suicide to James' embarrassed financial situation[23], once again for no reason suggested anywhere in the sources; the most likely reason for his suicide is quite simply that if it is true he was discussing or thinking of marriage with another woman, in fulfilment of his promise to Frederica rather than from being in love or wishing to start again, suicide could very well have seemed to him to be the only way out; he had made a promise to Freddy to marry again but when the moment of truth came, he had absolutely no desire to keep it. He was still entirely in love with her and could not face up to the idea of sharing his life with another woman; and at the same time, he was not capable of breaking the promise made to his wife on her deathbed[24].

Lord Mansfield had written a short note to Earl Stanhope when the body was found. Philip answered on 6 March, although no time is given on the letter:

Although the apprehensions which I had entertained had in some degree prepared my mind for the horrible calamity which has taken place, I am too much overwhelmed by it to be able to write more than a few lines.

James' depression and recent behaviour had certainly given his family cause for concern, to such an extent that they seemed to have seen suicide at least as a possibility, but even if this were so, when it actually happened it came as a great shock. Earl Stanhope went to visit his mother in London (where she lived at 24 Upper Berkeley Street, Portman Square), and spent the day with her, presumably to break the news to her in person.

On 7 March Mansfield wrote again to Earl Stanhope, again from Kenwood, informing him that the coroner's jury had reached the following verdict: "Died by his own hands in a temporary fit of derangement". He asks the Earl to visit him at Kenwood to discuss the will of the deceased and other legal matters; Philip's answer is clearly agitated, with a lot of crossing out and rewriting in the letter (see Figure 8.10). He has no desire to visit Kenwood:

---

[23] E.g. Ellis, *Morning Star*, p.351.
[24] This is also made evident in James' copies of Freddy's last letter to himself, as described in the previous chapter, in which she made him solemnly swear he would marry again; this whole episode is deliberately omitted in one of the copies he made. It is as if he was trying to blot the promise out of his mind, although in the end, of course, he could not do this.

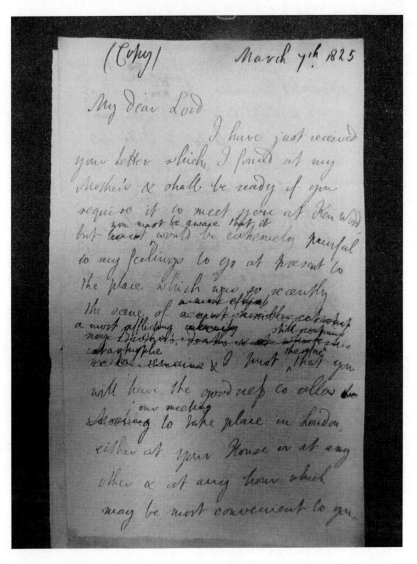

Figure 8.10 – Note from Earl Stanhope to Earl Mansfield

I shall be ready if you require it to meet you at Kenwood, but you must be aware that it would be extremely painful to my feelings to go at present to the place which was so recently the scene of a most afflicting catastrophe. I must therefore [ask] that you will have the goodness to allow our meeting to take place in London.

Mansfield answered on same day and asked him to go to Grosvenor Square on the following day at 1 o'clock. On 7 March the Earl also wrote to the Lord High Chancellor, begging to be excused:

As I have recently suffered a severe calamity by the sudden death of my brother, I hope that the House of Lords will be pleased to dispense with my attendance on Friday next, the 11th.

Letters of condolence addressed to the Earl were received from various different quarters. One of them, from George Pollock, says that he has "stupidly forgotten where it was that your brother received the wound of which he died". This must have been a mistake by the writer of the letter, as it was clear enough from the reports in the newspapers that James had taken his own life. Such letters were not only received by the family; General Graham received the following words from Lord William Russell[25];

Poor Stanhope, what a sad and unexpected ending to our former gay companion. It is to be regretted he did not end his days in the trenches of San Sebastian, for he met with nothing but disappointments and misfortunes afterwards.

On 16 March 1825, Philip wrote to the family solicitor, Alexander Murray:

I shall thank you to communicate to my eldest sister as her solicitor, but not as by my request, the melancholy event which has taken place and those provisions in the will which relate to herself. I am not in correspondence with her and I do not know her direction.

Most books about Lady Hester Stanhope tend to portray Philip as a cold and calculating person who rejected his sister; Hester becomes the victim after she had helped him so greatly earlier. As most (if not all) biographies of Hester tend to side with her in her various conflicts, this is only to be

---

[25] Quoted in Newman, *Stanhopes*, p. 199.

expected. Philip's reaction to Frederica's death two years earlier, however, the way he took care of his younger brother, and this detail about informing Hester, show us a much warmer and more caring person. In the end, however, it was Lady Hester's physician, Charles Lewis Meryon, who first informed her of the death of James, in a letter written just four days[26] after the tragic event (avoiding the fact that James had taken his own life, at least for the moment).

> It was but a few days since that I wrote to your Ladyship to say how strong my forebodings were touching the Colonel's health; but I did not think that I should so soon have had to communicate intelligence worse than forebodings, intelligence indeed of so melancholy a nature that, although I know you to be always desirous of at once learning without periphrase the full extent of any misfortune that befalls you, still I can hardly fulfil my duty on this occasion. [...] Your brother quitted this world two days ago [...] Of his last moments, as they have been related to me by Wheeler, who just now left me, I will say more when next I write; but at present I refrain from enlarging on a subject which, I fear, will be so painful to you[27].

Since Meryon returned to England for the second time in 1820, he had seen James on several occasions, and in 1822, the Colonel had sent him a letter promising him £100 towards his expenses if he were to return to Syria to look after Hester. Meryon implicitly trusted the promises but was rudely awakened from them when he heard of James' death:

> In the disposition of mind that the Colonel then shewed, there can be no doubt he would have bound himself by deed to the performance of his promises. But I took them to be as valuable as if put on parchment, and did not awake from my dream until the 5th of March 1825, when I was about to quit England to rejoin her Ladyship, when

---

[26] The dates do not quite fit in; according to the fair copy of the letter, it was written on 9 March, four days after James' death, although in the footnote added in 1862, Meryon shows he was aware that James died on 5 March. The date in the fair copy (which is not the original) might rather reflect the date when the letter was sent.

[27] In a footnote added in 1862, Meryon wrote the following words about James Stanhope: "Born 7 Sep 1788, married July 9 1820 Frederica Louisa daughter of the Earl of Mansfield. Hanged himself 5 March 1825 in an outhouse at Caen Wood, Hampstead".

Count Ludolf, the Neapolitan Ambassador, called on me and told me
Colonel Stanhope had committed suicide[28].

When Lady Hester heard the news, she quite literally locked herself up
in the house at Djoun, and never left the premises again[29]. In the letter she
wrote to Meryon, in reply to the news of James' death, dated July 1826[30],
she wrote simply "I received yesterday your letter of the 29th of March[31].
Alas, alas, alas! More I cannot say". The letter then continues as if nothing
had happened, full of trivial news and instructions.

According to Kirsten Ellis, Hester regretted her rejection of James on
hearing of his death, which seems quite reasonable:

James's suicide devastated Hester ... She blamed herself bitterly for
not reaching out to him more, and for their rift of recent years, but
especially for not writing to console him after hearing of his wife's
death, an act that had gone against her natural instinct[32].

On 30 March, James' half-sister Griselda Tekell wrote to her half-
brother Philip, the Earl. She was at the time living with her husband in
Morlaix, in Brittany in NW France.

The death of our poor departed brother, I was indeed in some
measure prepared for. I was causively alarmed by a letter which I
received from him last December, and then thought the symptoms he

---

[28] Meryon, *Additional Memoirs*, p. 169.
[29] Cf. Meryon, *Memoirs* Vol. I, pp. 96-97 (footnote): "In 1837 she said to me, 'I have
never been out of the doors of my house since my brother's death. For five years I
have not been farther than the outer door, once with M. Lamartine, and once to the
bench at the first door with the Americans. Since that time, I have not seen the
strangers' garden, nor your little room; for, if I should put my head outside of my
own court, I should certainly fall into such a passion with some of the people, that it
would make me ill'".
[30] The usually very careful Meryon did not record the specific day in July when the
letter was written.
[31] Meryon's own footnote in the manuscript states that "This letter communicated
the melancholy intelligence of her brother James's having committed suicide". The
letter informing Hester of James' death was actually written on 9 March, and made
no mention of suicide. There was either another letter written on 29 March (now
lost), which explained the details of his death, or Meryon was confusing the dates.
This shows how long to could take letters to travel from England to the Lebanon; in
this case over a year.
[32] Ellis, *Star of the Morning*, p. 351.

described augured serious danger; and although I subsequently heard of his being much better, an anxious apprehension still clung to me, but I had not the remotest suspicion of his mind being in a disordered state, though he had once or twice mentioned that he suffered under a depression of spirit.

You are now the last survivor of those whom I have loved from my childhood[33], for poor Hester has, as you well know, estranged herself from us all.

Griselda appears not to have had any children, unlike her sister Lucy[34]. She had beautiful handwriting and her lengthy, well-structured and elegant sentences show that of all six of the third Earl's children, Griselda was the one who wrote best and seems to have taken the best advantage of whatever education they all had.

James' will is a bound volume consisting of fifty-seven pages, including the Codicil and other additions[35]. The original will is dated 17 February 1823, shortly after the death of Frederica. One of the main points is that James' sister Hester Lucy Stanhope should be paid an annuity of £1,500; he insists on this payment, stating that if there is not enough money for it from his own legacy, the money should come from his estates in Lincolnshire. He also leaves an annuity of £500 to Griselda. If James Banks were to die before his father, the annuities were to be increased to £2,000 and £1,000 respectively. James' other sister Lucy had died in 1814, but her children were not forgotten; there is a stipulation in the will that whenever his son James Banks came of age and inherited the estates in Lincolnshire (until such moment held in trust by the Earls Stanhope and Mansfield), a single payment of £10,000 should be made to Lucy's children (although there is no clue as to their names or even number).

In a codicil dated 7 January 1824 at Kenwood, the following is added:

I, James Hamilton Stanhope, desire that in the event of my decease previous any second marriage, that the sum of ten thousand pounds sterling shall within two years of the death of Lady Banks, be paid to and for the sole use of Miss Elizabeth Barnett as a mark of my affectionate regard.

---

[33] Charles died in 1809, Lucy in 1814 (presumably in childbirth or shortly afterwards, as she is buried with her "infant son") and now James in 1825.

[34] Cf. *Journals of the House of Commons* vol. 71 (printed by H M Stationery Office, 1816.) p. 971, where pensions are assigned to Griselda, Lucy and Lucy's children.

[35] Lincolnshire Archives, RA/4/F/1.

This shows that as early as January 1824, just one year after Frederica's death, there seems to have been some plan for James and Elizabeth (Lizzy) Barnett to marry, and at the same time a suspicion or prediction on James' behalf that he would die before being able to go through with another marriage.

The idea of his early death remained with him, as on 29 March 1824 he made another addition to the will, this time concerning minor details:

> In case of anything ever befalling me suddenly, besides my regular will, I wish these little things to be carried into effect.
>
> I bequeath to my beloved boy all that belonged to his blessed mother and my letters to her, particularly her last letter and my account of her last illness. In that he will find my wishes and my blessing is on his compliance. I leave him my locket with her hair and beg him to wear it for ever. I wish to be buried in my wedding ring. The ring with Mr. Pitt's hair I wear, to Miss Murray. The other ring of two hands, to my brother Stormont. It was the last gift of my dear Charles, and our hearts were equally united. Let him be the same to his brothers and sisters. I leave my watch and all on it to my son – the chain was his mother's.
>
> …
>
> I of course wish to be buried at Chevening, by the side of Freddy, and the only record I wish to have upon my tomb is that I was not unworthy of being her husband.

Included in the Stanhope documents at the Kent History library is a very formal enquiry as to which clauses in the will may be implemented and which not; no addressee is specified and neither are the senders identified, although the executors were clearly involved in the questions asked. The document is not dated, although it must logically date from after James' death, when the clauses in the will were to be enforced.

The position of James Stanhope's possessions was defined mainly by his inheriting, in 1819, the manor and lands of Fulstow, and the manor and lands of Marsh Chapel, both in Lincolnshire, from Sir Joseph Banks. Colonel Stanhope had no real estate to his name except for the land and houses he had inherited in Lincolnshire, and as the legal document states, "nor is his personal property very considerable".

The document goes on to explain that the £10,000 left to Miss Barnett may be raisable from his property but was not to be paid until two years after the death of Sir Joseph's widow Mrs. Banks, who was still alive, when the Lincolnshire estates would be in the possession of James and Frederica's son, James Banks Stanhope, if living. The will apparently made no provision as to the application of the rents from the estate or for the education of his child. The problem was where the money for these legacies and annuities was to come from, as James Banks Stanhope was the technical owner and Lady Banks the tenant. The document in the collection states that "your opinion is requested on behalf of the Earl Stanhope and the Earl of Mansfield"; as said above, no addressee is specified, but we may assume that it was a lawyer of some description. The questions are written with a space between each one, although these spaces are still blank and there are only some words pencilled in to the left of the questions, presumably as draft answers, to be enlarged upon in the space provided. This was either never done, or done in another copy which is now lost. The first questions read as follows:

1. Whether the personal estate of Colonel Stanhope is liable to the payment of the two annuities to his sisters.
   Answer in pencil – It is not.
2. Whether these annuities commence immediately or only from the time the infant shall be in possession of the Lincolnshire Estate?
   Answer in pencil – Immediately.
3. Whether the <u>present</u> personal estate of the testator is liable to the two legacies of £10,000 each to the children of Lady L Taylor and to Miss Barnett or either of them?
   Answer in pencil – Not at present, but at Lady Banks' death.
4. Whether Fulston and Marsh Chapel estates shall be exempt during the life of Colonel Stanhope's son from the annuities to the Ladies Hester Stanhope and Griselda Tekell?
   Answer in pencil – They will be exempt.

Given the legal standing of the estates, and the fact that Colonel Stanhope was not wealthy (he had no known financial troubles but could hardly be described as rich), we must doubt whether either the legacies or the annuities were ever paid. We have no information about this from either Lucy's children or from Griselda; Lady Hester's debts were already considerable and did no more than increase until her death, in poverty and misery, in 1839.

In conclusion, while it is true that James Hamilton Stanhope was born into a privileged class of society, he was unlucky right from the start. His father was eccentric in many ways, which under certain circumstances could have led to an interesting childhood, but in this case the third Earl was a distant and authoritarian father; the mother of the three boys was cold and unloving too. One by one James' elder half-sisters and two brothers escaped from the tyranny they perceived at home, and lived on the charity of William Pitt the Younger to survive. When Pitt died in 1806 this too came to an end; James was with his uncle when he expired.

James joined the Navy at the age of fourteen or fifteen, and then the army with his brother Charles; he saw little or no action until he was appointed Aide-de-Camp to Sir John Moore in the morning of 16 January 1809. A few hours later his brother had been killed in the battle, and his commander in chief died in the evening of wounds received on the battlefield. Just as with Pitt three years earlier, James was present when Moore died. His position as Aide-de-Camp did not last even twenty-four hours.

He enjoyed relative success in the rest of the Peninsular War, although he missed out on the success of Salamanca because he had chosen to accompany General Graham back home. Back in the Peninsula, once again his star seemed to be rising until he received a severe wound at San Sebastián in 1813. The musket ball that lodged in his shoulder blade was never extracted, and caused him severe pain for the rest of his life.

In 1816 there was an other traumatic event in James' family life. His father was dying and James went to see him, to bid his last farewell, but the Earl refused to see him and died alone. The effects that this refusal must have had on James were no doubt worse than those of the death itself.

The period from 1817 to 1823 was probably the happiest in his life. He entered into politics and seemed to be making a modest but contented living. He had fallen deeply in love with Frederica Louisa Murray, the eldest daughter of Earl Mansfield; the feeling was mutual and the couple were married in July 1820. Their love was profound, intense and deeply religious, as is evident from their letters to each other.

James and Frederica became the parents of James Banks Stanhope in May 1821, and after a miscarriage towards the end of the year, Freddy was pregnant again in 1822. The baby was due in 1823, but it became clear that the mother would not survive. The baby too died after a few days. All James' happiness vanished. Before she died, Freddy had made both her husband and her parents swear that he would marry again. Her excessive insistence on this point would have fatal consequences.

Both James and Lord and Lady Mansfield seemed to have felt obliged to act on the promise they had made to their wife and daughter, respectively. James clearly had no wish to marry again, but as a man of his word he felt that he had to keep his promise to Freddy. It was no doubt the Mansfields who came up with a new bride; a member of the family who James had met in 1819, when travelling with them, Elizabeth Barnett. Just before the dinner at Kenwood at which no doubt the marriage was to be announced and planned, James saw no other way out; he could either marry and be unhappy (and no doubt he felt this would be deeply unfair to Miss Barnett too), or break his promise to Frederica on her deathbed. He took his own life.

While it is pointless to wonder what might have happened if Freddy had not forced James and her parents into making this promise (she of course did so with the best of intentions, she did not wish James to spend the rest of his life alone, and also seemed to have a spiritual concern, as if he would fall into a life of sin if he didn't get married again), it is also true that this same promise had a fatal effect on the person she thought it would most benefit.

As requested in his will, James was buried next to his wife; his own inscription is much shorter than hers, but much longer that he ordered in his will. It can be seen on the side of the monument, leaving the main front entirely for Frederica. The text is as follows[36]:

IN THE SAME TOMB IS INTERRED LIEUTENANT COLONEL THE HONOURABLE JAMES HAMILTON STANHOPE, THIRD SON OF CHARLES EARL STANHOPE, WHO DIED 5TH MARCH 1825 IN THE 37TH YEAR OF HIS AGE. HIS AFFLICTED RELATIVES WOULD HAVE FELT A MELANCHOLY SATISFACTION IN COMMEMORATING THE MANY TALENTS AND VIRTUES WHICH ADORNED HIM, BUT IN LAYING HIM BY THE SIDE OF HIS BELOVED WIFE, WITH NO OTHER RECORD THAN THAT HE WAS NOT UNWORTHY TO BE HER HUSBAND, THEY OBEY HIS LAST INJUNCTIONS.

James Banks Stanhope also had a plaque inscribed at the Guards' Chapel in Wellington Barracks in London, with the following words[37]:

---

[36] The inscription is recorded incorrectly in Janet Bromley and David Bromley, *Wellington's Men Remembered* Vol. 2 (Barnsley, 2015), p. 310; the words "He was not unworthy to be her husband" are omitted, resulting in an incomplete and meaningless sentence. The date is given as 6th March; the photograph of the inscription on the DVD accompanying the book is somewhat blurred (it is reproduced in this same poor quality by Glover, *Eyewitness*), but the date thereupon is without doubt 5th March, the date when James died. Although not incorrect, the phrase "in the 37th year of his age" is confusing and could easily be understood as saying he was actually 37.

[37] Bromley and Bromley, *Wellington's Men*, p. 310.

PLACED BY JAMES BANKS STANHOPE IN MEMORY OF HIS FATHER, LIEUTENANT COLONEL THE HONOURABLE JAMES HAMILTON STANHOPE, THIRD SON OF CHARLES EARL STANHOPE, BORN 1788, DIED 1825. 1ST GUARDS 1803 – 22. HE SERVED WITH THE 3RD BATTALION IN SICILY, 1806-7, AND WAS ON THE STAFF AT CORUNNA. HE WAS AIDE-DE-CAMP TO GENERAL THOMAS LORD LYNEDOCH KB, APR. 1810 – OCT. 1812, AND WAS AT BARROSA, THE ASSAULT AT CIUDAD RODRIGO, WHERE HE WAS WOUNDED, AND AT VITTORIA. HE WAS DEPUTY ASST QUARTERMASTER GENERAL, AND SEVERELY WOUNDED AT THE FIRST ASSAULT ON SAN SEBASTIAN. HE WAS ON THE STAFF AT BERGEN-OP-ZOOM, AND WITH THE 3RD BATTALION AT QUATRE-BRAS AND WATERLOO.

The plaque was destroyed by a German bomb in 1944.

CHAPTER NINE

WE THAT ARE LEFT BEHIND

When James took his own life in 1825, he left behind his young son, James Banks. The little boy had lost his mother at the age of two (and was probably too young to have been much aware of his loss), while his father committed suicide when he was four. After this deeply traumatic start in life, he was looked after and brought up by his grandparents, Frederica's parents, Lord and Lady Mansfield, and also by his uncle Philip Stanhope, the fourth Earl. The relationship between the two families was not good (James Banks was now all they had in common), and the child's interest was often neglected by the warring factions. Very little is known of his childhood; he was apparently sent to Oxford University but the experience was not successful, and it is not known whether he actually obtained a degree or not. He inherited the estates in Lincolnshire that had previously belonged to Sir Joseph Banks, and was such a successful and popular landlord that he was prevailed upon to stand for Parliament for Lincoln County. He was a Member of Parliament from 1852 to 1868, when he retired, arguing that "Lincolnshire might be represented by some of my young friends who are very anxious to get into the House, instead of by myself who for some years have on the whole rather wished to get out"[1].

The Stanhope archives include two interesting documents related to James Banks[2]; the first is an address to the electors of the Horncastle Division in Lincolnshire, printed on black-edged paper. The text reads as follows:

> Gentlemen,
> We are all suffering under a great calamity. I have lost one who was my adopted son[3], in whom all my hopes and my affections were centred.

---

[1] Cf. Newman, *Stanhopes*, p. 200.
[2] U1590 A18.
[3] Edward Stanhope, to whom he had left the Revesby Abbey estate in life.

You have lost the best member that Lincolnshire ever had. Edward Stanhope destroyed his life by over-work in this Winter Session, fighting on your behalf and doing all he knew for our Constitution and our Country. It is not enough to respect and to mourn him, but it is the duty of all who hold his principles and who honour his memory to do all they can to elect a Conservative as his successor.

Remember, that if you elect a Radical you may in a short time undo all the good work that Edward Stanhope did in the last 20 years, by hard work and at the cost of his own life.

Remember, that by voting for a supporter of Mr. Gladstone you are enabling that minister, according to his late Home Rule Bill, to divide the Empire, to place the loyal Protestant minority in Ireland under the foot of the priest-ridden majority; and while giving them almost uncontrolled power in Ireland, to keep 80 Irish members here to vote upon every English subject, to decide the fate of Ministries, and practically to rule the Empire.

Our new candidate – Lord Willoughby de Eresby – has shown by his plucky fight at Boston that he is not an inexperienced politician; his name is well known in Lincolnshire; he has already borne his share in the affairs of the County; he comes of an old and respected Lincolnshire family who for centuries have played no mean part in the history of the County. His opinions are the same as Edward Stanhope's, and I can confidently recommend him to you. You must forgive him if, in the short time in this unexpected election, he is unable to make the acquaintance of you all, or even to address meetings in all parts of the constituency.

I will now write a few words on my own behalf. I have been in this County for fifty years; forty years ago, with the assistance of many kind friends, I gained a great victory and my name is probably still known among you. As an old man of 72, whose eyesight is failing and who is no longer able from imperfect health to speak and work for the cause that I and Edward Stanhope have always fought for, I now ask you, as a final favour to do all you can to elect a Conservative in the place of him whom we now mourn.

Always yours very faithfully,
J. Banks Stanhope
Revesby Abbey, Boston, 28th December 1893.

While all opinions and ideas should be understood in their context and not judged according to today's prevailing train of thought, I think that

James Banks' comments on Ireland show a deeply bigoted nature (although as he remained in politics so long there were clearly plenty of others who thought like him). Politicians in all countries cover up truths and exaggerate by nature (if they don't, they never get into office), but to refer to the Irish as a "priest-ridden majority", and deplore the fact that they should rule in their own country, even in pre-independence days, is hardly respectful, and to say that they almost rule the Empire is such a huge exaggeration as to be almost comical.

The second document in the collection is a speech by James Banks Stanhope at Tennants dinner, Revesby, on 4 January 1894.

> My friends,
> For fifty years there has generally been a Stanhope in this room, and I feel there ought to be a Stanhope here today. Had Edward Stanhope been alive he would have asked me to take his place and I am sure he would wish me to be with you today. I am here with the permission of the executors, and by the wish of Mrs. Stanhope.
> In touching upon Edward Stanhope I am obliged to talk a great deal about myself, because for a great many years Edward Stanhope, Revesby and myself have been so interlaced that it is difficult to separate them. I must now take you back several years; when Edward Stanhope was a boy of fifteen I heard with pleasure that he had taken high mathematical honours at Harrow, and I was glad the same year at my full confidence in him, and as you know me well and can rely on me, I think you may place full confidence in him also.
> Probably by Mrs. Stanhope's kindness I shall occasionally be here, and whether my years be many or few, I shall always have but one feeling, that good fortune and happiness may attend you, and that the confidence that has existed between landlord and tenant may always remain undiminished. May God bless you.

The speech is written out in elegant handwriting; at the end James Banks added the following words, in what can only be described as a scrawl: "Dictated by me evening of 4th from memory to Hastings Brooke who made it more accurate".

James Banks Stanhope (see Figure 9.1) played a significant role in the history of the so-called Chatham[4] Vase (see Figure 9.2). The Vase is a

---

[4] Chatham was the noble title given to William Pitt the Elder; it passed to his eldest son (and not to William Pitt the Younger), who died without issue and the title fell into disuse after only two holders. The history of the vase herein is taken from Jacqueline Reiter, *"A felicity inexpressible": The Chatham Vase*, available online at

Figure 9.1 – James Banks Stanhope

https://englishhistoryauthors.blogspot.com/2016/08/a-felicity-inexpressible-chatham-vase.html

Figure 9.2 – A replica of the Chatham Vase

sculpture commissioned by Hester, Dowager Countess of Chatham, in 1780-1 to commemorate her husband William Pitt the Elder, First Earl of Chatham. It was sculpted in the shape of a Grecian urn by John Bacon, the same man who designed Chatham's monument in Westminster Abbey. The urn was erected at Burton Pynsent, Somerset, which Lady Chatham used as her house until her death. Lady Chatham was the maternal grandmother of all the third Earl Stanhope's children, and Lady Hester lived for a time with her at Burton Pynsent. The lines on the pedestal (largely weathered away now, but still just about legible) read:

> Sacred to pure affection, this simple urn stands a witness of unceasing grief for him who, excelling in whatever is so admirable, and adding to the exercise of the sublimest virtues the sweet charm of refined sentiment and polished wit, by gay social commerce rendered beyond comparison happy the course of domestic life and bestowed a felicity inexpressible on her whose faithful love was blessed in a pure return that raised her above every other joy but the parental one, and that still shared with him. His generous country with public monuments has eternised his fame. This humble tribute is but to soothe the sorrowing breast of private woe.

This tribute was apparently written by Lady Chatham herself, with a little assistance from her son William Pitt the Younger. Pitt wrote to his mother on the subject on 20 April 1780:

> All my feelings with regard to the paper enclosed I need not express. I am sure I should be far indeed from wishing to suggest a syllable of alteration. The language of the heart, of such a heart especially, can never require or admit of correction. May it remain as it deserves, a lasting monument of both the subject and the author.

After Lady Chatham died in April 1803, her son John, second Earl of Chatham, was forced to sell Burton Pynsent for financial reasons. He made sure, however, to take the Vase away before selling the property. Where it went after Burton is not known; presumably the Vase spent the time packed away in Chatham's attic.

In 1831 it was taken to Stowe House, although it was sold at auction in 1848, and then in 1857 it was sold again and purchased by James Banks Stanhope. The Vase moved on one more time, when it was bought by the seventh Earl Stanhope in 1934, and taken to Chevening, where it still remains (the original is kept in the house).

James Banks never married, and intended to leave Revesby within the Stanhope family, as this is what he believed Sir Joseph Banks would have wished. He left it first to Edward Stanhope, the second son of the fifth Earl, but Edward died before him. When Edward's wife Lucy died too, in 1907, the house passed to Richard Stanhope, the youngest son of the sixth Earl, who was killed in 1916 in the Battle of the Somme.

The current Revesby Abbey is the third building to be called such and is Grade 1 listed (see Figure 9.3). The house was designed by renowned Scottish architect William Burn as commissioned by James Banks in 1843 and building work finished in 1845. This means the construction of the house took less that two years, to build over 65,000 square feet, which is quite astounding. The house is called Revesby Abbey as it was built on the site of a Cistercian monastery; in 1538 the Duke of Norfolk wrote to Thomas Cromwell to inform him that the abbey was "in great ruin and decay" and so it was destroyed like so many others under Henry VIII.

Figure 9.3 – Revesby Abbey

Richard Stanhope's widow, Lady Beryl, lived at the Abbey, using it as a medical supply unit in the First World War and training many of the best racehorses in the country in the stable block. In 1931 Lady Beryl announced that the Abbey would be closed and she would move into a cottage on the estate. In 1953 a large amount of the contents of the house were sold off. Lady Beryl died in 1953 and the house was again passed on. In the 1950s the Abbey was used for American air force accommodation and then in the 1960s for RAF personnel stationed at the nearby East Kirkby Airbase. In 1977 an application was made by the owner to demolish the Abbey and the vote was very close, but then in 1981 the council advised the owner to apply for demolition again, suggesting they would vote for demolition, although the owner did not apply. In 1987 English Heritage used statutory power of entry to start emergency repairs; this was one of the very first times this power was used and cost the owner £119,000. Over the next twelve years the house passed hands and planning was approved for various things such as huge number of flats and a house retreat. The present owners bought the Abbey in 1999 and are in the gradual process of restoring it[5].

As for the rest of the Stanhope family, James had two elder brothers, Philip and Charles. As we have seen above, Charles was killed at the Battle of Corunna on 16 January 1809, at the age of twenty-three. He was unmarried and had no known descendants. Philip in due course became the fourth Earl Stanhope (see Figure 9.4), and had three children (Philip Henry, who became the fifth earl, George Joseph, who died at sea at the age of twenty-two, and Catherine Lucy Wilhelmina, who by her second marriage became the Duchess of Cleveland and later wrote a biography of her aunt, Lady Hester Stanhope). The line of Earls Stanhope ran through to 1967, when the seventh and last Earl died childless, bequeathing Chevening to the nation. The house and estate are owned and maintained at the expense of the Board of Trustees of the Chevening Estate, to serve as a furnished country residence for a person nominated by the Prime Minister, so qualified by being a member of the Cabinet or a descendant of King George VI. The nominee pays for their own private living expenses when in residence. Government departments also arrange privately with the Trust to conduct official business on the Estate.

James' sister Lady Hester Stanhope is one of the best-known members of the Stanhope family. She never went back to England after she left in 1810, and never saw James again after they parted on 7 April. When she heard of James' death she quite literally bricked up her house (leaving only a small doorway for servants to fetch supplies) and never left it again until her death in 1839. Doctor Meryon visited her twice more after James' death; from the surviving documentation we get the impression that he would have

---

[5] Cf. http://www.revesbyabbey.co.uk/history.html. The current owners also host "Paranormal Nights" at the house as it is being restored, mainly for ghost hunting groups and associations.

stayed until the end, but Hester insisted he leave. She died alone and in extreme poverty.

Figure 9.4 – Philip, the 4th Earl Stanhope

She was buried quickly, given the hot climate, by the American missionary William McClure Thomson and the British consul, Mr. Moore, in a vault in her garden together with the remains of her lover from 1820, the Frenchman Captain Loustaunau. The vault soon fell into ruin, although the tomb was still visible in 1970. In 1988 the bones of Hester were found (there were other bones in the grave, which were no doubt those of Captain Loustaunau) and reinterred at the British Ambassador's summer residence in the village of Abey on 2 February 1989. In 2004 they were dug up again and on 23 June her ashes (presumably the bones had been incinerated or ground) were scattered over her garden in Djoun[6].

What happened to the tomb has never been made clear. Some sources say it was destroyed during the Lebanese Civil War, which broke out in 1975; and indeed it can hardly have been in place in 1998 for the bones to have been so easily found and removed. The only plaque now remaining in Lady Hester's honour is to be found in the parish church of St. Botolph's, just outside the Chevening estate. It reads:

TO THE MEMORY OF LADY HESTER STANHOPE, ELDEST DAUGHTER OF CHARLES, THIRD EARL STANHOPE AND THE COUNTESS STANHOPE AND NIECE OF WILLIAM PITT THE YOUNGER. BORN 12 MARCH 1776, SHE DIED AT DAR DJOUN, LEBANON, ON 23 JUNE 1839. HER REMAINS WERE RE-INTERRED IN THE GARDEN OF HM AMBASSADOR, BEIRUT, AT ABEY ON 2 FEBRUARY 1989.

An additional inscription was later added underneath:

FINALLY HER ASHES WERE SCATTERED AT DAR DJOUN ON 23 JUNE 2004

Lady Hester had openly had various lovers (Michael Bruce and Captain Loustaunau being the best known), but never got pregnant by any of them. It would be something of a coincidence for all her lovers to have been sterile (Michael Bruce later got married and had children, although Hester was probably past child-bearing age when she met Loustaunau), so we can only conclude that Lady Hester herself could not have children.

---

[6] Lady Hester's biographer Kirsten Ellis claims that in fact the monks from Deir-el-Moukhalles had then gathered up her ashes and now keep them in an urn in the monastery. It is not explained how they managed to gather up ashes that had been scattered over a garden, which from the appearance of the photographs of the ceremony consisted more of sand and stones than grass.

As for Michael Bruce, on his release from prison in Paris (where he was sent for his part in the famed escape of Count Lavalette) Bruce returned once again to England and despite his father's opposition, married Marianne, the daughter of Sir George Dallas and widow of Sir Peter Parker, in 1818. They had two daughters and one son; both girls died young (Marianne was born in 1819 and died of scarlet fever in 1832, while Emma, for whom no exact dates are known, died of adenoiditis). Their son Michael was born in 1823 and lived until he was sixty.

Many years later, in a letter from Doctor Meryon to Michael Bruce in 1849 (they never quite lost contact and as Meryon grew older, his mind wandered more and more to his days of adventure and he was quite happy to converse with his old rival in their autumn years), he sent him a copy of some verses which he had written for Lady Hester to comfort her in her loneliness after Bruce's departure in 1813. Bruce answered and invited Meryon to dinner. Meryon makes no mention of meeting Bruce in his own letter, and so Michael's invitation to him to have dinner together is all the more surprising. At the time Bruce was 62 and Meryon 66; after all the unpleasant times they had been through in their youth, it is most curious that so many years later they were still in touch and seemingly on friendly terms. There are no records that I have been able to discover that tell us whether or not Meryon accepted the invitation, although I would be inclined to think that he did. It would have been truly fascinating to listen to their conversation and hear how they reminisced about former times. Michael Bruce died in 1861.

Charles Lewis Meryon, Lady Hester's physician, with whom James had had dealings, after he returned from Djoun for the last time in 1838 lived in Rye until the age of ninety-four. In 1845, despite opposition from the Stanhope family, he published the trilogy entitled *The Memoirs of the Lady Hester Stanhope*, and a year later a further trilogy called *The Travels of the Lady Hester Stanhope*. Charles Lewis Meryon had three children, two of whom died childless. His only legitimate daughter, Eugenia, never married and very little is known of her life; she died on 7 December 1889. The fruit of his affair with the French opera dancer Narcisse Chaspoux was the artist Charles Meryon, who never married either; despite his frequent visits to brothels and prostitutes, there are no claims that he ever had any offspring. Charles Lewis Meryon's only natural descendants are via Lucy Meryon, the Doctor's daughter born in 1810 and raised by his sister Sarah Meryon and her husband William Holloway, at least until Meryon's return to England in

1817. Lucy married William Gilbert[7] in 1837 (while her father was away) and had three daughters with him; Elizabeth, Juliet and Ann, born in 1838, 1840 and 1841 respectively.

Lucy Gilbert died in 1845 and her widower then emigrated to Australia with the three children. This was the start of the Meryon family history in both Australia and New Zealand, the only natural descendants of Charles Lewis Meryon. Ann married Robert Bennet Webb in 1870; they had seven children, prolonging the family tradition of using the same names as their ancestors and using surnames as Christian names. Thus, Lucy Webb was born in 1871, Charles Meryon Webb in 1872 (he died in 1875), Anne in 1874, William in 1878, Juliet in 1880 and Edward Meryon in 1882. Edward Meryon Webb married Beatrice Bartlett in 1910 and through their daughter the family is still thriving today (although the surname Meryon has been lost in this branch of the family). Anne Gilbert Webb married Henry Newman Barwell in 1902 and had four children, the descendants of whom are also still alive in Australia, although once again the surname Meryon was lost.

Finally, as for James' other two sisters, Griselda Stanhope married John Tekell but they never had any children. She died in 1851.

The earldom was passed from father to eldest surviving son; the seventh and last Earl had no children, but the others before him all had children apart from the eldest son who would succeed to the earldom. I have not followed these descendants through except in one case (Lucy Stanhope, one of James' half-sisters), but no doubt some or many of them have descendants still living today. As stated above, the line of first-born males (i.e. those who inherited the earldom) became extinct in 1967, on the death of the seventh Earl.

Lucy Stanhope married the local apothecary Thomas Taylor, in 1796, and died on 1 March 1814, at the age of thirty-four. When researching outside the main line of descent of the family information becomes very hazy. Lucy apparently had a child who died before his first birthday, called Thomas Taylor (like his father). She is buried in the Stanhope Crypt at St. Botolph's next to Chevening, together with her husband, the baby who died and another daughter[8]. Thomas and Lucy had another child in 1798, who they called William Stanhope Taylor. William fought at Waterloo[9], as did

---

[7] The marriage is recorded in *The Gentleman's Magazine* Vol. 163, p. 88, for 20 November 1838: "At Newenden, Kent, William Gilbert esq. of Hippenscomb, Wilts, to Lucy-Elizabeth, daughter of C.L. Meryon esq. M.D."

[8] Cf. https://es.findagrave.com/memorial/83330996/lucy-rachel-taylor

[9] At the time of writing this chapter, the medal which William was awarded for his part in the Waterloo campaign was for sale at

James Hamilton; that they met is shown by a letter from James to Lady Henrietta Frances Spencer, written from Montmartre on 3 July, two weeks after Waterloo:

> I lost my cook in the bustle but have replaced him with an English groom, which in my new capacity is more useful. I have also increased my stud, but a beautiful little pony I had I gave to my nephew who is just out to join the 4th and who made his beginning on the 18th.

William Stanhope Taylor married Lady Sarah O'Brien, daughter of the Marquis of Thomond. Their eldest son, Stanhope B. Taylor, was killed at the mutiny in Jhansi, India, in 1857. William and Sarah also had a daughter in 1831, called Elizabeth Lucy Taylor, and two daughters more (Mary Hester Taylor in 1833 and Adelaide Francis Taylor in 1841). The names show that they were very much aware of the Stanhope family history. The descendants of these three daughters no doubt had far-reaching families, but I have decided to focus on just one branch of the family to show how the descendants of the Stanhope family are still alive today, although possibly unaware of their noble heritage. William Stanhope Taylor (whose name follows the common nineteenth-century custom of using the mother's maiden name as the child's second name) had another son in 1844, named George John Pitt Taylor, showing again that the family history was still very much alive. William Stanhope Taylor died at Tunbridge Wells in 1858, and is buried in St. Paul's churchyard (see Figure 9.5).

George John Pitt Taylor married twice[10]; his first bride was Elizabeth Bannerman Burnett, with whom he had five children; Sarah Lauderdale Pitt Taylor in 1870, in Canada, Violet Mary Pitt Taylor in 1871, in Edinburgh, Sybil Violet Thomond Pitt Taylor in 1873, also in Edinburgh, Desmond Stanhope Pitt Taylor in 1876, in Aberdeen, and Ernestine Hester Pitt Taylor in 1877, in Fife. The names clearly show that the family at this stage were still very much aware and proud of their ancestry, from the Stanhopes and Pitts. Elizabeth Bannerman died in 1877, although the dates are somewhat confusing; her date of death is given as 23 February 1877, whereas Desmond Stanhope was born on 12 December 1876. This would of course leave no time for Elizabeth to recover from the birth of her fourth child, get pregnant again and have Ernestine Hester, whose date of birth is given as "c. 1877". There is clearly a mistake somewhere, although it is not

---

https://www.british-medals.co.uk/british-medals/single-campaign-medals/waterloo-ensign-4th-reg-foot-and-later-main-beneficiary-edited
[10] I am grateful to genealogist Jane Hewitt for her invaluable help in this section.

significant for my present purpose. George John married Eliza Ellen Russell
Davies in Paddington, Middlesex, on 3 October 1878, but even though she
was just twenty-three years old they had no children.

Figure 9.5 – The grave of William Stanhope Taylor

Of George John's five children from his first marriage, Sarah Lauderdale died unmarried in 1956, Violet Mary died just ten days after she was born, and Ernestine died at the age of thirteen. Desmond Stanhope married Jessie Barbara Ross and had two children, one in Scotland and one in Canada, where they presumably emigrated.

Sybil Violet Thomond Pitt Taylor married Frederick Peter Schipper on 21 April 1900 at St. Margaret's church in Westminster. Frederick is described as an actor and his father as a publisher. Sybil's father, George John Pitt Taylor, was a captain in the 78th Highlanders. Frederick's stage name was Robert Minster (see Figure 9.6); he was widowed in 1909 and died in 1932. Sybil and Frederick had two children; the younger of the two was the last to bear any traces of the Stanhope/Pitt family ancestry in his name (his name was Robin Schipper, but according to the family tree he was also known as Prof. Robin Stanhope); he was also an actor and died young in 1937. Sybil's eldest child was John Frederick Minster, the first of the family not to be called either Stanhope or Pitt. He was born in 1901, became a theatrical producer and died in Oxford in 1966. He married Barbara Hunter Cochran-Carr in 1939; she too was an actress. They had one child – Roger Michael Hilary Minster, born in 1944. Also an actor, known as just Hilary Minster, his best-known role was General Erich Von Klinkerhoffen in the sitcom 'Allo 'Allo! from 1984 to 1992. He died in 1999. He had four children, all of whom are still alive today[11]. No doubt there are other descendants from other branches of the family who are not aware of their history; I found this one particularly interesting because all the above people are direct descendants of James Hamilton Stanhope's sister Lucy.

---

[11] I tried to contact them just to inform them that they were in fact descendants of the first, second and third Earls Stanhope, but received no reply; they no doubt thought I was a crank in search of money.

Figure 9.6 – Robert Minster

BIBLIOGRAPHY

Black, Jeremy. *The British Abroad: The Grand Tour in the Eighteenth Century.* Stroud: The History Press, 2003.

Brett-James, Antony. *General Graham 1748-1844.* New York: St Martin's Press Inc., 1959.

Bromley, Janet & David. *Wellington's Men Remembered.* 2 vols. Barnsley: Pen & Sword, 2012 (Vol. 1) and 2015 (Vol. 2).

Bruce, Ian. *The Nun of Lebanon: the love affair of Lady Hester Stanhope and Michael Bruce; their newly discovered letters.* London: Collins, 1951.

Bruce, Ian. *Lavalette Bruce.* London: Collins, 1953.

Bryant, Julius. *Chevening, A Seat of Diplomacy.* London: Paul Holberton Publishing, 2017.

Bury, Charlotte. *The Diary of a Lady-in-Waiting.* 2 vols. London: John Lane, 1908.

Childs, Virginia. *Lady Hester Stanhope, Queen of the Desert.* London: Weidenfeld & Nicolson, 1990.

Cholmondeley, R. H. *The Heber Letters.* London: The Batchworth Press, 1950.

Clinton, Henry. *A few remarks explanatory of the motives which guided the operations of the British army during the late short campaign in Spain.* London: T. Egerton, 1809.

Day, Roger. *Decline to Glory, A Reassessment of the Life and Times of Lady Hester Stanhope.* Salzburg: University of Salzburg, 1997.

Dolan, Brian. *Ladies of the Grand Tour.* London: Flamingo, 2001.

Ellis, Kirsten. *Star of the Morning: The Extraordinary Life of Lady Hester Stanhope.* London: Harper Press, 2008.

Esdaile, Charles. *The Peninsular War: A New History.* New York: Palgrave Macmillan, 2003.

Fantin des Odoards, Louis Florimond. *Journal du Général Fantin des Odoards: Étapes d'un officier de la Grande Armée.* Paris: LCV Services, 2008.

Gibb, Lorna. *Lady Hester: Queen of the East.* London: Faber & Faber, 2005.

Glover, Gareth. *A Staff Officer in the Peninsula and at Waterloo: the Letters of the Honourable Lieutenant Colonel James H. Stanhope, 1st Foot Guards, 1809-15.* Godmanchester: Ken Trotman Publishing, 2007.

Glover, Gareth. *Eyewitness to the Peninsular War and the Battle of Waterloo: The Letters and Journals of Lieutenant Colonel the Honourable James Hamilton Stanhope, 1803 to 1825, recording his service with Sir John Moore, Sir Thomas Graham and the Duke of Wellington.* Barnsley: Pen & Sword, 2010.

Glover, Michael. *A Very Slippery Fellow: The Life of Sir Robert Wilson 1777-1849.* Oxford: Oxford University Press, 1978.

Gotteri, Nicole. *Le Maréchal Soult.* Paris: Bernard Giovanangeli, 2000.

Grose, Francis. *The 1811 Dictionary of the Vulgar Tongue.* London: C. Chappel, 1811.

Guscin, Mark. *Sir John Moore, 1761-1809: Una historia desconocida del general británico que murió en la batalla de La Coruña en enero 1809.* La Coruña: Arenas Publicaciones, 2001.

Guscin, Mark. *Lady Hester Stanhope (1776-1839): Reina de Oriente, Leyenda en La Coruña.* La Coruña: Arenas Publicaciones, 2008.

Guscin, Mark. *A Very Good Sort of Man: A Life of Doctor Charles Lewis Meryon (1783-1977), Physician to Lady Hester Stanhope.* Brighton: Sussex Academic Press, 2017.

Guscin, Mark. *Las Coruñas del Mundo.* La Coruña: Arenas Publicaciones, 2019.

Hague, William. *William Pitt the Younger.* London: Harpercollins, 2004.

Hamel, Frank. *Lady Hester Lucy Stanhope: A New Light on Her Life and Love Affairs.* London: Cassell & Company, 1913.

Hamilton, Anthony. *Hamilton's Campaign with Moore and Wellington.* Troy, N.Y.: Press of Prescott & Wilson, 1847.

Hare, Augustus J. C. (ed.). *The Life and Letters of Maria Edgeworth.* 2 vols. London: Edward Arnold, 1894.

Haslip, Joan. *Lady Hester Stanhope.* London: Cobden-Sanderson, 1934.

Hayworth, Peter. *Soult, Napoleon's Maligned Marshal.* London: Arms & Armour Press, 1990.

Healy, Róisín. "Suicide in Early Modern and Modern Europe". In *The Historical Journal* 49.3 (2006), pp. 903-919.

Hibbert, Christopher. *Corunna.* London: B. T. Batsford Ltd, 1961.

Hibbert, Christopher (ed.). *The Recollections of Rifleman Harris.* Moreton-in-Marsh: The Windrush Press, 1970.

Hibbert, Christopher. *George IV.* London: Penguin Books, 1976.

Hibbert, Christopher. *Wellington: A Personal History.* Reading, Massachusetts: Addison-Wesley, 1997.

Hill, Joanna. *Wellington's Right Hand: Rowland, Viscount Hill.* Brimscombe Port: The History Press, 2011.

Jamieson, John. *An Etymological Dictionary of the Scottish Language.* Edinburgh: Alexander Gardner, 1818.

Kieran, Brian L. *Corunna 1809: Sir John Moore's Battle to Victory and Successful Evacuation.* Milton Keynes: AuthorHouse, 2011.

Lavalette, le Comte de. *Mémoires et Souvenirs du Comte de Lavelette (1879-1830).* Paris: Mercure de France, 1994.

De Léocour, Béochet. *Souvenirs.* Paris: Librairie Historique Teissèdre, 1999.

Maurice, J. F. *The Diary of Sir John Moore.* London: Edward Arnold, 1904.

Maxwell, Herbert (ed.). *The Creevey Papers, a Selection from the Correspondence and Diaries of the late Thomas Creevey M.P. born 1768 died 1838.* 2 vols. London: John Murray, 1904.

Meryon, Charles Lewis. *Memoirs of the Lady Hester Stanhope, as related by herself in conversation with her physician; comprising her opinions and anecdotes of the some of the most remarkable persons of her time, in three volumes.* London: Henry Colburn, 1845.

Meryon, Charles Lewis. *The Travels of Lady Hester Stanhope, forming the completion of her Memoirs, narrated by her physician.* 3 vols. London: Henry Colburn, 1846.

Meryon, Charles Lewis. *The Additional Memoirs of Lady Hester Stanhope* (ed. Mark Guscin). Brighton: Sussex Academic Press, 2017.

Napier, George. *Passages in the Early Military Life of General Sir George T. Napier.* London: John Murray, 1884.

Napier, William. *History of the War in the Peninsula and in the South of France from the year 1807 to the year 1814.* New York: J. S. Redfield, 1844.

Napier, William. *Life of Charles Napier.* London: John Murray, 1857.

Napier, William. *Life of General Sir William Napier KCB* (ed. H.A. Bruce MP). London: John Murray, 1864.

Le Noble, Pierre. *Mémoires sur les Opérations Militaires des Français en Galice, en Portugal et dans la Vallée du Tage en 1809.* Paris: Barrois l'aîné, 1821.

Newman, Aubrey. *The Stanhopes of Chevening.* London: St Martin's Press, 1969.

Oman, Carola. *Sir John Moore.* London: Hodder & Stoughton, 1953.

Parkinson, Roger. *Moore of Corunna.* Abingdon: Book Club Edition, 1976.

Patterson, John. *The Adventures of Captain John Patterson.* London: T & W Boone, 1837.

Penny, N. B. "English Church Monuments to Women who died in childbed between 1780 and 1835". In *Journal of the Warburg & Courtauld Institutes* XXXVIII (1975), pp. 314 – 332.

Poser, Norman S. *Lord Mansfield: Justice in the Age of Reason.* Montreal: McGill-Queen's University Press, 2013.

Robertson, Scott. "Chevening Church". In *Archaeologia Cantiana* Vol. 16 (1886), pp. 114-126.

Robinson, John Martin. *The Travellers Club: A Bicentennial History.* Marlborough: Libanus Press Ltd., 2018.

De Rocca, Albert Jean Michel. *Mémoires sur la Guerre des Français en Espagne.* Paris: H. Nicolle, 1814.

Schaumann, August Ludolf Friedrich. *On the Road with Wellington: The Diary of a War Commissary in the Peninsular Campaigns,* translated and edited from the German by Anthony M. Ludovici. London: William Heinemann Ltd, 1924. Reprinted by Greenhill Books, London, 1999.

Shelley, Frances. *The Diary of Lady Frances Shelley.* 2 vols. London: John Murray, 1912.

Smith, Jack C. et al. "Marital Status and the Risk of Suicide". In *The American Journal of Public Health* (1988), pp. 78-80.

Soult, Jean de Dieu. *Mémoires du Maréchal Soult, Espagne & Portugal,* texte établi et présenté par Louis et Antoinette de Saint-Pierre. Paris: Hachette, 1955.

Stanhope, Catherine Wilhelmina (Duchess of Cleveland). *The Life and Letters of Lady Hester Stanhope.* London: John Murray, 1914.

Steevens, Charles. *Reminiscences of my Military Life.* Winchester: Warren & Son, 1878.

Vogelsberger, Hartwig A. *The Unearthly Quest – Lady Hester Stanhope's Legacy.* Salzburg: University of Salzburg, 1987.

Watson, J. Steven. *The Reign of George III 1760-1815.* Oxford: Oxford University Press, 1960.

Wilson, P.W. *William Pitt the Younger.* New York: Doubleday, Doran & Company, Inc. 1930.

Woodward, Llewellyn. *The Age of Reform 1815-1870.* Oxford: Oxford University Press, 1962.

INDEX

In this index I have not included the names of people who are present throughout the book, such as James Stanhope himself and his wife Frederica Murray. Neither have I included the names of people who are mentioned just once and have little or no bearing on the story.